MEADS

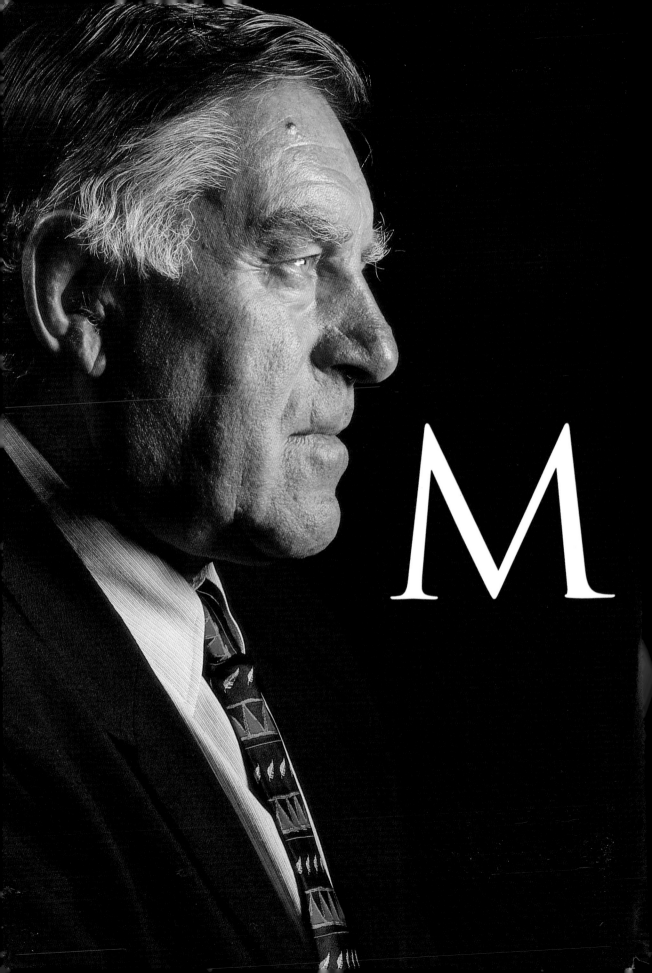

M

EADS

BRIAN TURNER

Hodder Moa Beckett

Front Cover Photos
Top: Colin Meads — All Black for the ages. Various team photos from 1957–71. NZRFU Photos
Middle right: On the burst for New Zealand, 1971. Peter Bush
Main photo: Colin Meads, 2002. Harper Photographics

Back Cover Photos
Colin Meads at home on the farm, Te Kuiti, 2002. Photosport

Pages 6–7
Meads disputes lineout possession in the first test of the 1969 series against Wales at Lancaster Park,
Christchurch. The All Blacks, from left, are: Ian Kirkpatrick, Brian Lochore, Tom Lister, Alan Smith, Brian
Muller, Meads, Ken Gray and Bruce McLeod. Barry Durrant

Pages 8–9
Characteristic charge by Meads against Wales at Cardiff Arms Park in 1963. In support are, from left: Allan
Stewart, Wilson Whineray, Waka Nathan and Kel Tremain. Fotopress/Morrie Hill

Page 10
Meads at full stretch in a lineout against Northern Transvaal, 1970. News Media Auckland

Pages 14–15
Meads pictured next to the lone pine tree on his Te Kuiti property. The tree is surrounded by natives of one
kind or another. It grew from a Christmas tree that neighbour farm worker Andrew McDonald had given
Colin and Verna Meads. Photosport

A catalogue record for this book is available from the National Library of New Zealand.

ISBN 1-86971-041-X

First published in 2002 by Hodder Moa Beckett Publishers Limited
[a member of the Hodder Headline Group]
4 Whetu Place, Mairangi Bay, Auckland

Reprinted 2002
Reprinted in limp edition 2005

Designed and produced by Hodder Moa Beckett Publishers Limited
Scanning by Microdot, Auckland
Printed by Toppan Printing Co., Hong Kong

This book is dedicated
to my wife Verna

CONTENTS

ACKNOWLEDGEMENTS

My thanks to Verna and Colin Meads for being so open and friendly and helpful. And to a heap of others for information and reminiscences. There are a great many people all over New Zealand who have a lot of time and admiration for Colin Meads and the Meads family. I want especially to thank — in no particular order — Noel McQuilkin, Wallace Bain, Stan Meads, Alex Veysey, Sir Brian Lochore, Sir Wilson Whineray, Fred Allen, Chris Laidlaw, Victor Simpson, Chris Herbert, Barry Becker, Donny Cameron, Taine Randell, Jeff Wilson, Anton Oliver, Ox Wightman, Bryan Williams, Ric Salizzo, Laurie Mains, Tony Gilbert, Ron Palenski, Brent Edwards, Sid Going, Martin Toomey, Peter Sinclair, Grahame Thorne, Paul Dwyer, John Dowling, Warren Alcock, Kip Brook and Spiro Zavos.

Thanks, too, to Warren Adler and Kevin Chapman of Hodder Moa Beckett for subtly cajoling and watching over me.

In the course of this project, I read a number of books on New Zealand rugby; books on tours and individuals. Alex Veysey was especially generous in giving me access to his 1974 bestselling biography *Colin Meads All Black*. Among other books that proved helpful were: Chris Laidlaw's *Mud in Your Eye*; *Lochore — An Authorised Biography* by Alex Veysey, Gary Caffel and Ron Palenski; *Cavaliers in South Africa, 1986* by Doug Laing and Kip Brook; Ron Palenski's *The Jersey*; Keith Quinn's *Legends of the All Blacks*; and *On the Loose* by Josh Kronfeld and Brian Turner.

Brian Turner
May 2002

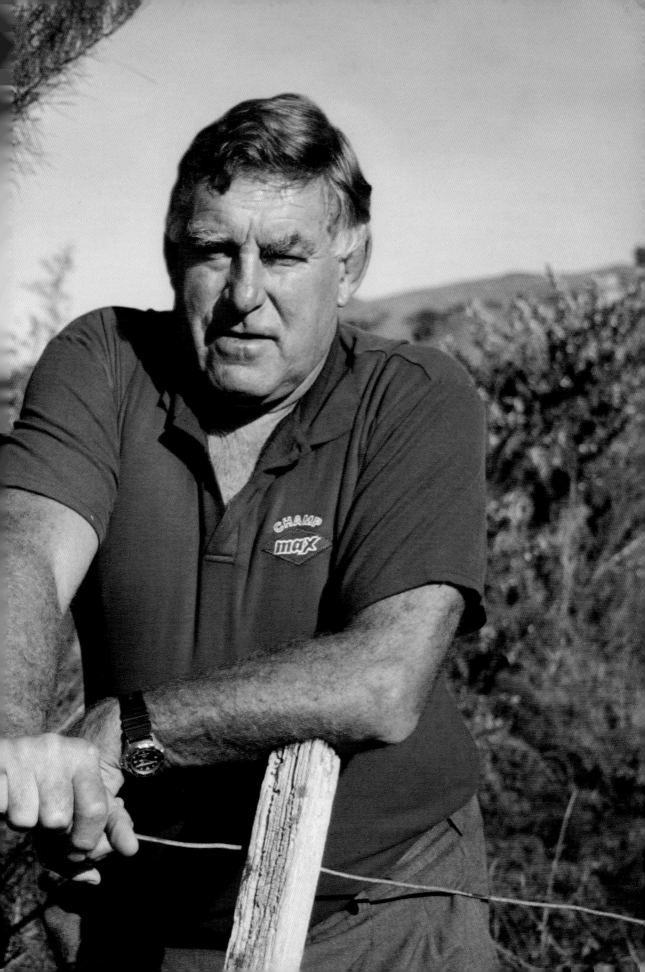

PREFACE

The names Colin Meads and All Black are synonyms, or very nearly so. He was a legend in his playing time, and the legend has, if anything, grown. That in itself marks him as a rare figure in New Zealand life. There are few New Zealanders with an interest in sport who are unaware of the stature of the man they call Pinetree.

Meads was an immensely talented All Black. Most see him as the greatest player ever to wear the silver fern. Throughout an All Black career spanning three decades, from the mid-1950s to the early '70s, he was either feared and respected or adored and admired wherever he appeared in the rugby-playing world.

However, the player the French called *Le Monstre Sacre*, one often termed a rugby colossus, has always been known as decent, genuinely helpful and self-effacing.

The man himself is somewhat bewildered as well as amused by the non-stop attention he has received over the years since his All Black debut in Sydney in 1957.

Honours galore have been bestowed upon him: he holds the record for the most number of games for the All Blacks (133 games), followed by stints as an All Black selector, then manager, before overwhelmingly being voted by the public as New Zealand's Player of the Century in 1999. Just about all the tributes that could be given to a rugby player have been awarded to him.

Yet it is not only rugby that has recognised him. Awarded an MBE in 1971, exactly 30 years later Meads was chosen as a distinguished companion of the New Zealand Order of Merit, the equivalent of the old knighthood. Today Colin Earl Meads is New Zealand's second-most popular icon, after Sir Edmund Hillary. His face on the cover guarantees thousands of magazine sales. When *60 Minutes* profiled him for TV, they received one of their highest viewership ratings of the year. Commercial offers are sent to him each week.

While he does not seek attention, it invariably finds him. From *Holmes* to the *Herald*, his views on rugby, and New Zealand life in general, are frequently aired. Such is the public demand for his straight-down-the-barrel, not particularly 'PC' homespun wisdom, that he has speaking engagements lined up for the next three years. Whether he's addressing over a thousand people at a flash Eden Park corporate do, or talking to a tiny rugby club somewhere deep in the heartland, Meads unfailingly delivers down-to-earth opinions on what *he* believes in — and he couldn't care less if his views clash with the prevailing mood of the day: 'If I'm old-fashioned, so be it. I'm not apologising.'

In his heyday, Meads acquired a reputation for being overly aggressive. Now and then he was accused of foul play. He bridles at that, mildly, and a wry smile momentarily passes over his face. He himself contends he never started rough stuff, and that most of the incidents that marked and at times marred one aspect of his career resulted from provocation, or were simply retaliation. The overwhelming majority of players who played with or against him agree.

Rugby folk the world over speak of Meads in tones approaching awe. He was, by common accord, one of the fittest and most agile tight forwards ever. As his playing mate, close friend and long-term All Black captain Sir Wilson Whineray said, 'I could rely on Colin to play for the whole 80 minutes without letting up. There was no one better, no one more reliable. No one more committed to the team effort. I admire him enormously.' Of course, Whineray's view, initially, was formed as a consequence of his on- and off-field experiences with Meads over 30 years ago. For a more recent opinion, the 2001 All Black captain and hooker Anton Oliver responded regarding the name Colin Meads: 'All Black or, to put it another way, hear the name Meads and one immediately thinks, All Black.'

Everywhere you go in rugby you meet people who both admire and respect Colin Meads. They admire and respect him for his playing ability, for his loyalty to the game of rugby and to his friends; they admire him for his vast contribution to both club and provincial rugby, as well as to the All Blacks; for his support for schools, colts and Maori rugby; and for his long involvement in coaching, captaining, selecting and administrating at all levels. But he is also admired for his great contribution to charities and, in particular, to New Zealand's Intellectually Handicapped Children's Society, known nationwide as the IHC.

In fact, his entire personal collection of All Black jerseys has almost disappeared, gifted as prizes for numerous charity fund-raisers. He has seen such gestures as one way of reciprocating and saying thanks to the wider community that has supported him, his wife Verna, and their family of five, in the course of his long career.

Colin Meads may not have set out to play his life on a world stage, or to play many parts, but he has played major roles nationally and internationally, especially in so far as his lifelong part in world rugby is concerned. Meads doesn't see himself as having been a 'colossus' of rugby — as many have described him — for such an assessment strikes him as overly grand. It makes someone as modest as Meads feel sheepish. But he has come to accept, albeit reluctantly — 'sometimes I wonder what all the fuss was about, I really do' — that he is seen as something of an icon in New Zealand sporting circles and that there's little he can do about it now.

For Fred Allen (All Black coach 1966–68), though, the reason for 'the fuss' is simple. 'To me, Colin Meads was the greatest rugby player ever. There's been no one better. They threw away the mould when they made Pinetree.'

PART ONE

—◇—

'An All Black —
and a good one'

'[It] reminds me of the time when I first encountered Keith Murdoch, that very good Otago prop. I'd hardly ever met him, but I'd sure heard a lot about him. We all had. Keith had a reputation for liking his beer. In 1969, so the story went, he was down to play in an All Black trial in Dunedin, but beforehand he'd been drinking with some fishermen and he ended up on a fishing boat. It was on the weekend and the trial was down for the Tuesday. Keith probably had had some rum among other things and he went to sleep on the boat. The skipper cast off in the early hours of the morning and went off to sea fishing. He was intent on being away for a week or two. All of a sudden, Keith had become a cook on a fishing vessel. Keith's mum got phone calls asking where he was — no one knew. So he missed out that year.

'Right, come 1970 and he's in the All Black trials — in Lochore's team, I think. I was captain of the other. I'd been playing rugby for a long, long time, and yet I hadn't come up against this character before. I'd heard about him all right. The word was he fixed up all situations that occurred on the field. In the trial — and I'm not sure if Lochore, BJ, actually got him to do this or not — but Murdoch was told to stand just behind me in the lineout and every time I went to jump he just pulled my arm away. After he'd done that a couple of times, I said to him, "Hey, you do that again and I'll knock your head off." The bugger, he chuckled and looked at me and said, "Have a go."

'That put me on the spot. All these stories came flooding back, stories about how tough and rugged Keith was. People said, "Don't mix with that fella, he'll kill yer." I thought, ooh, hell, that's nice . . . and I'm captain of this team. Here I am telling this guy I'll knock his head off and, usually, if you told some young

Games legends are made of . . . the second All Black trial of 1970 at Athletic Park. 'Probables' captain Colin Meads — Keith Murdoch (inset) no doubt on his mind — disputes lineout possession with Alan Smith. Others in the frame are, from left: 'Jazz' Muller, Jake Burns (1) and Ron Urlich (2).

PETER BUSH

fella that, that was enough. Not this time. I told Keith two or three times to stop it and he kept saying, "Have a go." I reckon BJ was grinning down the back of the lineout. So I often thought back to my time with Whineray when he'd have asked me to fix some fella up . . . so I turned to Jazz Muller, one of my props, and said to him, "Jazz, get this b———", but Jazz would have none of it. He spluttered, "Aw, no, no, hell no, not me." Then I turned to Jake Burns, the other prop and he said, "Geez, I'm having enough trouble holding the scrum up, let alone bloody well belting Murdoch. You look after yourself."

'I thought, well, I'm a great captain, aren't I? I used to do what I was told. Now I realised I'd got myself into a position where I had to do something about it. Here I was thinking, in three weeks time I'm going to be touring South Africa, Keith's probably going to be there, and he'd be thinking, "This Colin Meads, he's all piss and wind." The question for me was, what do I do? So I planned it, decided to wait until about three minutes from fulltime, and then when I dong him it'll have to be good, for if he's as tough as they say he'll get back at me before the end. I'll have to make sure he goes down and doesn't get up. So I waited until it was their throw-in, so that Keith had a job to do, and I thumped him. It was a beaut. I thought I'd broken all the bones in my hand. Keith reeled back several yards. I'm saying to myself, "Fall over, fall over for Christ's sake." He didn't; he shook his head and rejoined the play. I thought, oh, dear, think quick now, Pinetree. Whineray would have called the team around him. So I called them in. We used to have a saying — Whineray would say, "You've got a sore elbow" — and that meant we could get the Zambuck out and we could discuss something. So I said to Muller, the nearest to me, "Jazz, you've got a sore elbow." The idiot, he said, "Have I?" What a captain. So I had to convince Jazz. So we got Jazz to feign a sore elbow and I got the team in and I gave them a lecture. I said, "I've just had a message from the selectors." Now that was plausible because they stood on the sideline and sometimes delivered messages during a trial. "They want to see the ball spun around. There's only three or four minutes to go, but they don't want the ball kicked out at all. What's more, if you do kick it out, you're in trouble from me, too; I've got a little problem up here. But the selectors want to see it run around."

'Now the only one who really queried me was Bill Davis. He asked, "But what if we're behind our own goal-line?" I said, "Just kick the bastard as far down the middle of the field as you can, but don't you kick it out. Right?" A lineout with our throw-in was okay. I'd do the calling and, by hell, they were long throws to the second five-eighth, or right to the back, and I'm Willie-ing away as fast as I can with this Murdoch chasing me. He was stalking me. I could see it, that there was going to be trouble here.

'The final whistle went and, boy, the relief. I thought, well, I've done what I told him I would. And then I looked up and saw Keith coming straight towards me. I started to shake. I grabbed a couple of our blokes and said they'd better stay close for a moment or two. "There could be a bit of trouble here." But, no, they evaporated, were gone. Keith came up and put his hand out. I grabbed it and shook it hard. He said to me, "By the way, your king hit is not working." As quick as a flash I said, "It was just a warning."'

—◄○►—

1.

KING COUNTRY MAN

A lot of King Country people
would bridle and say, 'No, he's
not a Southern Man, he's a
King Country Man.'

THESE DAYS, WHEN COLIN MEADS RIDES INTO BUSTLING TE KUITI, NO HUSH
DESCENDS ON THE TOWN. NO WHISPER SPREADS EITHER. PEOPLE DON'T STOP TO STARE,
DON'T STEP ASIDE TO ALLOW HIM UNIMPEDED PASSAGE. THERE'S NO DEFERENCE TO SPEAK
OF. BUT FOR ALL THAT HE'S LONG BEEN SEEN AS A FRONTIER-LIKE, STRAIGHT-SHOOTING
MARSHAL, NOT BIG BAD COLIN, A MEAN DESPERADO.

The middle-aged and the elderly locally have seen and known him for so long that
he's simply a comfy fixture, respected and often admired, and although for many
of his contemporaries, especially in King Country rugby, his feats made him
legendary, he's not doted on anymore. As for the young, it's hard for them to really
put him and his rugby and other achievements in perspective. Meads may have
done more than any other local to put Te Kuiti on the nationally conscious map, but
understandably the young, most of them, only have hazy impressions of that. It's
partly a case of the common observation, as King Country Rugby Football Union's
CEO Ox Wightman puts it, of a 'prophet having little honour in his own patch'.
And, 'Hell,' says Wightman, gesturing to the walls of the union's offices, 'there's
virtually nothing on the inside or outside of the building to indicate that this is the
home of one of the greatest All Blacks ever. I want to do something about that.

He's been taken for granted, and that's wrong.' Wightman believes, as a recent arrival in the job, that Meads and his legacy need to be given greater prominence. 'As far as this union's concerned, or should be,' says Ox, 'he's a Messiah.'

Verna Meads laughs quietly about such matters, about Colin's place in the district. I suggest that there's nothing truly disrespectful, or unappreciative, about the community's attitude towards him, maybe just the usual one about familiarity breeding . . . and so on. I suggest that maybe Colin Meads is, in today's New Zealand rugby world, more Southern than Northern Man, a bit laconic, dry, inclined to twinkle and chuckle; fond of understatement and averse to gush and glitter. She nods, 'That could be right. They seem to like him down there. In Otago and Southland, Colin's sometimes said it's almost like he's being welcomed back home.' And in Canterbury, too, says Verna, the 'Canterbury Rugby Supporters' Club has always been right behind him. They didn't like the way he was treated after he came back from the Cavaliers' tour of South Africa in 1986.'

Colin considers that the Southern Man characterisation is 'a fair assumption, but a lot of King Country people would bridle and say, "No, he's not a Southern Man, he's a King Country Man."'

However, Meads does go down well in what is sometimes called the heartland of New Zealand rugby. In Ranfurly, in the pure and rarefied air and, sometimes, eerie spaces of the Maniototo. This is country which has produced New Zealand and Otago rugby players to be reckoned with — names such as Hore, Kreft, Smith, McAtamney and Kearney among them. Down there they feel that Meads has always understood the value, importance and needs of grass roots rugby in New Zealand, and they're not convinced that all of the so-called Flash Harrys and well-heeled sharpies up north do. 'Tony Kreft and others got Colin down to talk to us,' says Barry Becker of Oturehua, 'and he was hilarious. No bullshit. He talked to us for the best part of an hour and a half. Kept sipping on his glass. "Excuse me," he'd say, "just need to lubricate my throat." Piney's glass just happened to be a jug.'

So in the rugby heartlands, where rugby's roots arguably went deepest, Meads was and remains an icon.

If not at home on the farm with Verna and their five children — Karen, Kelvin, Rhonda, Glynn, Shelley — or off elsewhere on rugby matters, Colin Meads' home away from home was, in the majority of cases, on the grounds of Rugby Park or in the clubrooms of the Waitete Rugby Football Club, about a kilometre out of town south of Te Kuiti on the road to Rotorua. Colin's father, Vere, who only ever had time for social rugby himself as a youngster, in 1964 began his long stint as joint club Patron with another of the club's stalwarts, Wilf Derby. When the club's Golden 50th Jubilee was celebrated in 1981, Derby had been Patron, first with A. McQuilkin (another dominant Waitete club name), since 1951.

The club's earliest members were notably keen and zealous. In 1935, club member Len Kawe was the first King Country player to make an international side when he was a member of the New Zealand Maori side on a tour to Australia. By 1936, the year Colin was born, Waitete's motto, THE GAME ABOVE THE PRIZE, began to be used. It reflects the moral spirit of the times and was no doubt meant to be pointed and salutary. Colin Meads himself smiles at mention of it, not because he disagrees with the sentiments inherent in it, but because, as he notes, it's not always easy to take one's eyes off the prize, usually the winning of a game.

In 1937 a grandstand was built on Rugby Park but it wasn't until '39 that funds

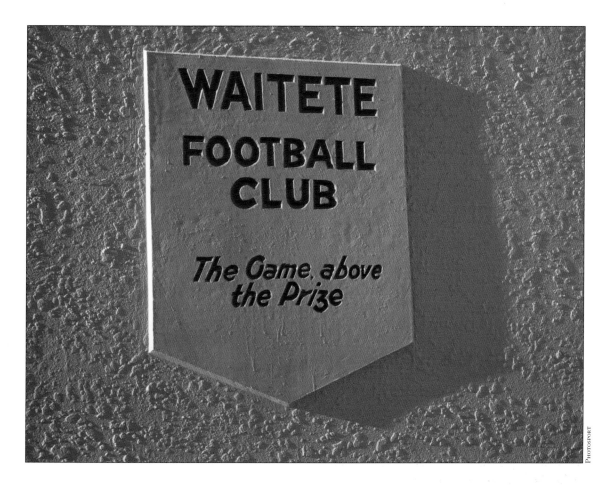

WAITETE
FOOTBALL
CLUB

The Game, above the Prize

Photosport

Etched in stone, the Waitete club motto: The Game above the Prize.

were raised to build the club's own training shed. That year the club held its first Annual Dinner and ran an evening featuring dancing, cards and various other items of entertainment. Then Gala Opening days were held to mark the start of the 1939 and '40 rugby seasons. Events included: seven-aside matches; 'basketball girls' on the No. 2 field; field events for footballers; inter-club 110 yards sprints and relays; and goal-kicking competitions. All competitors had to wear full football gear, and the basketballers had running events too. According to the editor of the 50th Jubilee programme, one Verna Meads, the opening days were 'just like a Carnival'.

There was a 'Ladies versus Men' football match, three-legged races for footballers and 'Lady' partners, the ladies 'comprising a wondrous bevy of beauties'.

'Points were allotted for events and handsome cups presented. Profits were for Patriotic purposes. The parade was led by the Municipal Band.' All this took place in the shadow of impending war, and was indicative of greatly different, possibly more stoic and community-orientated times. It was a far cry from the rugby world — club, provincial and international — of today.

Rugby was played at Waitete until mid-1940 and then the club went into recess until the winter of 1944 when junior and third-grade teams were entered in the local competition, but it wasn't until 1947 that the club put the 'lean years' behind it and won 'practically every Trophy . . . in the Sub-union competition'. In 1948 the changing and shower building at Rugby Park 'was extended a further 12 feet' and the showers 'proved a great asset' for both club members and visiting teams alike.

When Colin Meads was a boy, not only was it seen as natural to want to play rugby, it was expected. His earliest memories are of the encouragement he received from the former All Black, Ron Bryers, a schoolteacher in Taumarunui. To Meads, and scores of other King Country rugby stalwarts, Bryers seemed to coach just about every team going, and in Meads' last year at primary school he was in Bryers' rep team.

Meads had a taste of inter-provincial rugby as a schoolboy and liked it. He played at Te Kuiti High School and 'at about the age of 16, I got in the King Country juniors'. Ron Bryers was coach of that team too, and Meads saw him as a motivator and a mentor. 'He was a big man,' says Meads, 'a New Zealand Maori rep and a lock.' Two years or so later, as a 19-year-old, Meads played his first game for King Country seniors against South Auckland Counties. Later, Meads learned that the North Island selector, Jack Finlay, was at the game. During the match, Meads found himself in the first five-eighth position about 15 yards out from the goalposts. 'The halfback threw me the ball and I thought, "What the hell do you do now?", so I let go with a dropped kick. It wasn't a good one, but it went over, just.' Meads also scored a try in the match, which he had forgotten about. Finlay told the then New Zealand selector, Jack Sullivan, a former star All Black back, that Meads was a boy with 'a ton of potential'.

Ask Meads if he has a mental picture of himself that dates back to 1955, and he says, 'I'd have been a tall, skinny, gangling fella; I wouldn't have been 14 stone.' After another couple of games for King Country he was chosen to play in a North Island Colts trial match prior to the selection of a New Zealand Colts team to tour Australia and Ceylon.

Meads reckons that his height more than anything else probably helped with his selection for the New Zealand Colts in 1955. That, and the advocacy of the journalist Cedric Gray, then working for a paper in Palmerston North where the colts trials were held. Gray and Meads had played together for King Country juniors — Gray as a talented but physically slight inside back — and Meads thinks Gray was behind the paper publishing photographs of him. 'I'm sure that helped,' says Meads, although he didn't think of it that way at the time.

J.J. (John) Stewart, still quite young as Meads recalls him, was coach of the colts team. Reflecting on his career, Meads thinks this was the making of him. He saw Stewart as a 'great coach. He used to say to me, "When you get the ball, your first instinct should be to run with it. Bugger everyone else, run. It should be like an electric shock, psshaw." Up until then, when I got the ball, I used to look around, wonder what to do with it, or who to give it to.'

The tour to Ceylon was a marvellous experience for Meads. The team played in Melbourne, Adelaide and Perth before boarding a ship for a two-week passage to Ceylon, a truly exotic place to Meads. For a rather gauche young farmer from the backblocks in the central North Island, sailing away from New Zealand was exciting. Meads said he was one of a number of 'unknowns, a bunch of bumpkins'. He still chuckles about the voyage: 'Two weeks on a boat. It's unheard of nowadays. It was a glorious experience. Hot as hell, of course. JJ [Stewart] was the ideal sort to have as coach of a team of young guys like that.'

When they returned, JJ was asked who he thought were potential All Blacks. Meads recalls that he named four, 'and I wasn't one of them. So ever since, I always keep reminding him of that. It was one of my greatest incentives, to prove that blighter wrong.'

Meads en route to Ceylon in 1955 with J.J. Stewart's New Zealand Colts team . . . 'a tall, skinny, gangling fella'.

NZ RUGBY MUSEUM

To Meads, in 1955 he had made only 'a small niche' for himself in rugby. He had played only two or three games for the King Country, partly because the selectors 'wrapped me up in cotton wool, didn't play me against the Maori, nor another match, because they were scared I'd be knocked around'.

In 1956, the Springboks were imminent. The rugby fraternity was abuzz, and most provincial players dreamed of going out and toppling the Boks. Meads was one; already he felt the burning desire he was to carry in him all his life, which was to humble South Africa at rugby. To him, All Blacks versus Springboks matches were the pinnacle of a rugby player's career. Somewhat to his surprise, in 1956 he was picked to play in a regional All Black trial. He wasn't bulky enough to lock the scrum, so he played as a loose forward and surprised both himself and others when he made the North Island team. How, he wondered, had he got in and Bill Clark of Wellington missed out?

Meads' selection probably owed much to the fact that Jack Finlay was coach of the North Island side. Years later, Jack Sullivan, former All Black and later chairman of the NZRFU, told Meads that no matter how well he played they were not going to pick him for the All Blacks; 'they were never going to put me in against the Springboks at that age'. Meads thought that was fair enough.

How young is too young to be picked for the All Blacks and test rugby? Meads' view is that 'every player is different, physically and mentally. You can mollycoddle young fellas too much and that doesn't help. The younger you learn the longer and the better it stays with you.'

Meads returned from Wellington and the giddy heights of inter-island rugby to the bedrock realities of a King Country competition full of all 'those old guys who had been there for years . . . and they were lining me up and asking what I'd learnt. They wanted new input. My outlook had changed and I was seen as a means of introducing something new. Of course,' and Meads finds this awfully amusing, 'I had to ask myself, what did I damn well learn?'

To the young, eager Meads, rugby at inter-island level and above was still very much a foreign country called Mystification. 'In the King Country we were still in the Ice Age when it came to lineouts, for instance. We never had calls, hell no. The wing just threw it somewhere near where the halfback was standing. That would do.'

In the dressing room before practice for the inter-island match, coach Jack Finlay said to the forwards: 'Right-o, we've got Tiny White, and we know he's good. His photo's on the programme and he's the All Black lock . . .' Whereupon Meads says he was thinking, 'Geez, he's my idol' . . . 'and we've got Nev MacEwan, but in the first three lineouts, no matter where they are on the ground, we're going to throw the ball to Colin Meads. Well . . . I could see this was a tactical move to blunt Bob Duff and Tiny Hill, but even so I was in awe of all these players and I was a bit taken aback.'

Meads, no great fan of sports psychology, knew he was being thrown in at the deep end, but for all that, he didn't see himself as a young novitiate in need of counselling. He simply vowed to do his best in the job that was asked of him. The wing, Ron Jarden, a man whom Meads was 'terribly impressed by', sidled up to Meads and asked him how he wanted the ball thrown in. 'Do you want a fast one or a lob?' asked Jarden. Meads blinked. 'Just throw it in,' he said to Jarden. This was Meads at his ultimate keep-it-simple approach. He had never had experience of fast or slow throws, or lobs. He just did his best to grab what came along. Jarden took Meads aside, 'was very helpful', said, 'Just come over here for five minutes.' Meads said he didn't want any special treatment and spluttered, 'Aw, no, just throw it.'

Meads was at number seven in the lineout. He often wonders what they thought of this young guy from, where? 'Hell's teeth,' says Meads, 'Jarden persisted. He wanted to know whether I wanted the ball thrown so it moved across, or lobbed, and I didn't have a clue. It was a big learning curve for me. We went and had some practice throws, and I said to Jarden that I didn't want a slow lobby one and that I would be happy with a brisk throw across the top, not too

Meads and Nev MacEwan locked the All Blacks' scrum in nine tests between 1958 and 1962. They first appeared in the same side, though, in 1956 in the inter-island match at Wellington. On that occasion Meads, the tyro, was a loose forward . . . and major ball-winner.

MEADS FAMILY

high. I'll never forget those first three lineouts.'

Meads was marked by Canterbury's John Buxton who actually got in the test team. Meads says, 'I never thought he was much of a player, really.'

When Meads got back among his team-mates in the King Country, he may not have felt like a seer bringing marvellous new tricks and profound information, but he was required to deliver the goods. So he related his experiences with Jarden and others and from that day on King Country lineout rugby was never the same again. Meads saw King Country rugby as full of hard bushmen who played to win and 'knocked the hell out of each other in the process. There were some skilful backs but generally it was a pretty bruising, brutal sort of game up front, and that was the way it should be as far as they were concerned.'

After his first inter-island match, Meads began to think more seriously about the game of rugby football. It was, in many ways, a case of never such innocence again. It made him realise the deep importance of tactics. 'I didn't feel guilty, I just felt embarrassed. Here I was, not even in my twenties, telling hardened King Country players in their late twenties and early thirties what had happened and what we should be doing.'

The impression of the inter-island game that lingered with Meads was that the game was faster than he'd thought it would be. Nevertheless he felt up to it as he was, in his words, 'quick and mobile then. I got my hands on the ball quite a bit. And the first three lineouts put me right. I thought, "Christ, playing with these jokers is a piece of cake." And I was lucky; the first three lineouts were all on Jarden's side of the field. If I recall right, Tom Katene may have been on the other wing, and not renowned for being much of a lineout thrower. I must say I breathed a sigh of relief too, for I'd been thinking that it was all right talking about it, but actually doing it and getting it right during the game is another thing.'

There was another significant aspect of Meads' experience of playing that inter-island match at Athletic Park: from that time on, he saw that he began to have a serious input into King Country rugby. It was a contribution that, in the end, was to become monumental. The next year he became an All Black, went on tour, came back, and the same cry went up every time: 'Tell us what you learned.' Meads realised that he had been unofficially appointed a 'tutor for my own union. I would be able to say that I'd been watching Ron Hemi hook, and little things like how Ron wanted the halfback to put the ball in. I'd see Ron taking a new halfback aside and telling him to turn the ball a little this way or that.' The point Meads makes is that, now and then, the little thing can amount to a lot, at a particular time, and that there is an accumulative effect. Also, he could see clearly that new discoveries of the sort that Colin Meads, fledgling star, could transport and make known to the wider rugby world were not being made in the King Country.

Up until this time, Meads had played mainly by instinct. Now he started to scheme more, to observe more carefully. Young players should be keen to absorb. You get the feeling from Meads that he thinks it makes sense for the young to be respectful and possibly a little deferential towards the older, more experienced players, because he thinks they learn more that way, and as a consequence are less likely to make foolish decisions.

By 1957, the 20-year-old Meads' outstanding form could no longer be overlooked by the All Black selectors. After a rousing final trial, he heard his name called out for inclusion in the All Black tour party to Australia. Here is how Alex Veysey, who wrote the bestseller *Colin Meads All Black* in 1974, describes Meads' first encounter with the black jersey and his performance on the tour.

> When he was given his first All Black jersey to put on for a team photograph before the team left, Meads gripped it tightly, stared at it and said, 'It's mine.' The feel of the black on his back was warm. There was power in it. In that jersey with its white fern across its heart he could believe, actually believe, that he was an All Black. It was not with any sense of self-achievement or self-importance that he regarded himself in the all black strip. There was born within him that day that which, above all things, was to make him the player he became. It was

The legend is born. Saturday, 18 May, 1957 and Colin Earl Meads makes his official debut for the All Blacks against New South Wales at Sydney. Meads actually played in the tour opener against Illawarra, a match which was never accorded first class status.

RON PALENSKI COLLECTION

The All Blacks perform a haka in Australia, 1957. Meads is third from right, wearing headgear.

MEADS FAMILY

pride. A bursting pride which found its expression in many ways and which, rather than diminishing through the years, grew and grew. When he shrugged into his black jersey for his fifty-fifth test match it possibly meant as much to him as it had when, as a shy backblocks boy, his chest heaved and his muscles swelled in his first New Zealand gear. It became almost an obsession in Meads that while he wore his country's uniform no circumstances would quell his spirit.

On this tour Meads played in nine of the 13 matches — excluding his New Zealand debut at Wollongong — and he scored five tries. Five matches at lock were in partnership with Tiny, Peter Burke and Nev MacEwan, and although he had the size and the capacity to play at lock he was also regarded as the team's real 'loosie' in the test teams, playing both tests from the side of the scrum and the back of the lineouts. This was in the days of no replacements — that most archaic, not to say cruel, piece of legislation — and Meads was loose forward under instruction as a back in case of injury during a test. He had to practise throwing in from touch for five minutes every day and the coach with the team, Dick Everest, most optimistically and fruitlessly tried to encourage Meads to learn to dive tackle. It came to pass that the New Zealand centre Frank McMullen [later an international referee], was injured during the second test. That most ubiquitous of players Pat Walsh went from wing to centre and Meads took his six feet four and 16 stone off to the wing, there to meet the dashing, delightful and determined Australian Alan Morton. Pat Walsh's instruction to Meads was succinct: 'If he gets the ball keep inside him and squeeze him towards touch. If you get the ball run straight through him.' The wisdom of Walsh's advice may be judged by the fact that Meads scored a try. Or it may be cancelled out by the fact that Morton scored one too.

Of more consequence than scoring a try in the test, whether as wing, lock, loose forward or hooker, was that this tour gave Meads a great foundation from which to build his playing career. And it is in this that he sees Australia as an ideal launching pad for new All Blacks . . . 'I feel terribly sorry for players who, selected for the All Blacks for the first time, have to play that first test in a home series. Without actually being thrown to the wolves — because, after all, he is an All Black because he is good enough to be one — he does not have the advantage of the fellows who fall into a tour of Australia. This tour gives a young player the chance to settle into All Black routines and demands. It gives him an idea of what All Black rugby is all about before the tension of a test. In Australia he may have three, four or five games against teams of no great consequence so that when the test comes he is working smoothly within team tactics.'

In those days the All Blacks operated a 'sophisticated' lineout calling system: hands on skin; hands on heads; one hand on, two hands on. And so on. Meads said they all used to stand there 'and glare at the halfback because he would give the signals'. To Meads, once he had learned his own team's signals, it became a challenge to

The match programme from Meads' first test, against Australia at Sydney in 1957.

work out the opposition's. Thinking about the opposition's moves was a good way of trying to gain an advantage through a greater awareness of the whole picture.

What developed here — and Meads doesn't want to be boastful — was that by the time he had returned from the All Blacks' tour of South Africa in 1960, he was virtually captain and coach of the King Country side. While Neil 'Curly' Neilsen was officially the coach and selector, Meads took the training. Such would never have happened, in Meads' view, in Otago or Wellington or Auckland, but in King Country, yes. Meads saw Neilsen as a fine fella, one who occasionally 'wanted to fight the world. He had a heart of gold and he just loved King Country.'

Playing for the All Blacks helped Meads become more organised and better at organising, as he sees it. Which was why he played such a wide-sweeping role in

King Country rugby for such a long time. He was, to all intents and purposes, captain and coach of King Country, for virtually all of the time from 1960 to 1972, although he says he 'never had the label coach'.

Meads took the training and was, especially in his early years, 'a fitness maniac. We always liked to have a few beers after training, which was fair enough. But I used to say that if you were going to have a few, you were going to have to earn them. If I ran the guts out of some people, then I was always able to do it myself. I applied some of the things I'd experienced in the All Blacks; and we'd do our team drills. We had a good team, particularly in the mid-sixties. Apart from me and Stan, we had a front row that could handle anyone in New Zealand. There was Bill Wordley, who played for the North Island, Howard Paiaka and Rocky Parr . . . real hard men who wouldn't run away from anyone. If anything they were a bit the other way; they liked a bit of how's your father if it got that way. We were in good company. If anyone tried to get at Stan and me, these guys would look after us.'

The King Country rep side, and King Country rugby generally, 'became a part of your life', says Meads. 'But that didn't mean that we backed off when we played against each other in club games. When I was playing for Waitete, we used to have some real dust-ups against each other. I even got sent off a couple of times. In many ways I deserved it. But we often laughed about it among ourselves. I can remember one day playing against a chap named George Peake. It was a vital, tense game against Kio Kio. There had been a couple of scuffles — I'm not sure if I'd been involved — and at one stage George was in our side of a ruck or maul and the whistle went. I just gave him a push with two hands and told him that he was a cheatin' bastard and that he was to get on side. George tripped, fell over someone else and knocked the referee over, so he got up and sent us both off. It was all a chapter of accidents. The ref was a bit of a hothead too, and he was worried about the game getting out of control.

'George, a loose forward, and I were mates in the King Country team. It was quite hilarious, and when we were in the dressing room somebody brought out half a bottle of whisky — now I never drink spirits — but on this occasion George and I sat there and drank it and got a little bit drunk.'

While Meads was in the All Blacks, the style of play King Country adopted was greatly influenced by the methods of the All Black coach of the day. He says that when he first got involved with the King Country side, it was mainly 'rugged stuff up front and then a bit of bash, wallop in the backs. We had a big winger, Rangi Paki, and we used to bring him in outside the first five-eighth. We told him not to pass the ball but to have everyone on. We would start another phase from where he went to ground. Then when Fred Allen started coaching the All Blacks, we went along with his style and King Country played the open, running game.'

Meads really enjoyed playing in the King Country side because he saw it as having a great spirit. What that meant was that the team played hard on and off the field. They were a spirited lot. Anyone who played King Country knew they had had a game.

Noel
MCQUILKIN

Someone who knows Colin Meads as well as anyone, and who admires him unreservedly, is Noel McQuilkin of Te Kuiti. McQuilkin, currently coach of the New Zealand Divisional team, played rugby with Meads for both Waitete and King Country. McQuilkin himself has made a huge contribution to King Country rugby. He took over as coach of the King Country side after it had finished second bottom of the second division in 1989. In 1991 the team beat Bay of Plenty to gain promotion to the first division. In 1992 the side battled to sixth in a nine-team first division competition but thereafter had great difficulty hanging in, didn't have a big enough playing base, lost a few key players, and was relegated from the first division in 1996. It's a familiar, and not happy, New Zealand provincial rugby story. 'It was inevitable, really,' says McQuilkin, 'given the way rugby has gone. King Country's gone from being a sort of Cinderella to a kind of Ugly Sister.' He doesn't mean that disparagingly, but the comment vividly draws attention to painful realities. 'In the smaller unions — in the more sparsely populated areas — you probably get a good team every twenty years.'

McQuilkin has watched Meads for longer than he cares to remember. 'He's made a huge contribution. He's worked his ring out for Waitete, for King Country, and for New Zealand rugby. He's never moaned, but the return to him financially has been pitiful really, when you compare Colin's contribution with that of a great many others. Colin told me not long ago that, "You know, Noel, this is the first year for ages that I'm going to have to think about paying my tax."'

'You won't find many knockers, although a few have taken him for granted. And there were always a few guys waiting to line him up, sort him out. Stupid buggers wanting to have a crack at him.'

McQuilkin thinks Meads was a terrific influence for King Country. Teams Meads had control over trained hard. 'He believed in players being extremely fit and hard. "Keep going, keep going."

I can still hear Colin saying that. We trained until we were buggered and then Colin said we could have a couple of beers and go home.' Noel says he never saw anyone get the better of Meads at training. 'He had a dog, though, who gave him a run for his money.' Here McQuilkin begins to laugh loudly. 'He had this dog, see, that he'd named Skip after the captain he'd admired so much, Wilson "Skip" Whineray. One day the dog misbehaved and Colin gave it a couple of whacks with a stick, but Skip was having none of that. He grabbed the stick and tore it out of Colin's hand.'

A former representative coach and, like Meads, a great servant of the King Country union, Noel McQuilkin is unstinting in his praise of Meads.

'But tough, I've never seen anyone as tough and uncomplaining,' says McQuilkin. 'I'll give you an example, one among many. Colin broke his toe. It was swollen and a bit bloody. He wasn't supposed to be playing. The pressure from his boot got too much, so he cut a hole in the side of it and carried on playing that way. And another thing about Colin, which sticks in local minds, is that he'd play for the All Blacks in a test and within a few days he was back practising and playing club games for the Waitete club. He was great like that.'

McQuilkin enjoyed going away on rugby trips with Meads and in more recent years recalls being with him overseas with an unofficial New Zealand Youth side. In Belgium they shared a room where no towels were provided. 'Colin got into the shower and when he came out, he dried himself with a sheet and pillow slips. No mucking around. In London, we were shown our room, which was on the third floor and there was no lift. And then, when Colin went to use the toilet, it was so small he couldn't shut the door — his knees were poking out into the room.

'He was so disgusted he went downstairs straight away and told the proprietor that we wanted a decent room on the ground floor or we were out of there.'

2.
MOST DEVOTED FAN

'At the time, I just thought he'd play for a few years and then we'd just be farmers.'

Verna Lang was nine when her family — parents Bill and Kathleen, older brother Donald, and younger siblings, Janice and John — moved into Te Kuiti where her father became a stock agent. Until then he had managed a farm at Te Anga, 40 miles away. Verna thinks her parents moved because they thought it would be better for their children's education. Her father soon became very friendly with Colin's father, Vere Meads. Vere and Bill were so friendly, she remembers, that 'people called them twin brothers'.

Verna met Colin at Te Kuiti High School. They were in the same form but in different classes. She played basketball — netball today — and her team often went along to support the rugby team in which Colin was prominent. Verna says: 'I don't remember much about Colin at school, but after leaving I can recall speaking to him in the street in Te Kuiti. So he must have made enough of an impression for me to think him worth noticing.'

After leaving school at the end of the fourth form, Verna worked in the office of the Ford Garage in Te Kuiti. Later, when she was 17, a girlfriend encouraged her to see more of Colin, 'and that's when the romance started', she says.

When they were 21, they got married in Te Kuiti. As Verna says, perhaps

MEADS FAMILY

*Family wedding group,
5 October, 1957.
From left: Vere and Ida
Meads, best man Stan
Meads, Colin and Verna,
bridesmaid Janice Lang
(Verna's sister) and
Verna's parents Kathleen
and Bill Lang.*

hinting at a portent of things to come, 'We got married at the end of the rugby season and before shearing started.' Verna can't recall Colin ever actually asking her to marry him; they 'just started planning to get married'. When Verna told her parents, her mother said she 'thought it was going to come sooner or later'.

Verna never had serious thoughts of a career of her own, although for a time she 'quite liked the idea of being an air hostess'. She felt, though, that she would have been deemed too tall. Also, she'd heard some nursing experience was required, and she wasn't keen on that.

A slight smile spreads across Verna's face when she reflects on her marriage to Colin Meads. 'I thought I was marrying a farmer who just happened to play rugby in his spare time. I knew he was very keen on rugby . . . he had been away to Ceylon with the New Zealand Colts in 1955, and he made his first trip away to Australia with the All Blacks in 1957.' So she agrees that the extent of Colin's involvement in rugby didn't exactly steal up on her. 'But I didn't realise it would ever escalate to the extent that it has done. He was an All Black for 15 years. There are All Blacks today who have played more tests than Colin, for these days it seems that just about every game is a test, but no one has played more games for New Zealand. I don't think anyone ever again will play for the All Blacks for that many years.

'At the time, I just thought he'd play for a few years and then we'd just be farmers.'

Verna and Colin's first child, Karen, was born in 1958. 'Thereafter,' says Verna, 'I was a mother with great regularity. Our first two children were 11 months apart, and so were our third and fourth. Then there was a nine-year gap before Shelley came along.' Bringing up young children is daunting, but Verna says she was 'very lucky' in that she had 'marvellous local support when Colin was away. Colin's parents lived within calling distance' and her own parents lived in town and were always ready to help. The members of the Waitete rugby club were right behind the Meads family too. As Verna says, 'Colin couldn't have made all those trips if it

Verna at home with children Karen, Kelvin, Glynn (in her arms) and Rhonda just prior to Colin's departure on the 1963–64 tour of the British Isles, France and Canada. The tour lasted four months.

MEADS FAMILY

hadn't been for the support from the Waitete members, who did some farm work when Colin and brother Stan were away. They also provided financial assistance. The club ran crown and anchor evenings, and then had a farewell party at which they would present Colin with a suitcase which had a cheque in it for the amount he was allowed to take out of New Zealand. While he was away, Colin's parents paid me his regular wages. At that time, it was below the award wage — it was a family farm and money was scarce.

'When on tour, Colin spent a lot of his money buying clothes for the kids. On one of his first trips away, to Japan in 1958, he saved his money and bought me a washing machine when he came home.'

When Meads was away for three to four months, Verna divided her time between Colin's parents and her own. On his return she moved back into their farmhouse and he went back to work on the farm.

Verna remembers that Kelvin, their second child, was about 11 months old when Colin went away to South Africa in 1960, 'and he didn't know his father when he came back. I couldn't leave the two of them alone in a room together. Kelvin would scream his head off. Colin would go to pick him up and pacify him. It was the worst thing he could have done. I know other All Backs had similar problems. The same thing just about happened with Glynn when Colin went away on the 1963–64 tour of the British Isles — Glynn was about the same age Kelvin was when Colin went off to South Africa — and Glynn didn't want much to do with Colin when he came back either.'

Ask Verna if she quickly came to see herself principally and simply as the wife of a famous All Black and she says 'No'. She knew he was becoming 'quite famous', and she enthusiastically went to most of Colin's club and King Country representative games, but because she generally couldn't afford to go to more than the tests that were held in Auckland, she wasn't aware of the extent to which he was becoming a commanding figure in the eyes of rugby folk throughout New Zealand. But she was amused to learn that prior to the 1960 tour, in a competition inviting rugby followers to write in and pick their All Black team, one young woman had chosen Meads for every position. 'I remember there was a photo of Colin reading this in a paper in the street in Wellington, or wherever the trials were being held, and laughing like hell. I read the write-ups of games and realised that he was playing well, but the paparazzi photographers were not around in those days, like they are with today's equivalent of Colin, Jonah Lomu. They've got Jonah up there on a pedestal, so much higher than the other All Blacks. I can't recall thinking it was ever like that with Colin.'

Verna knew Colin was an exceptional player, and saw him as the best around, but she wasn't going to be heard praising him in the presence of others. She says he never assumed he was an automatic choice for the All Blacks. 'Whenever a team was due to be announced, he was on tenterhooks. Is he going to get in? To Colin and me the worst thing that happened was when people came up and said, "Aw, you're a certainty." It made him even more anxious. Secretly, I never doubted he'd be picked.'

Perhaps surprising, to some, is Verna's assurance that she wanted to see Colin continue to play for the All Blacks for as long as he had a strong desire to do so. To her, Colin had 'a God-given gift', and she didn't feel she had 'the right to step in and say he couldn't use that ability. I'd like to think he'd have supported me if I'd had something like that. When I look back now, I think that my gifts were probably bringing up the children. If it hadn't been for me, he couldn't have done what he's done.'

Suggest that there are many people who see the likes of Verna as saintly, and that many saw her as extremely selfless and excessively tolerant, and she says she never saw it that way. She disagrees with those who allege that people who devote their lives to sport in the way that great figures like Colin Meads and others have are overly selfish, and she is adamant she has never shared such thoughts. She lived from one season to another.

'That's the way our life evolved. I never sat down and thought, "He's been playing for 14 years, it's time he gave it up." But looking back now, with the benefit of hindsight, I can see our lives were a bit different. Certainly if I hadn't had all the local support, we couldn't have done it. I remember Kelvin Tremain saying to Colin once, that he never got the amount of support, financially and in other ways, that we did. Kelvin moved around a bit, whereas Colin didn't; and the Waitete Club were just so proud to have All Blacks like Colin, then Stan, in their club, that they provided whatever help was required. And it wasn't just Waitete; other clubs in the King Country pitched in as well. They all put their hands in their pockets. So did the local drinking clubs; so did local people. Then the local mayor in Te Kuiti would arrange a farewell and a welcome home for them.'

In the early years of their marriage, Verna seldom saw Colin actually playing test rugby. Increasingly, though, she heard about his exploits and read about them. The Meads boys, Colin and Stan, were perhaps Te Kuiti's most famous celebrities in days before the term was in vogue. Not that they were ever comfortable with the term 'celebrity', and they would have cringed if they had been described as 'personalities'.

For Verna, Colin's fame didn't bring any more money, didn't lessen the amount of work she had to do around the home, caring for and bringing up their children. But she remembers with pleasure getting their first television set, 'a black and white repossessed one that we got for next to nothing' in 1967.

Year in, year out, while Colin was on tour, whenever Verna went in to Te Kuiti, she was stopped every few yards by person after person wanting to know if she had heard from him: 'How's he getting on? How's the team going? What's it like over there? Did you hear the last game?' She shared their enthusiasm 'and responded in kind'.

For Verna, while life was often far from easy, she says that she has 'benefited a great deal from Colin's involvement in rugby'. When the All Blacks, who had toured South Africa in 1960, were invited to play a match in Invercargill to raise funds for a new grandstand, Verna flew down. It was the first time she had visited the South Island. In 1971, Colin was one of seven All Blacks invited to play for an International XV against England as part of the English centenary celebrations. Pam Lochore and Verna

The match programme for the RFU's centenary match against a President's Overseas XV in 1971. Verna Meads made the trip to England for the celebrations — her first venture out of New Zealand.

39

went along on the trip. The Hogg family in Wellington paid her fare. They thought it was time she had a trip away. There have been many overseas trips since — to the UK a number of times, to South Africa three or four times — all because, says Verna, 'Colin's been an All Black'. Overall, Verna feels that she has been 'adequately recompensed' for the times she had to remain at home while Colin was away being an All Black.

For years Verna felt anonymous in public when in the presence of Colin Meads. And so, most likely, did others in the immediate vicinity of him. It's often that way for family and friends of famous people. Verna found this amusing more than irritating.

As for her view of the place of women — wives and partners — in the elite rugby scene, she sees it has 'having gone from one extreme to the other'. She cites the fuss the press made over forty years ago when it was learned that the wives of Ross Brown and Don Clarke were in Australia while the All Blacks were on tour. Verna says it was seen as 'shocking'. Contrast that, says Verna, with when the All Blacks were on tour in the mid-1990s. It was decided the team needed to regroup and sharpen its focus, and wives and partners were asked to stay away. One of the women was adamant she was going along and no one would stop her. Says Verna, 'I look at it this way. For today's players, rugby is their job. They are overseas playing rugby for New Zealand, and if the womenfolk can't organise themselves to do things together, or singly, while the men are doing their job, then there's something amiss. I don't think the women should be looking to live in the men's pockets. I think it's more likely to hinder rather than help the men do their jobs.'

Verna is astonished by the number and the frequency of the cost-free telephone calls that players and officials make home these days. She laughs now at 'the disastrous call we had, screaming and yelling and shouting at one another' when he

Verna, with children Karen, Rhonda and Glynn — along with other wives of All Blacks — await the arrival home of the 1967 team at Auckland airport.

rang on his 21st birthday when on his first tour with the All Blacks in Australia in June 1957. This was two days after he had scored his first test try in the second test at Brisbane. He played part of the game on the wing because Frank McMullen had been injured. Meads could have been excused for feeling at a bit of a loss, more remote than he had ever felt on the farm back home. But the one thing Meads the rugby player liked to do most was run like hell with the ball, and this he did.

After their shouting match on the phone in 1957, Verna recalls they vowed never to make phone calls again while Colin was away touring, and they never did until he became All Black manager in the 1990s. 'But,' says Verna, 'he did write twice a week when he was playing on tour. That was very good, for Colin. There was nothing very evocative, though, for he was never much for description.' As for, 'today's young women,' Verna thinks they 'have so much going for them. They've got all this lovely money; they've got all the trips, but they need to watch that they don't look to take up too much of the players' time when they're away. Now that rugby's a job, they have to be mindful of the need to keep their distance and remain fairly self-reliant.'

For all of rugby's so-called advances, Verna 'still feels that Colin played in a better era. The only thing that's better about rugby today is the money. Colin and his team-mates lived on the smell of an oily rag in comparison. When they played there were dinners after matches. The wives and partners go along these days. When Colin was on the NZRFU Council, I accompanied him to test matches and the rugby union paid for my travel costs and accommodation. It struck me how different things were. Colin had told me that at post-match dinners in his playing days, both teams mixed at the tables — one All Black, one Frenchman, and so on — and this meant they socialised and became friends. But when I went along as a councillor's wife, it was obvious that the All Blacks sat with their wives and partners. I had no problem with that, but they did not mix with the opposition. Often, All Blacks would get up before dessert was served and go off to a nightclub. The opposition might just as well have not been there.' Verna shares Colin's view that the advent of professionalism has brought losses as well as gains, and that rugby is in danger of becoming more of a business than a game.

Verna has fond memories of staying at the home of Willie John McBride near Belfast when Colin and Willie were guests on a speaking tour of the UK in 2001. She also recalls a three-week speaking tour in 1999, when Colin, Willie and Frik du Preez made a series of fund-raising appearances in South Africa. This tour was organised to raise funds to provide a satellite security service to help protect white farmers who were being killed on their farms in southern Africa.

Verna is emphatic: 'I can't imagine the current All Blacks being friendly enough with their opposition to have the sort of contact that Colin and his team-mates had. He made some great friends. We exchange Christmas cards and letters.' On one trip to the UK, she remembers going to the Cardiff Rugby Club and meeting 'half a dozen members of Welsh teams Colin had played against, maybe more, and he has met them several times since. I'm sure that sort of thing would be unheard of today.'

Verna has long been a great fan of rugby. 'Exceptionally so when Colin was playing. I used to love watching him run with the ball. I'd stand up and scream and yell and shout.' Somewhat surprisingly, Colin was unaware of his wife's vocal enthusiasm. Neither of them had watched a game together until 1976, the year after he stopped playing rugby. 'When we went along to the game at Taumarunui, he was astounded. I think he was embarrassed too. He kept looking at me and saying, "Stop that, stop that," and I just flung his arm away. Afterwards I think he came to accept that that was me and didn't take any more notice.'

What is it about the game that Verna likes so much? She found it exciting, and she particularly liked what she always thought of as 'Sunday rugby. Early and late in the season matches featuring Harlequins or Barbarians teams — and the King Country Foresters and Olympians. These teams played purely for the love of the game. They had invited name players and the games were always to raise funds for some worthy organisation. I loved them.'

She didn't like dirty play, and was contemptuous of a few local players who always tried to 'bring Colin down a peg or two when he came back from playing in the All Blacks. I think they were out to make sure he didn't get too big for his boots, as they saw it. There was one lady, locally, who would run up and down the sideline shouting, "Kill him, kill him," and waving her umbrella. Given who it was, I could laugh about that. But I never liked seeing players getting kicked.'

Verna knew from the way Colin used to talk that he had a reputation as being a very hard, uncompromising player; and, in some circles, as a dirty player. She knew that Wilson Whineray, as All Black captain, thought that a captain 'couldn't be seen to be breaking the law'. She knew of his occasional request: 'Piney, can you deal with this problem I've got.' Colin's reputation as a rough, tough nut 'probably started from that', she thinks. 'Possibly Brian Lochore may have been in the same mould as Wilson, in regard to not wanting to engage in rough stuff, although Wilson was a university boxing champion, so he could handle himself. And I've no doubt Brian could, too but Brian would be less likely even than Wilson to deal to anyone, I would think.'

Does that side of Colin Meads' rugby reputation truly reflect his character and behaviour generally? 'No,' says Verna, 'I have never known him to get involved in a fight outside of rugby.' And while she has never seen Colin as physically aggressive generally, she says, 'The Meads as a family are very fiery, and at one time Colin would blow his stack — not so much now as he used to — so as I came from a family that didn't do that, it took me years to learn to deal with it. For a time I took it personally. If something went wrong, I thought he was getting at me, whereas it was the matter itself, not me in particular. Things have a habit of going wrong on farms.'

Later, when Colin retired from rugby, Verna remembers that watching games made him extremely tense. He remained silent and concentrated, as if he was physically and mentally still involved in the actual game. But gradually he became more relaxed, even to the extent of singing out advice to the referee and commenting on what players were doing right or wrong. 'He's definitely mellowed,' says Verna, 'although he still clings to the belief that there's no point in playing if you don't go out there determined to try to win. He never liked being beaten, oh no, but a loss didn't leave him embittered.'

Like a true rugby fan, Verna has her favourite players among the All Blacks she has seen. For her, though, playing ability was far from the only criterion. If she liked a player a lot personally, he became one of her favourites. 'Kel Tremain was a great player. Wilson Whineray was very good. And Stan Meads; Stan was a terrific player. I don't think he ever got his dues as a player. He was in Colin's shadow all the time. And then Colin played on after Stan gave up, which meant he got forgotten about a bit. Colin had this tremendous respect for Stan's ability, but the fact that they were brothers didn't come into it. Colin's no sentimentalist like that. To hear Colin talk about Stan is to know that he found him terrific to play with. Stan has had a lot to put up with. I still have great admiration for him.'

When Colin was still playing, one incident had a big effect on Verna. She says the All Blacks were about to travel overseas, and she was spoken to by a lift attendant when in Auckland to farewell the team. The attendant said that when his sister was engaged to a chap who was picked for an earlier All Black side, she had told him she didn't want him to go, so he didn't. 'He told me,' says Verna, 'that later she'd said that she'd never regretted anything as much in her life. That remark made a deep impression on me, and it might have influenced me — or at least confirmed my feeling, that it would be wrong of me to try to stop Colin going away with the All Blacks.'

Verna found quickly that almost every time Colin appeared in the All Black jersey people were saying how well he had played. 'Even old Terry McLean, whom Colin didn't get on with all that well in his early days as an All Black, was later to write that pressures on Colin to retire were based on references to his age, not his ability, and that he should play and continue to be picked for as long as he was good enough.'

She says, 'To be honest, I was sad when he gave up playing for the All Blacks.' It is as if she saw him as some relentless, indefatigable, mighty warrior who performed great deeds on the field of play — not just for Colin Meads, but for his wife and family and friends within the King Country region, and for the small island nation, New Zealand, near the so-called bottom of the world. As if Colin strengthened New Zealand's identity by being at the forefront of a team, the All Blacks, who at that time were the only New Zealand sporting side who set the standard in their sport worldwide. 'I never enjoyed watching the All Blacks as much after Colin gave up as I had before,' says Verna. 'To me there was magic in watching him play, it was as simple as that.'

In Verna's view, the All Blacks had a very good team for several years when Colin was at his best. One or two newcomers appeared, but the team remained largely the same for a number of seasons, especially in the forwards. But there's no suggestion that players of his day were more virtuous, whatever way one looks at it. As Colin says, if substantial amounts of money had been available in his day, then many of the players would have been offering themselves to the highest bidders, just as many tend to today.

Verna was wary of journalists and their ability, as she saw it, to make things up or twist a remark and highlight it to attract attention. Journalists often rang Verna when Colin was off playing for the All Blacks, wanting to know what was going on, and for her opinions. She rarely knew details of what was happening on or off the field, and did not think it appropriate that she should be expressing opinions in respect to All Black rugby.

Media people rang her after the All Blacks had lost to Newport in Wales in 1963. Brian Lochore's wife, Pam, was also rung and was astounded and dismayed to find she had been quoted as saying she was glad the All Blacks had lost.

Talk to Verna and it is clear she is a stoical, stalwart person who unabashedly says she remains proud of Colin. 'He hasn't altered over time. He isn't big-headed, has no airs and graces. People admire him for that. Go to the Waitete clubrooms and they still gather around him.'

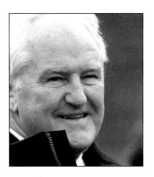

Wilson
WHINERAY

Wilson Whineray is a Knight, so honoured for his services to rugby and business in New Zealand. He lives in tasteful and, by Colin Meads' standards, opulent urban surroundings in the prosperous Remuera suburb of Auckland. Whineray speaks quietly; he is polite, gracious. He appears, on the surface anyway, mild-mannered yet hearty in a restrained sort of way. He comes across as tolerant, but one who respects and prefers to see evidence of discipline and drive. Whineray is familiar with the corporate and managerial world and is no stranger to the boardrooms of the country. Until recently, that made him unusual in sporting circles — and possibly unique in his rugby generation. Whineray has always been greatly interested in sport in general, as well as rugby in particular, but not consumed by such interest.

It is over to others to work out which of those traits and qualities he and Meads share, and to muse over why, and how, they came to hold each other in such high regard. The easy answer is their mutual rugby experiences. It also has a lot to do with their belief in the importance of loyalty to those who depend on you when the acid goes on.

Whineray likes Meads and has long regarded him as a good friend. They met, first, Whineray thinks, during a New Zealand Colts trial match in Wanganui. He was, he says, 'a city boy, a university boy' whereas Colin Meads was quite the opposite, 'long-limbed' and a bit gangly, clearly 'a country boy all over'. Contrast this with Whineray's build, tending to the stocky, a New Zealand Universities' boxing champion with both academic and sporting ambitions. They went on the Colts tour to Ceylon in 1955 and soon grew to respect each other.

Whineray and Meads were both selected to tour Australia as All Blacks in 1957. 'I'll never forget watching Colin when he pulled on his first All Black jersey. He vowed, gruffly, "No bugger's going to get this off me for a while."' Whineray says he felt there and then that in Meads was a man with far, far greater than normal resolve. Thereafter Whineray and Meads played together in most of the tests the All Blacks contested up until Whineray 'pulled out in 1965. But not Colin, it was if he played on forever.'

Meads soon became one of Whineray's most trusted lieutenants — minder, bouncer, athletic mammoth, mean but never mean-spirited. 'He was not so much humble, more self-effacing. Uncomplicated rather than simple, full of common sense. He never did daft things off the field and was always modest. Colin often wondered what all the fuss was about in respect to his abilities, and to lots of other things too, for that matter.'

Whineray found Meads an excellent tourist. 'Colin loved the off-field social life, the rugby friendships and camaraderie. He was friendly with nearly all of his most ardent on-field foes, the likes of Willie John McBride and Frenchman Walter Spanghero for example. And Frik du Preez.'

Whineray sees Meads and himself to an extent 'as creatures of another era' in so far as seeking to socialise and retain contact with many of those they played against. Both Whineray and Meads are 'grateful we played in our era. In many ways it was an age of innocence. Piney wasn't naive, though there were few less pretentious than him. I sometimes think today's rugby world tends to produce a few too many players for whom it's a case of just another day at the office. Modern players would think us loopy for playing for nothing. But I think rugby had to change and go professional or many of the best players would have gone to league.'

Reflecting, Whineray reckons that, 'When I was first All Black captain at 23, we were straight, unsophisticated. Today's lot may well be a lot more clued up.'

It is a pity, says Whineray, that so much attention has been paid to those games in which Meads figured in incidents deemed to have been overly vigorous physically. 'I think it has to be said that 99 per cent of Colin's games were good games — no murky stuff at all. And it needs to be remembered that there was always someone having a dig at him.' Whineray nods, implying that he and others found that tiresome, and that it was something that virtually no other player had to contend with to anywhere near the same degree. But he said it did give rise to a number of memorable and highly amusing incidents. For instance, when one England forward complained about Meads whacking him, Whineray heard Pinetree's gruff rejoinder, 'Stop pushing me and I'll stop punching you.' Then in the lineout in a game in Wales — Whineray thinks it may have been against Llanelli — he remembers the prop Ken Gray, who was being obstructed, saying to Meads, '"Colin, this prick's pissing me off. I know what I'd do if I was playing for Petone. What do I do here?" Unhesitatingly, Colin shot back, "Dong him." So Ken did, biff. All right I thought, but the trouble was it was right out in front of the main stand. I thought, Fancy going to Pinetree for advice. And I took Ken aside at the next opportunity and told him, "Jesus, don't ever do that again right out in front of the stand. You could get sent off and I'll have some juggling and explaining to do."'

Meads and Willie John McBride, the Irish captain, on the field 'were like chemical compounds that exploded', says Whineray. After McBride had belted Meads in the 1963 test at Lansdowne Road in Dublin, Whineray looked around for his number one lock and went back to find him down and 'bent like a staple. I said to him, "What's wrong with you?" I knew what had happened, told him to get to the next lineout somehow. When Pinetree arrived I heard him growl, "McBride,

PETER BUSH

Eight years after their 'Donnybrook' at Lansdowne Road, Meads and Willie John McBride were still like 'chemicals that exploded' on the field. Here, referee John Pring lays down the law to the two great warhorses in the first test between the All Blacks and the Lions in 1971 at Carisbrook, Dunedin.

what you've done is declare total war.'" Actually, according to Whineray, McBride hit the deck soon after, while Meads was still regrouping — honing his senses — and it's thought that Skip may have been responsible.

Whineray hasn't forgotten, either, about when Stan was felled in a lineout against the Springboks at Eden Park in 1965. It was just before halftime. He went to Stan and asked, 'How are you, Snow?'

Stan mumbled, 'Not too good.'

'I told him to take his time, even though we were waiting for him to come and join a scrum. Then a shadow fell over us. It was Pinetree. "How are you, Snow?" Same answer as before: "Not too good." Piney's response was blunt and immediate. "Well, you'd better get good in a hurry. We've a scrum to set and we've not gone back before and we're not going back this time."'

Whineray says the Meads brothers were wonderful together, and formidable when pitted against each other too. Stan was smaller, but pound for pound he was just as tough and he played above his weight. In Whineray's opinion their slavery around the farm was one of the reasons why they were apt to turn up for early training half a stone or more below their ideal weight, Stan especially. 'But both were a captain's dream on the field. They had flair as well as technical excellence, and they played full out for the whole 80 minutes. Just like Tremain and Gray. We had a terrific pack of forwards like that.'

Whineray has never lost his respect for Colin Meads and is one among many who sees the irony in the fact that Pinetree's contribution to New Zealand rugby has been greater than his return, personally, 'not that Colin has ever worried over much about that as far as I have seen'.

3.

THE HARD MAN

'I was mean in the sense that I wanted to win and thought we had to win when wearing the All Black jersey.'

FOR OVER 40 YEARS, COLIN MEADS HAS BEEN SEEN AS PERHAPS THE MOST DOMINANT FIGURE IN ALL BLACK RUGBY. REFERENCES TO HIM HAVE CARRIED MYTHOLOGICAL OVERTONES. SOME HAVE DEPICTED HIM AS LIKE JUPITER PRESIDING OVER THE ROMAN GAMES. CAN WE ASSUME, THEN, THAT MEADS KNEW OF HIS REPUTATION AND FELT BOUND TO ACT ACCORDINGLY?

No, he says that he was mostly unaware of the extent to which the lore surrounding him was developing. The 'legend stuff', as he puts it, has often amused him. When there have been signs of trouble at the Waitete club, for instance, Meads has sometimes been summoned to intercede and douse the flames. 'But I've never been a scrapper; I've never had even the slightest inclination to want to get into a ring. The likes of Fergie McCormick saying I was a mean man when I pulled on the jersey with the silver fern on it just added to the myth. I was mean in the sense that I wanted to win and thought we had to win when wearing the All Black jersey. But I wasn't like that otherwise.'

What Fergie McCormick said was that Meads was 'a terrible man with the silver fern on. He regarded the All Black jersey as pure gold.' All Meads will agree with there is the last bit.

However, there is a common thread through all of the stories about Meads as a player and a man, and that is his oft-stated remark that all he's wanted, in so far as rugby's concerned, is to be remembered as an All Black, 'and a good one'. There's stern affirmation in Meads' voice as he nods, feels the phrase is worth repeating: 'That's right, an All Black — and a good one.'

It is a measure of just how good an All Black Meads was that few New Zealanders have ever been better known.

It is often said, in the field of advertising, that 'name recognition' is all. That would seem to be true in a great many cases: ask yourself what we associate with Speight's, Kentucky Fried or McDonald's, and most people will come up with the right answers. Ask most people the length and breadth of New Zealand who or what 'Pinetree' is and a high percentage will be in no doubt that Pinetree is Colin Meads, and that his field is rugby.

That recognition is, in part, indicative of the importance of rugby football in New Zealand. But it is also a tribute to Meads himself in the sense that his is a name that is well known outside of sport.

So where did the name come from? Meads recalls that when away in Japan with the New Zealand Under-23 rugby team in 1958 — captained by Wilson Whineray — Roger Boon and Ross Brown of Taranaki said that he looked a bit like a bloke they'd known who worked in a sawmill in their locality. Meads says, 'They told me, "He's gone. Died. There's got to be another. You're it. Pinetree." To be honest,' says Meads, 'I wasn't overly impressed initially, but the minute they saw I was sensitive about it, I was gone. The name stuck.'

Within a few years, not long after Meads had become an All Black, and was quickly establishing the reputation that would make him a legend, one of his favourite team-mates, Kel Tremain, started calling him 'Piney'. So that's what he became in the All Black camp.

Later on, when Meads was a selector, then manager of the All Blacks, 'some of the younger ones — I think Mike Brewer and his lot might have started it — called me "Tree".'

All over New Zealand you can find rugby folk referring to Pinetree, or Piney, or Tree. Some even refer to 'The Tree'.

'I don't mind what they call me,' says Meads, 'and anyway there wasn't a lot I could do about it. I answer to any of them now.' There's a pause, then a chuckle: 'I've been called a lot worse.'

Those who played with and against Meads found him formidable. Willie John McBride said he was a 'big bugger'. Meads himself doesn't mind having been seen as formidable: he also likes to think he was seen as fit, skilled, loyal, fair . . . and a few other things as well. A loyal All Black who had an almost fanatical reverence for the All Black jersey and a deep pride in playing for New Zealand.

While he may have been fairly big in his time, he would certainly not have been big by today's rugby-playing standards. Meads never really saw himself as big, he saw himself as big enough, but only just. He hopes he was, and is, big in other respects. Big-hearted, perhaps, uncomplicated, fair-minded and generous-spirited.

He can see why he got the 'hard man' reputation but thinks that many so-called 'hard men' in life generally like to get involved in fights. 'But, I've never been like that; never been one of those who, when he's got a few drinks aboard, becomes aggressive. My advice to people is, "If you don't get happy when you drink, don't drink". I hope

Meads poses with a member of the All Japan side at Fukuoka, 1958. The NZ Under-23 side, captained by Wilson Whineray, beat the Japanese in all three 'tests'. It was on this tour the famous 'Pinetree' nickname was born.

Peter Bush

I was a hard man in rugby, but the image doesn't apply to me outside the game. I played for the team. Sometimes that meant I got involved in some hard stuff. Remember, in my playing days — it's different now with the linesmen and TV replays — your team could lose out if you allowed certain tactics to continue.

'Any hardness I might have possessed naturally may well have been added to by the nature of the team talks we got. I often got told that if I thought I was a good lock, then I'd better remember I was marking a guy who some thought of as the best in the world. And the coach would say that he wanted to be able to look me in the eye after the game and see who is the best. We certainly got encouraged in that way.'

Meads aimed to leave the field believing that he was at least the equal of those he'd played against. Now and then he came off a ground thinking that he'd not done quite enough. And he found that playing for King Country against, often, stronger opposition was in some ways harder than playing for New Zealand. 'It was easier playing for the All Blacks a lot of the time. I remember playing for King Country against France in 1968. The French had that great player Walter Spanghero. He could play as a loose forward as well as a lock. He was a big, strong bugger, and that day he gave me a helluva bath. He was one player I couldn't rip much ball off — I couldn't upset him too much. It wasn't all beer and skittles for Colin Meads. I got my share of hidings; I got done over.

'When I was playing in France in 1967, the media were building up a huge image of the lock Benoit Dauga. He was France's answer to the question of how to beat the All Blacks. The French selectors picked the two teams that played us before the test. The papers were full of references to, and pictures of, Benoit Dauga, but he didn't play against us before the test, he was a reserve. After each game,

Tête-à-tête at Christchurch. Meads and Kel Tremain are the trouble-shooters here against the French in Christchurch, 1968.

Fred Allen — who could be a cruel, aggressive little so-and-so — would come up, look around, and give you one in the ribs. Then he'd say, "Can you handle that? Do you think you can handle that?" There'd be a twinkle in his eye. He'd be asking if I could take it from Dauga. What do you say? If I'd said, "Yeah, I can," he'd have said, "You skiting prick." If you were non-committal, he'd say you were a gutless so-and-so. You couldn't win. I'd generally say something like, "Well just line him up, get him on the field, I'll see how good he is then."

'I was getting really annoyed by Fred, and by the time the test came round I'd had a gutsful of Dauga. In the test, I did a 'Willie-away' move and got tipped over at the back of the lineout. One of the French put the boot into me and cut open the back of my head. It was a good one, too — a big gash. As I struggled up and went to the sideline, all I could think of was Dauga. Dauga Dauga Dauga, that's all that was in my head. It was HIM. I came back all bandaged up. All I could think of was, "I'll get even with that big bugger. I'll do him." At the first opportunity I plastered him. I whacked him so hard I actually cut my hand open. That turned septic too. Hygiene in those days was . . . well, it didn't really exist.

'After the match I had to get that stitched up too. I had 17 or 18 stitches in my head. Fred Allen reckoned my backside twitched every time the needle went in. That's probably right since there was no anaesthetic. It was a pretty casual affair all round compared with today. The French wandered in and out of our dressing room — we all did that in those days.

'That night we all went to the after-match dinner. No one in our side had more than a few words of French but somehow or other we communicated — we had some great times. I had a towel round my neck because the wound was weeping, so that made me look a sight. Benoit Dauga came over. I'd cut my hand on his teeth and broken his nose. He was stammering, trying to find the words to ask me a question. Pierre Villepreux, their fullback, helped out. He could speak good

Strong men

Stories were rife throughout Meads' career about just how strong he was. It was implied, if not stated outright, that in Meads' time, no one was stronger. Pinetree never agreed with that. There were, he is adamant, many others who were just as strong or stronger. The Welshman, Rhys Williams, who came to New Zealand in the 1959 Lions side was, says Meads soberly, 'a terribly strong man. He was easily one of the best locks I played against. You could not upset him. Johan Claassen of South Africa was no cream-puff, and certainly a great player. Keith Murdoch was mighty strong; Ken Gray (pictured) too. For a tall prop he had a very strong back. He was a clever man too. Ken died in his sleep in November 1992, aged 54. He'd had a medical the week before. It was a great shame, and a shock.' For the record, Gray played 24 tests and 50 games for the All Blacks from 1963–69.

Sports Digest

English. He told me Dauga wanted to know why I'd belted him. I was astonished and pointed to my head. "That's why. The dirty so-and-so . . . I was getting even for that." Villepreux explained and Dauga raised his arms and spluttered, "Mais, non . . . non . . . non. Plantefol . . . Alain Plantefol [Dauga's locking partner].'"

When he looks back now, Meads 'blames' Fred Allen for his needling during the build-up. Dauga represented all the French forwards in Meads' eyes. Meads saw him as a formidable lineout opponent. He was, says Meads without a hint of malice, 'a big, ugly bastard'.

Meads believes he was typical of his era in many respects. 'I always considered myself a fair player,' says Meads, 'even though I was sent off for allegedly kicking Chisholm at Murrayfield. I didn't and wasn't kicking at him. I kicked at the ball. I admit I retaliated at times, and that didn't help my image. It got me into a bit of strife.'

As an example he refers to the incident involving David Watkins when the 1966 Lions were in New Zealand. Meads has seen a bit of Watkins in ensuing years and sees him as 'a good little guy'. But he was 'a cheeky little bastard in those days. Tap kicks had been recently introduced and that changed things. Watkins tap-kicked and I charged. I nearly charged it down but just missed it. As I went past, this little fella give me one in the guts. I thought, "You dirty little . . ." so I give him a backhander. Well, he went down and did he put on an act. The referee saw it, the crowd saw; they booed me. Mine was purely a reflex reaction. The press gave me stick . . .'

Stan Meads says he was right there with Colin and saw the whole thing. His version is the same as his locking partner's. 'Frank Laidlaw, the Lions hooker, made a great fuss. I saw him as an instigator in a way — it was noteworthy that he was one making a great fuss prior to Colin being ordered off at Murrayfield a year or so later — and Watkins' performance was pure Hollywood.'

On the issue of unacceptable play generally, Meads says sardonically, 'I've played against players that you didn't want to fall over in front of. There were a lot of players at top level who would kick the proverbial out of you. I never condoned that, and I never did it. I saw it as cowardice. And I copped a fair bit of it.'

Down the decades all players and coaches have agreed that test rugby is no place for the meek or mild. As recent assistant All Black coach Tony Gilbert said, in test football, when things got tough, unless a forward held his own, at the very least, then the opposition lost respect for him. Meads agrees. 'I was impressed,' he says, 'by the way the young Canterbury lock, Chris Jack, stood up to Mark Andrews of the Springboks in 2001.'

Meads accepts there's not so much 'skullduggery' going on these days. In his time he says 'you had to do something about it to stop them winning the ball illegally; if you didn't, then you came second.'

During Meads' career, referees didn't see a lot of the rough stuff that went on. He doesn't want to give himself a medal for duplicity, but he admits that, 'We were clever; we waited until the ref was standing on the other side of the lineout. Often, though, they did see what went on, but a lot of the time they operated on the old Pat Murphy [a leading test referee of the day] theory, "Why are you getting hit? I must be missing something." I sometimes said to the ref, "If you don't stop him doing that, there'll be trouble." To which the response would often be, "Oh, no, oh, no, we'll fix it. I'll catch him, I'll have a look at him." And then you sometimes got a couple of penalties for no reason.'

All of which makes one wonder, what happened when Meads engaged in mischief of his own? Meads replies, 'Well, once, early on, Tiny Hill taught me a great lesson. I took a swipe at Tiny and he waited until there was about a minute to go and he floored me. He winded me and I was doubled over groaning and moaning, and then the final whistle goes. Tiny came up to me laughing and said, "Good one, eh? Told yer I'd get yer." Served me right for pushing him. He'd lowered the boom on me properly.'

Different countries had varying perspectives of the Meads image. Notably, for a long time he was never quite the legend in Australia that he was in rugby circles elsewhere. He tended to have saved his greatest performances for other nations in other places. In fact, a significant number of rugby folk in Australia were hostile towards him. Meads says that for a time that was correct, he was not popular in certain circles in Australia. What did it was his part in the awful leg injury sustained by the superb halfback Ken Catchpole in a test at Sydney in 1968. 'That incident,' says Meads, 'was one of the things that tarred me. Of course, I felt sorry for Catchy, but I never felt guilty about it. Those were the days when we were getting a lot of ball, and on the times when the opposition got it, Waka Nathan was cutting across and spoiling their efforts to run it. So Catchy was ducking back into the forwards — if he did it once, he did it half a dozen times. And this was in the first half. The Wallaby forwards gathered around him and kept the ball.

'We got the message from Fred Allen, "For Christ's sake, put the little b———— on the ground, then see if he wants to keep coming back in amongst you, you big, soft, so-and-sos." Fred wanted us to ruck. He thought Catchy was contributing to killing the ball. Eventually, after halftime, we caught him again. I grabbed one of his legs and gave it a yank to tip him up. Unfortunately, his other leg was trapped and he ended up doing the splits. The ruck collapsed, I was still hanging onto his leg and muscles got severely ripped. I honestly didn't know his other leg was pinned.

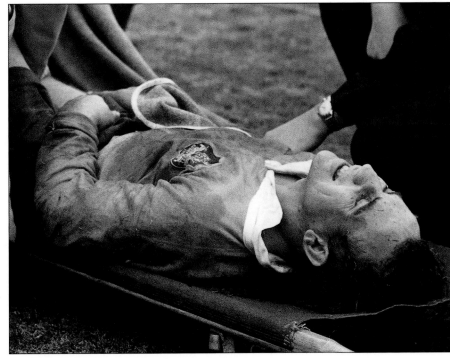

Ken Catchpole is stretchered off the Sydney Cricket Ground in 1968. Says Meads of the controversial incident, 'Of course, I felt sorry for Catchy, but I never felt guilty about it.'

'I always saw Catchy as a good little guy. I went across to a testimonial dinner for him some years ago. I think over $300,000 was raised for him. It was a big affair. One radio station's announcer rang me a few days before the dinner and said his advice was not to come. I said I'd been sent tickets, why shouldn't I go? He said that the crowd would "boo hell out of you". My response was to say that it was all the more reason why I should go. I went over and was asked to say a few words. What they were wanting me to do was apologise. I didn't. I was extremely sorry for Catchy, for what happened. I remembered actually going to Tonga with a charity team a couple of years later and Catchy was there playing with us. Playing extremely well, actually.'

When Meads was in his prime, the All Blacks were said to be the hardest and most competitive of all international rugby sides, but in these respects the men in black have become progressively less dominant over the past 10 to 20 years. Meads' view is that rule changes over the years took much of the harder physical aspects out of the game. He also thinks it is a 'mental thing too. People now think that in order to get strong, gymnasium training is essential.' Meads thinks this may have been overemphasised. And while he doesn't set himself and his brother Stan up as the ultimate 'how to get fit for rugby' models, he is sure it helped to have had to cut a hundred acres of scrub by hand each summer. It was 'terribly hard work, and you used every muscle in your body — or so it felt. We had to walk the hills, balance in awkward spots, use our shoulders and arms to cut the damned stuff with slashers. Our work made us hard physically. Now they get helicopters in to spray scrub, or great big bulldozers with huge rollers that crush everything.'

It would be wrong to assume that Meads pines for days when there was no alternative to work the way he and Stan did; no alternative to digging post-holes with shovels and setting the posts in with a rammer. But he is certain that as farming in New Zealand has changed, so has New Zealand rugby. He also agrees that the uncritical, and with some, obsessive preoccupation with gymnasium training that was the fashion up until recently has changed for the better. Meads says, though, that we have a habit of inventing new words and terms for much the same things that occurred before. 'We used to say we did a lot of running, now they talk of "aerobic fitness". It's easy to fool me.' One smiles and thinks, not likely.

In regard to fitness for rugby, Meads thinks the work needs to be tailored to fit the individual. 'If we can use Sean Fitzpatrick as an example. No one was tougher than Sean, no one was harder. He was rugged. He did his gym work and really worked at everything he did. He was a great trainer. What I'm saying is that in many cases, it is an attitude thing. Sean did the running too. Now that he is away from playing rugby, it is noticeable that he's getting smaller. Presumably through not doing the work that he used to. But no one came tougher or harder than him.'

Fitzpatrick recognised, and accepted, one indisputable fact, says Meads, that there are no short cuts to fitness for rugby. In his own case, Meads admits that in the last two years of his rugby-playing epoch, when he played club rugby solely, 'I was taking short cuts and the standard of my rugby reflected that. While a lot of people were saying, "Aw, he's still playing well," by hell it was hard work for me, and I couldn't last out the games the same.'

Yes, one says, that is no doubt true. But he was a pretty old bloke to be playing senior rugby, so it is no wonder some might say that. It highlights one fact: for as long as he played, Meads never saw himself as too old to play rugby up to a standard equal to and often better than anyone around him on the field. Sternly he says,

Forget the gym . . . tough, unrelenting farm work meant Meads was always one of the fittest players in first class rugby.

'Of course, no All Black can afford to take short cuts.' Ask him if he ever left the field feeling so completely shattered that he felt he couldn't give any more, and he struggles to think of more than one or two examples, and they are vague recollections only. He never felt utterly spent when coming off the field: 'It's about half or three-quarters of an hour later, after you've showered, that you feel completely poked. Often it hits you in stuffy rooms at after-match functions. There were a few times during my career that I had to leave functions and go outside and recuperate. After the second test against South Africa in 1960, at Newlands in Cape Town, there was a huge, packed function. I had to get out; I was buggered, and there was Johan Claassen sitting in the stand. We had a talk. I told him it was too hot and muggy inside.'

As for the day after, Meads seldom had to struggle to get up and under way. Occasionally he had a few sore spots — 'bruises from kicks in the backside and elsewhere' — and in such cases he found that the best thing was to go for a run.

Nowadays the players are more likely to be found in the local swimming pool. Not Meads: 'I was always a believer that water was bad for you because it softened your muscles. Someone had told me that once, said that going swimming would take your edge away. If we stopped over for a day or so in Hawaii en route to the northern hemisphere, we were warned about the dangers of too much swimming. "Keep out of that bloody water," is what we were told. Now they have pool sessions to relax the muscles.'

Meads admits to being a little superstitious. His wife Verna says, 'a big bit'. When in the UK in 1963, at Newport in Wales, a game that the All Blacks lost, Meads says they had been training hard. 'I was feeling a bit stiff, so the night before the match I was talked into having a rub. It was in days when masseurs did not travel with the team as they tend to now.' The locals arranged for Meads to go along to a guy who worked on the Welsh team. He was said to be 'the best in the world', says Meads. 'They told me a rub from him would work miracles: loosen up my arms, legs, shoulders, the works. So I had the full rub, and the next day we lost. I vowed and declared I would never have another rub in my whole life, and I never did, before or after a match.

'I often had a sore back, so I put capsicum on it. That made the area warm. I put a bit of oil on first so the capsicum didn't burn. But I never let a masseur touch me. I always got another player or the baggage man to apply it. Mac McKenzie, a really nice guy, was one. He was our baggage man on the 1963–64 tour of the UK and he always put the stuff on before I went out.

'I never warmed up before games, either. I always thought the haka was the best warm up, because the opposition would be standing there freezing cold. I didn't like to warm up in the dressing room or run down the corridor as some players did for up to 10 minutes. They were buggered by the time they got out on the field.

'On this topic, I always quote shearing, for in my opinion it's the hardest work you can ever do. You don't see a shearer going over in the morning and shearing five sheep just to get his gear right. I think it is a silly idea running about for half an hour beforehand when you are going out there to run your guts out anyway.

'I think there are more muscles pulled and tendons torn today than there ever were in my playing days. Lifestyle has a lot to do with it. We walked or ran everywhere. If we went out to the back of the farm to shift some sheep, we could be away three hours. Now people drive just about everywhere.'

When Meads went for a run, mostly he consented to remove his farm boots and pull on a pair of sandshoes. But one year he was suffering from shin-splints. The doctor in Te Kuiti told him that all his running on the roads probably wasn't helping him. He advised Meads to run in his working boots and to run on grass around the farm. He remembers going home to find his 'old man had a big mob of bullocks in the front paddock and I went out with a torch to have a run around this paddock. It was the flattest one we had on the place. These bullocks spooked and took off, and three or four flattened fences later, they stopped. That was the last time I ran in boots in the dark on the farm with a torch.'

So when Meads concedes he had his 'silly superstitions', he says he wasn't the only one. Kelvin Tremain always cleaned his boots at the ground whereas Meads made a point of always cleaning his before midday in the hotel. Meads refused to start to get changed until half an hour before the game. 'If the game was at two-thirty, I would not take my shirt and tie or anything off until it was two o'clock.

Nowadays they are all out ages before running up and down the field. To me that is unnecessary, but I would never want to interfere with modern players.'

There was no one telling Meads and his team-mates what to do in respect to warm-ups and what to eat. He remembers that 'Mac Herewini always used to have poached eggs on toast between 10 and 11 in the morning before a test. He never had breakfast. We are silly buggers you know; we all have our little idiosyncrasies. I read an article a few years ago that said that too much sugar was bad for us. But then I remembered reading one in a women's magazine in the 1960s which said that sugar was the quickest way of getting energy into our bodies, that it was better than glucose. I was sitting at home getting ready to go to rugby and I'd read the article a few minutes before. So instead of putting two teaspoons of sugar in my cup of tea, I put in four. I had a great game that afternoon and from that day on I put four in every time. I didn't mention it to anyone else, but when I was away with the All Blacks I'd be putting six or seven or eight in. It was like syrup, terrible. But that was my last drink before the game. We weren't allowed to drink during the match.'

This brings Arthur Lydiard to mind. Meads recalls Lydiard, the great athletics coach, talking to the All Blacks about 1959, and telling them that their last drink should be three hours before they played. Which is one of several reasons why Meads has watched today's on-field water carriers with amazement and amusement verging on incredulity at times. For instance, when he watched the All Blacks playing the Springboks at Christchurch 'a couple of years ago, we kicked off. Springboks penalised, Andrew Mehrtens comes up, kicks a goal and out come the runners with the water-bottles. Gee, the boys were thirsty, they had been going for 30 seconds. It seemed like half the team had a swig.'

In South Africa, Meads says players sometimes craved a drink during a game. The heat and dust was well-nigh intolerable. Mouths would be full of dust, but there was no water at halftime. 'If you were quick you grabbed two quarters of orange.'

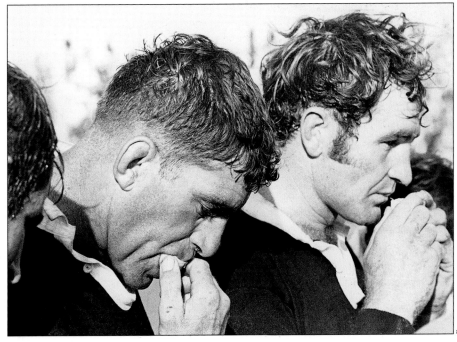

No water at halftime in Meads' day . . . 'if you were quick you grabbed two quarters of orange'. Meads and Ian Kirkpatrick in South Africa, 1970.

PHOTOSPORT

In the days leading up to a test match, Meads ate what he liked. He had no fads. Apples and oranges in the dressing room, a few beers after training. Meads can remember coach Fred Allen saying that 'two or three beers was okay. I can remember Fred coming up to me, stabbing a finger at me and alleging, "You've had four." "No, no, Fred, I've only had a couple." This was after training, around midday the day before a test. We didn't go out on the Friday night and have any more.'

Ask Meads if there were heart-rate monitors in his day and he looks blankly at you: 'What are they?' He can't ever recall checking his pulse-rate. And he laughs when he hears people talk of the need to find that 'extra competitive edge'; to him that is just another way of saying working out ways to get the drop on your opponent.

If Meads had a good game he was always thinking, 'What did I do beforehand that might have contributed to that?' He washed his laces at home and had one pair of boots, the old square-toed jobs. 'Then in the 1960s we started getting sophisticated. We had two pairs of boots, lightweights and heavyweights. Nowadays, they just take the sprigs out and put in a different set to suit the ground conditions. Not us, our sprigs were tacked in. We did have short and long sprigs, though. And when I was playing as a loose forward I used the lightweight boots; the heavyweights had bigger sprigs and I used them when playing lock. We had long-sleeved jerseys and, from time to time, I wore headgear. I wore it for the best

Them's the breaks

On the 1970 All Black tour of South Africa, in the game against Eastern Transvaal, Meads was kicked while lying on the ground and his arm was broken. This was tragic because, as Lochore said later, Meads had been great in the past, but here 'He was something to behold . . . just stupendous', and would have been absolutely 'dominant' in the tests.

Meads hadn't got the telegram he usually got from Verna before he ran out to play against Eastern Transvaal on 8 July. She'd been at the Waitete Club and had forgotten. For one with his superstitions, this was a bad omen. He should have known better: instead of running onto the field last, as was his practice, he ran out second, behind Lochore. He did that because he'd been made vice-captain. It wasn't a decision he agreed with. 'I thought that was stupid, me being made vice-captain. Chris Laidlaw or Ian MacRae would have been a more sensible choice. But the team said to me I had to go out second because I was the v-c. They were having me on.'

For all but one other match in his All Black career to that point, he'd run out last. The only other time he'd not been last was against Scotland at Murrayfield in 1967, and he'd been ordered off. Says Meads, 'Then, I thought I was running out last but I wasn't. Bill Davis was in the toilet.'

So it wasn't so much, as others had claimed, that he thought that if he ran out last New Zealand would lose, it was that he thought something would go wrong. Did it ever.

After being deliberately kicked in the game against Eastern Transvaal, Meads went to the sideline. He knew something was not right with his arm. He says, 'It was tingling and the doctor that examined it said he couldn't tell what was wrong. And then he said he didn't think it was broken. I thought, I'm not going off if it's not broken, I'd be a wimp if I went off just because someone had kicked my arm.'

One is reminded of Chris Laidlaw's remark, made on a television documentary in 2001, that players were 'more irrational in those days'. Even now Meads doesn't see his decision to return to the field as irrational. In those days part of a whole season once after I'd ripped half my ear off — that's what it seemed like — in a tackle. I had my normal run of cauliflower ears, which made me wear the headgear off and on.'

In the 1950s, Meads remembers, 'the flanker Bill Clark used to wear white headgear and he stood out, so I went and bought a set. But the coach said to me, "You get rid of that white headgear; you're offside half the so-and-so time, and you're sticking out like a sore toe." So I got rid of it. But I was willing to try anything. We used to wear shoulder pads, mainly to try to look as big as others. A few had other reasons for wearing them, though. Take Tiny Hill. He said the pads weren't to protect him, they were to protect others. Tiny had these bony shoulders and if he hit you in a tackle without his shoulder pads on you got hurt far more than when he was wearing them.'

Vaseline around the ears and elsewhere, yes, but sweatbands, no. 'I couldn't stand them,' says Meads. 'I always tell young players to massage Vaseline into their ears an hour or so before a match to soften them up. It stops the ears getting hard. You don't ever want to have to drain your ears. Once you drain them you never stop having problems with them; they get big and hard. I never drained mine.'

Outside the rugby season, Meads liked to drop in to the Waitomo Club in

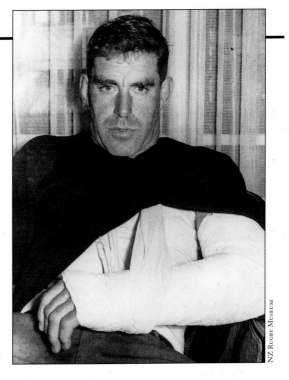

replacements were allowed but a doctor had to be called to verify a player would be unwise to continue. But Meads soon discovered that something was badly wrong. He couldn't hold onto his prop's shorts properly. The prop was Jake Burns. 'I said to him, "Look, I'm no help to you." Jake was struggling like hell anyway and with me not being able to pull him in, it was hopeless, so I suppose I should have gone off.'

When waiting for the broken arm to heal, Meads was desperate to keep himself fit and trained hard. He had various guards made for the arm and the last one, made in Cape Town, was 'just brilliant'. He found he could put it on easily and it felt good running around. Meads said, 'I can play with this.'

The referees were asked and they said that before they would let him play, they had to be convinced he couldn't use the guard as a weapon. He was granted permission from referees and the South African Board. 'How they thought I was going to use it as a weapon,' says Meads, 'I don't know.'

When he recommenced playing on 12 August, Meads said he'd only play in the Wednesday games. But the selectors — there were four of them, including Meads — had him play the next five games and then named him in the test team. In hindsight, Meads now thinks that, 'In fairness, I probably shouldn't have been in it.'

59

Te Kuiti on Friday evenings. 'We always used to tell politicians, that if they ever wanted any help, they should come to the Waitomo Club on a Friday afternoon and they would get all the advice in the world.'

The talk was about stock and stock sales, this breed and that; about politics and politicians of the day; about cricket, and, especially in Meads' company, about rugby players and rugby generally. A perennial topic was who and what made a good All Black. Meads saw scores of players who were good All Blacks at home, but not so good on tour. An example of the latter was Mac Herewini. To Meads, 'Mackie was a brilliant footballer, but two weeks away from home was all he could stand. I think a good All Black is one who can tour, enjoy himself, then line up once and possibly twice a week and give his all. Many can, some can't. There are all sorts. I remember Derek "Bluey" Arnold, a tough little joker, and a character. A good fella, good company, but inconsistent in his play. I wondered if he had it in him to be sufficiently dedicated to the cause.

'It's not easy. I remember Terry Lineen saying that the one thing he hated about rugby was the next game. Even if it was a social-type game, like playing for the Barbarians, the next game always seemed to be seen as the most important you'd ever played. That's what a man was always being told. He said he'd go back and play for his club, and the coach would be tearing into him and telling him it was the most important game they'd had all year.'

It's talk like Lineen's that fortifies Meads' long-held conviction that all great rugby players are resolute, resilient and aggressive. They have to be quick-thinking and quick on their feet, and skilful too — that goes without saying. They have to be as near indomitable as a man can be. And while Meads would never say that he saw himself that way, others did, thousands of them. That is a principal reason why he came to be seen as one of the icons of the game worldwide.

Meads says that coaches' expectations of the sort that bugged Lineen 'never worried me at all. It's a terrible game, rugby, one game you're playing in snow, the next it might be 30 degrees. You have to adapt. Some backs especially are good when it's dry and warm, but hopeless when it's wet and cold. You have to learn to handle all situations: Johannesburg one week, Dunedin the next is very much the way it is for the modern player.'

In a way, Meads was obstinate: he knew he was a marked man, and he relished the challenge that brought. He was Top Dog and, everywhere, from club rugby to the infernos of tests, a few players were bristling and growling, looking to humiliate him.

If Meads saw that some of his team-mates weren't fit enough, he told them so, bluntly. One result, at the Waitete club in Te Kuiti, was that now and then a couple of the fitter blokes would wait for him to arrive at practice. Then they would run with him, round and round the field in a protracted warm-up, intent upon exhausting Meads, hoping to hear him cry enough. As long-time friend and King Country player, coach and colleague Noel McQuilkin says with a triumphant laugh, 'No one succeeded.'

Fred
ALLEN

Both Fred Allen and Colin Meads make no secret of their admiration for each other's talents, and they also liked one another a good deal. Allen was All Black coach from 1966–68 and under him the national side went 38 games without being beaten. 'Even though I say it myself, I'm quite proud of that,' says Allen, now 82, and living in Auckland. No All Black coach thus far can point to such a record. Allen still follows rugby intently and often attends test matches with his old friend, former All Black prop Kevin Skinner.

Allen doesn't beat about the bush. 'To me, Colin Meads was the greatest rugby player ever. There's been no one better. They threw away the mould when they made Pinetree. He was an inspiration to the younger players in a side. He was a fanatic when it came to training and he always had this great will to win.'

But none of that, according to Allen, ever got in the way of Meads' essential modesty. 'He had a marvellous temperament; there was nothing swollen-headed about him. He was a fine rugby thinker with excellent ball-handling skills, and he could run fast for his size. Colin was no angel but I never saw him as dirty or vicious, just hard.

'Pinetree wasn't afraid to have his say anywhere, but he always listened to others too. A born leader but probably not exceptionally good as a coach. A lot of top players aren't. Look at Vic Cavanagh, Otago's coach of the late 1940s. Not known as a player but the best coach of all.'

Allen saw Meads as the greatest lock of all. 'He was a lock, no doubt, not a true loosie. To be a great lock you have to be strong, athletic and not shirk work; do road work, hill work. There are no short cuts. My impression is that some players today take a few short cuts, and they spend too much time standing around talking at practice. You don't need too many moves, but you have to get the ones you have right. It might be boring for some, but you've got to go over them again and again until they are right, and you've got to hang on to the ball. Players don't run on to the ball like they used to. Inside backs go too far and the gates close. One, two and spin the ball was our rule for fly-halves.'

Allen felt that Meads reflected the sorts of attitudes and disciplines men got from the army. 'I believed in disciplined play and the strength that comes from self-discipline. I think Colin saw it the same way.'

When on tour, Allen says, Meads came into his own. 'He was the ideal tourist — unlike that great little joker and excellent player Mac Herewini, say — because he didn't get upset generally and he never lost sight of the main purpose, to play and win rugby matches. Colin had no problem with hard training, he thrived on it. He got the balance right. For example, he liked a few beers, and so did a few of the blokes — Hoppy [Hopkinson] and Bruce McLeod for instance — and I had no objection to that. But I had one or two provisos. I used to tell them that I didn't want them getting on it in the day or two before a game, and I told them all in the team that they weren't to bleat if I got stuck into them at training. They had to be prepared to put the work in and no excuses.'

Meads was devoted to training. 'I was always impressed by that,' says Allen. 'No matter where we were, in hotels in Paris or Knightsbridge in London, Colin would get up between five and six in the morning and run five miles. He'd often drag a few younger guys along with him and then do everything he could to outsprint them at the end. He took Kirky [Ian Kirkpatrick] along once and wasn't too happy when he outsprinted him I can tell you.'

Meads had his own idiosyncratic ways. 'He made me laugh like hell every time we weighed in at airports. As he got on the scales he would be grabbing others' coats and bags. He may not have been that big by today's standards — he was 16 stone, though, and six feet four inches tall — but he was pretty big by the standards of the day. I used to say, "Colin, you don't have to do that. I know what you weigh."'

Allen saw no one tougher than Meads. He remembers him suffering a savage kick to the head during the first half of the test against France at Colombes Stadium in Paris in 1967. 'Piney thought it was Benoit Dauga who had done it. He took an unusually long time to get up and make his way to the next lineout. I was watching this intently and when, a bit later, I saw a lot of movement going on up and down the lineout, I said to those around me, "Oh hell, here it goes."'

'We had a Scottish doctor assigned to look after us and all he seemed to have in his bag was a bottle of gin. In the dressing room after the match he had a look at the gash in Piney's head. You could see he was concerned. "That'll need six or seven stitches at least. I haven't any anaesthetic; I think we'd better take you to the hospital." Piney would have none of that. "Do it here. Now," he said. I could see some of the players, Thorney and others, looking away and wincing and saying "Ooh" as the stitches went in. It looked like a huge and messy gash to me. Piney didn't say a word, not a sound.'

Meads, as recounted earlier in this chapter, tells the story a bit differently, and rather more stitches were required.

As Meads would say of instances when he was on the receiving end of brutal play, 'I just went back out there and got stuck into them, gave them hell.' That was true, indubitably, and tough as Meads was, Allen is sure 'There's no way they should have let Piney play in South Africa with a broken arm in 1970. That was just silly.'

'There's no way they should have let Piney play in South Africa with a broken arm in 1970. That was just silly.'
— Fred Allen

ROSS WIGGINS

Allen always felt allegations that Meads was a 'dirty' player were untrue and slanderous, and in part promoted by overseas media keen to ascribe New Zealand's general international rugby superiority as due as much to overly rough play as to genuine playing ability. He was appalled when Meads was sent off in the closing minutes of the 1967 test against Scotland at Murrayfield. 'For a start, the crowd didn't like Colin, possibly because he'd been pretty severe on some Scots players there back in 1964. I think crowd hysteria influenced the referee, Irishman Kevin Kelleher. Colin's head was all bandaged up as a result of the injury he'd got in Paris, so he looked a bit scary. But I'll swear on my deathbed that he didn't intend to kick the halfback Chisholm. I was just so sad seeing that big guy I liked and respected so much trudging off the field. Quite wrong.'

The other main disappointment of the tour, for Allen, was the cancellation of their fixtures in Ireland. 'I wanted the Grand Slam. We'd beaten England, Wales and Scotland. We'd have beaten Ireland too.'

Meads, unsurprisingly, agrees with that, and right from the outset he respected Allen for his knowledge and coaching abilities. Both Allen and Meads had deep resolve, saw eye to eye on what was required to play outstanding rugby. Both, too, hated even the prospect of All Black defeat. In a personal sense Allen was probably more vocal and fiery, and Meads less so, less demonstrative — except when in the heat of a game — but both had a similarly intense pride in the black jersey. They were men to be reckoned with and saw absolutely no easy way to success anywhere.

Meads is ordered from the field by Irish referee Kevin Kelleher during the All Blacks-Scotland test at Murrayfield in 1967. Watching on are: Bruce McLeod (2) and Ken Gray.

So what characterised Allen's coaching style? Relentlessness, no favourites, emphasis on mastery of the basic skills, logical patterns of play, a high level of physical fitness and good all round strength of both body and mind, and a willingness to put the team's interests first, always. Much the same as Meads, actually. In 2002, discussion with Allen shows that his views on these matters have changed little over the years. 'And you can't get away from the fundamentals — the three Ps, position, possession and pace.' He's not convinced there's enough work on the training field today, and he's concerned about the amount of dropped ball.

'In our day, to lose was a terrible thing. The players really felt it, none more than Piney. Do they feel a loss as keenly today? I'm not so sure.'

All along both Meads and Allen knew what powerful results one could get from channeling outrage, indignation and anger. It's not enough to get a few individuals going, 'you have to get the whole bloody lot going in the one direction. Then it's amazing what a force you've got.' As Allen says, 'They followed Piney. He was the ultimate pack leader.'

4.

LOCKED IN BROTHERHOOD

'We never worried about scrums.
We just fell into them, we had
such a long history of locking
scrums together. We knew each
other's games; we had a bond.
Stan was a natural, a real athlete.'

COLIN MEADS FINDS IT EXTREMELY AMUSING THAT LORE HAS IT THAT ON THE FARM HE USED TO GRAB A SHEEP HERE, A SHEEP THERE, SHOVE THEM UNDER ONE ARM, THEN PICK UP A FENCEPOST WITH THE OTHER AND MARCH OFF ACROSS ROUGH COUNTRY. THERE ISN'T MUCH TRUTH IN IT.

The myth came about, as he sees it, after he received a visit from a journalist and a photographer from the British Isles. It was dipping time on the farm. In those days, Meads' father Vere insisted that every sheep on their farm be dipped. 'Any sick sheep, if it couldn't come home, you either carried it or you cut its throat. It was either dipped or it was dead,' says Meads. The day the media men arrived, they caught Meads driving a big mob of sheep home to be dipped. Some of them were sick. It was a case of leave them or carry them. Meads had his photo taken carrying sheep, and the myth was born: Pinetree, the great, dark and fearsome All Black lock trains to savage visiting rugby players by carrying sheep under each arm on his farm in the wilds of backblocks New Zealand.

Of course, Meads is a dry blighter, and he admits it's likely one of the media types

Horse play. Colin's Aunt Lulu holds the reins for Colin (centre), sister Joan and brother Stan, January 1945.

may have asked him if carrying sheep was part of his training for rugby. 'I probably said, "Aw, yeah, I do it often. It's good for training." Not long after it was all through rugby circles in Great Britain and Ireland, Colin Meads training for rugby, carrying bloody sheep up and down hills. There were some stupid stories. Tony O'Reilly wrote that they used to go up the hills with ropes and ladders, lasso Colin Meads and bring him down for the winter, and harness him up for rugby.'

Put it to Meads that it was explicable if one subscribed to the view that he was the toughest rugby player on the planet, the roughest man alive, and he can see what is meant. But it didn't occur to him then. It was in the mid-1960s, and he and brother Stan were in the middle of a major development stage on the farm. Photographers and journalists used to visit the near-legendary Meads brothers and, says Colin, 'watch us work or train. And in the summer we used to cut scrub for three or four months of the year. In between times we'd have to do all the sheep work. Dad would get in a thousand hoggets, or a thousand lambs. They'd have to be drenched. He'd muster in the morning and we'd cut scrub until 12 o'clock and then do the lambs in the afternoon. There were photos of us working in the yards or with sheep.'

The Meads boys represented hard yakker, were seen as setting a standard which others, if they were to become great All Blacks, needed to meet. He says that when his mother and father first farmed the land adjacent to where he lives today, there was no electricity on the farm. They lived by lamplight and his father ran cows down by the main road into Te Kuiti. The monthly cheque for the milk and cream was essential. The Meads boys had to milk the cows when they got home from school, and before they went to school. When their father carted the cream down to the main road Colin and Stan got a lift with him and waited for the school bus.

Then, when he and Stan were no longer at school, his father bought the neighbour's property. More cows. The family gradually acquired more land. A lot of it was scrub-covered and the Meads boys, All Blacks by now, were clearing about 20 acres a year. That was all they could afford to do. One of the neighbouring families broke land in at a faster rate, presumably because they had access to more money. Vere Meads could not only see this, he kept being reminded of it by patrons when drinking at the Waitomo Club in Te Kuiti. When he was asked when he was going to clear more of his land, others used to have him on and say that Colin and Stan would never do it because they 'were too bloody interested in rugby'. Colin says that when their father told them about this ribbing, they said that they'd break it in as long as he got the money to buy grass seed and manure. Vere took his two sons along to State Advances with him and when asked who was going to break in the land, he pointed to Stan and Colin and said, tersely, 'They are.'

In the 1960s a tremendous amount of scrubcutting was going on in the King Country. Gangs of scrubcutters were everywhere, including Indians from Fiji. Just down the road from the Meads property was a gang of Maori fellas who were state of the art operators — they had the first of the chainsaws. Meads says there was an element of competition in it and 'when we got the loan from State Advances we just went mad. For the best part of two years, except for when we were playing rugby, we did nothing but cut scrub. We had Christmas day off and that was it. We got to the stage, Stan and I, that we were praying for rugby to come round. We could only cut to the end of February, then look to fine weather in March so we could get a good burn.'

Stan doesn't see himself as having been the equal of his older brother Colin as a rugby player but he is confident that he made a valuable contribution to both King Country and All Black rugby. King Country rugby folk hold the view that while Colin was a great player, Stan wasn't far behind him. They share Brian Lochore's assessment that Stan was underrated.

Stan says that while he and Colin were different personalities, on the field they had a similar tremendous will to win. They worked and trained very hard together on their farm, especially in the summer months leading up to each rugby season. Their sort of farming was far more arduous than farming is today. Stan says, 'We'd be carrying fenceposts up the hill; Colin might have three or four and me one or two, but that's neither here nor there.'

According to Stan, Colin never lost his desire to play for the All Blacks, was always excited by the prospect of pulling on the black jersey. 'And nothing gave him more satisfaction than beating the Springboks.' Says Stan, Colin had such a fierce will that he 'didn't believe he could be beaten, he didn't believe in even considering the possibility of defeat. So he hated losing, and at such times he was like a bear with a sore head.'

The Meads brothers locked the scrum together for the All Blacks in 11 tests in New Zealand between 1962 and 1966. 'Those games were very special for me,' says Stan. 'We'd played together so often for Waitete and King Country that we sort of knew instinctively what the other was going to do. I think we complemented each other quite well. He was more robust than me, no doubt about that, but I was a jumper whereas Colin wasn't really. He operated closer to the front of the lineout where you get involved in play differently.' One can sense there's a smile awakening beneath the folds of his face as Stan says that, as he assures me that he is not one to blow his own trumpet.

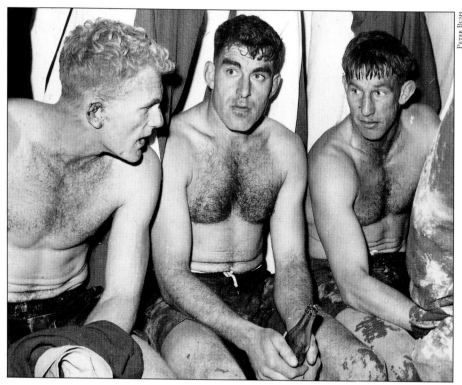

PETER BUSH

How did that one get away? Stan, Colin and Kel Tremain in reflective mood after the All Blacks' 16–19 loss in the third test of the 1965 series against the Springboks at Lancaster Park. New Zealand had lead 16–5 at halftime.

But others do: he played for King Country in 74 matches between 1957 and 1966. In 1961 he played on the side of the scrum for the All Blacks in one test against France at Eden Park. All told, Stan played 30 matches for New Zealand including 15 internationals. In a 126-match first class career, Stan Meads had unusually bad luck with injuries and illness. Possibly his most bizarre setback was when he was bowled over and pinned by a ram when drafting sheep on the farm in 1959. Major knee surgery put him out of rugby for all of the 1959 season. He played only nine matches on the 1963–64 tour of the British Isles and France before succumbing to a blood disorder and had an operation for appendicitis after the test against Ireland.

The Meads brothers farmed difficult upsy-downsy, steep, jumbly country, the sort of land that, if it was to be made farmable, could not be broken in unless a person was undeterred. Colin and Stan, one dark and one fair, both biggish for their day, were two such men who set out from near Te Kuiti — backblocks New Zealand in the eyes of many — to take on the might of the rest of the rugby world. In this sense, then, the Meads brothers represented a kind of colonial cockiness, a no-nonsense, unaffected, rugged latter-day pioneering quality, a never-give-in spirit. International opponents from over the seas found that these flint-hard, brawny buggers, could play. Not only were they relentless, wouldn't back down, they were highly skilled and rugby smart — cunning and prepared to go to the edge of what was allowable within the laws.

Stan Meads, while always an admirer of his brother's play, never felt overawed by him or inferior. They were their own men. 'I never felt hacked off by the attention he got, have never felt as if I lived in his shadow and it's irritated me when people have said I was concerned about that. There was no real sibling rivalry as far

PETER BUSH

Irrepressible. Colin (with ball) and Stan lead this All Black assault against the Springboks in the fourth test at Eden Park in 1965. New Zealand won the match 20–3 and clinched the series 3–1.

as I was concerned. Of course, we were competitive on and off the field — we competed when shearing sheep, for instance, but that is common enough and only to be expected.' The point Stan wishes to make is that they both had personal expectations of themselves. 'People often said that in many ways we were chalk and cheese, and that's right, we were. I had my ideas about farming and Colin had his, so we split the farm up and went and did our own thing. I was attracted to farming and wanted to be successful in my own right.'

Stan, mild-mannered and confident of his own abilities while being aware too of his limitations, says that one of the best pieces of advice he ever received was when he was playing under Wilson Whineray in 1961. 'I tried to bust across the line from a few yards out, like Colin used to. I didn't make it and Wilson took me aside later and said, "There's only one Pinetree. He's got his style, develop your own." That simple good sense helped me get to where I got.' As for when Colin was in his prime, Stan thinks that up until 1967–68 'he was awesome, supreme. After that maybe not so dominant, but of course I'd retired by then, so I wasn't there to see it first-hand.'

That Colin sometimes took matters into his own hands on the field and went right to the line between what was fair and what was a little too vigorous is acknowledged by Stan. 'He trod a fine line on a few occasions, no one can deny that. He did transgress. He'll admit it.' Stan laughs and says, 'And he liked to run the show if he could get away with it. Novice refs didn't have a show with Colin.'

Stan says his brother has done far more voluntary work for rugby and for the IHC in the King Country and elsewhere than he ever did, and that Colin's farm probably suffered as a consequence. 'But that was his business.' Stan put his farm first, in the main, felt he had to, although he notes that he 'put years into kids' rugby

69

MEADS FAMILY

Ken Gray flicks a pass up to Stan Meads during the third test against the Lions at Lancaster Park in 1966. The All Blacks won the match 19–6.

locally' during a time when there was 'obviously a real need for that'.

Stan is extremely modest. Records show that he was one of a group of six who spent about six years from 1967 onwards working on reviving junior rugby in the Maniapoto Sub-union, and in the last three years of that was junior rugby president. In 1974 he and Brian Cressy coached the Waitete under-18 side which was unbeaten that season. Then for the next five years he assisted with coaching the Te Kuiti High School First XV. In 1991 he was the Maniapoto Sub-union senior representative coach and, following an SOS in 1994, he took over as King Country coach of the NPC first-division side.

For his part, Colin always saw Stan as an outstanding all-round player. 'He was a leaper, too. A spring-heel. Pound for pound he was never one of the big ones, but he was very strong and he was an athlete. Stan was a far greater athlete than I was; he could give me 10 yards start in a hundred and beat me. He was unlucky with injuries; he had a cartilage out at one time too, and in those days it

Opposite page: Meads beats Lions skipper Mike Campbell-Lamerton to the jump in this lineout from the first test of the 1966 series at Dunedin. Other All Blacks, from left, are: Bruce McLeod (2), Ken Gray (3), Jack Hazlett, Stan Meads and Chris Laidlaw (9). Referee is John Pring.

Winning in the air

Meads says he was against lifting in the lineouts when it came in. He agrees that it has made for cleaner ball, but it has also created problems. He laments the loss of 'the great jumpers at five in the lineout. That was a skill. Some of the great locks I played with and against wouldn't be seen as so good now. This is the day of the big beanpole who is hoisted high in the air.' Meads preferred watching the likes of 'terrific spring-heeled jumpers like Ian Jones before lifting came in. Jones and John Eales — he was another — had an advantage gained from their skill. Nowadays the best lifter might make the difference.'

For Meads, one of the satisfactions of the old lineouts was that there was never any talk of guaranteed possession from one's own throw in. 'Nowadays, even though lineouts are being contested again to a greater degree than they were when lifting came in initially, there's still those who say that if the side that throws it in doesn't get the ball it's the poor hooker's fault. I think that's a ridiculous allegation. We had to put up with two fellas throwing the ball in, one good on one side of the field, one rough on the other.'

Many of Meads' team-mates have commented on Pinetree's jumping ability, or the lack of it. Some claimed that Meads didn't have to jump all that often, he merely waited until his opposites returned to ground and took the ball from them. He laughs at that and says it wasn't altogether true. The key to effective play near the front of lineouts in his day was, he says, working out who the ball was going to. If you could work that out you were in a good position to spoil things. 'Some great players gave it away. I remember marking Andy Haden early in his career. Now Andy became a very good lineout forward, but I remember marking him in a farewell match when I captained the President's XV against the All Blacks at Athletic Park in 1973. We won that. I could tell from Andy's stance that the ball was going to him. He used to get excited — he was a one-step man, take one step and jump. All you had to do was keep him out. I'd just move into the little gap he'd left and that mucked him up.

'I suppose I got pretty good at giving a player a little nudge just before he jumped. You could put a lot of players off with just a slight push. Often they'd miss the ball, or they'd take their inside arm away and then they'd give you the ball by pulling it towards rather than away from you. That said, it was a bit of a fallacy to say that I never jumped. I blame 'Monkey' Briscoe for starting that myth, when he said that if you were quick you'd get a matchbox under my feet.'

RON PALENSKI COLLECTION

meant a season off. Stan was looking forward to going to South Africa in 1967 and when it was called off he decided he didn't want to go back to the UK. I don't blame him, he had spent over half of the previous tour there either in hospital or recuperating.'

In Colin's view, Stan was the best lock he played with in New Zealand. When he thinks of outstanding locks, Meads thinks of Stan and Frik du Preez. They were, he says, very competitive, and neither were really big by modern-day standards. But both were very mobile and it was surprising, he says, how high they got up in the lineouts in days when lifting wasn't allowed.

What is Stan's take on the tales of his and Colin's legendary training regime? He thinks that, when compared with many in his day, the brothers trained consistently hard. 'Colin and I would have hacked it today, I've no doubt about that. We'd eat most of them as far as fitness goes.'

Colin supposes that he may have sacrificed a lot for rugby, but to him he 'never looked upon it as a sacrifice. It was difficult in some ways, and I guess I was a bit flippant when I said things like, "Well, the grass still grows while I'm away." We were lucky, Stan and I, because in our early days especially, our father was still very capable and he took over the running of the whole farm.'

And did Stan ever say to Colin words to the effect that Colin had stolen the limelight and left him with more than his fair share of the work? 'No,' says Meads, 'that never came up.'

But Colin Meads felt for his brother and saw him as amazingly stoical. 'It was horrendous, tragic really, the run of injuries and illness that he had. We seldom discussed his problems. They were plain. The only thing he ever said was that, after his experience in the UK in 1963, "Bugger it, I don't want to go back there." I think he would have been keen to go back in 1967 if things had panned out differently in '63.'

Colin Meads loved playing with Stan. They locked the All Black scrum together for eight tests in series against South Africa and the Lions in 1965 and 1966. 'We never worried about scrums. We just fell into them, we had such a long history of locking scrums together. We knew each other's games; we had a bond. Stan was a natural, a real athlete.'

But Meads never took his position, or Stan's, for granted. 'Against Australia in 1962, a couple of us got a big wake-up call when we were dropped from the second test and Stan took my place. So there was competition between us all right, but we never took it out on each other, we took it out on the other team. I think we were seen as a formidable pair for the King Country in those days.

'Stan and I played together for the North Island but never in All Black trials. We often laughed about that — even in the King Country trials, the cunning blighters would put us in opposing teams. Stan would be captain of one King Country trial side and I'd be captain of the other. Well, once or twice we actually biffed each other. After that there wouldn't be too much talk over breakfast on the Monday. Our mother would tell us to wake up. You can be sure that little brother never backed down to big brother.'

Chris
LAIDLAW

In a way, Colin Meads and Chris Laidlaw were alike: resolute and competitive; proud of their abilities and unwilling to be pushed around. Proud to be known as New Zealanders and proud of the All Black tradition.

In 1973 the outstanding former All Black halfback Laidlaw published a book called *Mud in Your Eye*. He sub-titled it 'A worm's-eye view of the changing world of Rugby', and it caused a stir. No one in New Zealand, and probably no one anywhere else, and certainly not an All Black, had examined and discussed and sometimes called into question so much about the ways in which rugby was played and administered.

Laidlaw set out to have a close look at all aspects of rugby, and that included its place politically and sociologically. Meads wasn't really interested in examining the latter. He examined his opponents and set himself high and rigorous physical and playing standards. He thought that was enough, the rest was above and beyond him, and he wasn't convinced of its relevance. But he would have understood and agreed, in the main, with Laidlaw's contention that team unity and purpose were easier to develop in Meads' day because the players' backgrounds were more common and interests were less varied. Also that Whineray had a group of senior 'loyal lieutenants' and Lochore was 'everyone's man'. Meads, though, resists the view that Whineray and, by implication, himself, were unwilling to take a more nurturing, caring interest in younger players, that they were unduly cliquish, possibly harsh. Meads accepts that mollycoddling, soft-soaping, wasn't their way, but won't accept that they lacked concern, understanding or compassion at appropriate times.

All this should be seen in the context of Laidlaw's view that on the 1963–64 tour the younger group of players — Bill Davis, Earle Kirton, Laidlaw, Ian MacRae, Derek Arnold — 'felt quite estranged'. Whineray was perhaps 'too much of a man's man and not enough of a boy's man', wrote Laidlaw. Meads' response would be to say that he and Whineray and their ilk were mighty hard on themselves, and that their example helped quickly turn boys into men. Meads had the feeling that the younger ones, Laidlaw and Kirton when they first joined the All Blacks, thought Whineray saw himself as superior. In Meads' view they were mistaken. And anyone who thought he, Meads, or Whineray, expected to be deferred to was mistaken too. 'I never understood that,' Meads says, puzzled. 'I always saw myself as one who tried to mix with the young guys. I think Bryan Williams would agree with that. He was a shy, young kid when he came into the team in 1970. He was the star, no doubt about it; unfortunately he never produced rugby as good as that anywhere else. I remember going to the room committee and saying, "I want to get to know this guy. I've not roomed with him. It's half way through the tour . . . he's so shy, quiet."'

By contrast, says Meads, 'you could never call Chris shy. I thought we mixed quite well with him and his age group. Perhaps the fact that Kel Tremain and I were friendly with Whineray was interpreted as meaning we were less interested in the others.'

Meads saw Laidlaw as typical of those All Blacks who like to win and want to win 'terribly well. Chris had a knack of knowing what to do. I can remember him telling Bunny Tremain, who was on the side of the scrum, to get us to screw the scrum left or right because he reckoned he'd score. And he did, the little bastard. We were clever enough to be able to move a scrum one way or the other — and that's not always easy. It was in a test match too. Laidlaw was what a team needs — players with brains, clever thinkers about the game.'

Meads won't go with the view that there's no place in top rugby for shrinking violets. 'Everyone's respected for what they are, or should be. Take Sid Going. He was the complete opposite to Laidlaw. Sid never drank alcohol; he wouldn't train on Sundays. But no one ever held it against him. Of course one wouldn't expect them to be close — they were so different — and there was the rivalry for their position. I don't think backs put their rivalry aside as readily as forwards do — forwards who compete for the same position are more likely to be good mates. That said, I never found either of them hard to get on with. I like to think I always got on fine with Chris.'

Laidlaw saw the 1960s as 'exclusively' Meads' and that his 'array of skills' was 'probably greater than any other player in whatever position'. He wrote, also, that the forwards — Meads, Tremain, Graham, Clarke, Whineray, Nathan, Young, MacEwen — with 'creative running and handling' had really 'raised the level of forward play' and that its 'likes had never been seen before'.

At the time Laidlaw wrote his book, he felt that Meads had given more to rugby physically and spiritually than any other living player. And that Meads' was 'an era where physical strength' counted 'above all else in the measure of both men and rugby players'. To Laidlaw, Meads was pretty dour and rather humourless when he played with him in the 1960s. Meads can see why he came across that way to some, but would say that that was often untrue too. It was an extension of his early shyness, and because he never saw himself as articulate. 'Me rubbishing the Varsity boys was just me and him playing our roles and wasn't meant to be taken seriously.'

Meads' ultimate articulate expression, perhaps even imaginative and artistic performances, were reserved for the rugby field. There he was creative, anything but dour in his play. For a lock forward he was exceptionally athletic and sometimes surprisingly innovative, and he could run, and never stop running.

Laidlaw says that when he first made the All Blacks and for a time after, as a young player, a novitiate in world rugby's hardest school, he felt he 'didn't have the right to speak' to Meads, and that Meads was a kind of 'Darth Vader' who could be pretty savage when it came to punishing opponents who crossed the line and tried to gain an advantage illegally.

Laidlaw saw and sees Meads as 'an enduring symbol of what our personality was'. For Laidlaw that, possibly, means pragmatic, unsophisticated and somewhat unworldly in a cerebral sense. Others tended to view Meads as representing New Zealanders' disinclination to overstate and overpraise, as preferring exuberant play rather than flashy personal displays both on and off the field. A bit of restraint, and reserve, and an unwillingness to openly seek acclamation was seen as preferable to the sort of public dramatics and orchestration that some sports notables engage in today.

In the early 1970s, Chris Laidlaw wrote that Meads 'had given more to Rugby physically and spiritually than any other player in whatever position'. Here, Meads has secured possession for the All Blacks against Western Province in 1970.

Ross Wiggins

5.

TAKING OFF THE BLACK JERSEY

'You don't so much retire today, you're told you're not wanted. That's professionalism. In my day, you'd say, "I'll go to South Africa in 1970 and then I'll retire."'

AFTER THE 1970 SOUTH AFRICAN TOUR, WHICH HAD LEFT COLIN MEADS AND MANY OTHERS CHAMPING, EXASPERATED, AND RUEING MISSED OPPORTUNITIES AND UNSAVOURY EVENTS, MEADS SAYS,

'An element thought I was over the hill. Not just me, others too. Rugby went in cycles in those days. There was a group of established All Blacks who picked their time to pull out. The game's not really like that any more. You don't so much retire today, you're told you're not wanted. That's professionalism. In my day, you'd say, "I'll go to South Africa in 1970 and then I'll retire." There was much more likelihood of your being picked. There tended to be a major clean-out after a major overseas tour. One had to think about careers, about getting on with earning a living. Chris Laidlaw and Brian Lochore probably came into that category.'

In *Mud in Your Eye*, Laidlaw writes that he saw Meads as 'a non-lover of publicity' and that 'newspapers and critics at large crucified him in 1971–72 for "not retiring"'. Laidlaw said he 'was infuriated at the attitude of so many who had elevated this sincerely simple man to such a position'.

Meads says it was true that he never sought publicity — he never had to, it

76

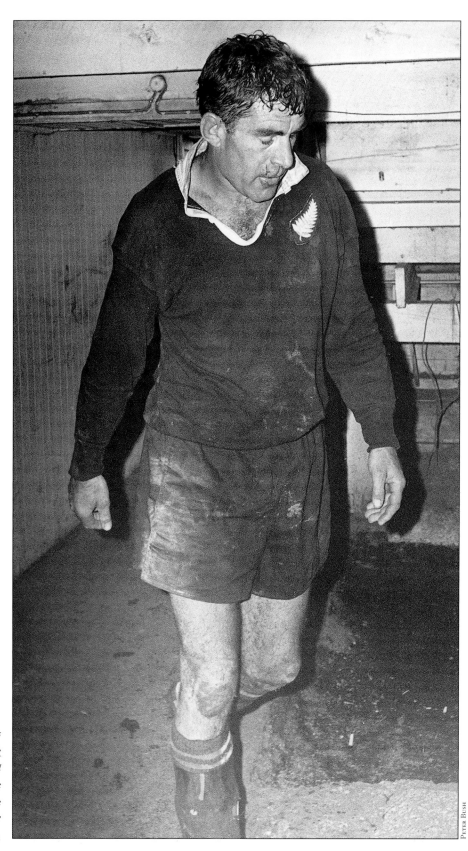

A dejected Meads heads for the Carisbrook dressing sheds after the All Blacks' loss in the first test of the 1971 series against the Lions. It was Meads' first test as captain.

PETER BUSH

RON PALENSKI COLLECTION

Meads, the reluctant skipper, watches on as Sid Going kicks over his forwards during action from the 1971 series against the Lions. Other All Blacks pictured are, from left: Ian Kirkpatrick, Peter Whiting and Richie Guy (3).

followed him, and occasionally dogged him too. The truth was that Pinetree Meads couldn't bring himself to stop playing. 'I thought, ah, I enjoyed rugby so much that, come the next year I'd just start training again and see where it took me. I enjoyed life in and around rugby; I enjoyed the company at the footie club, the Tuesday and Thursday nights of training and having a beer in the clubrooms afterwards — 10 o'clock closing had come in. I was the player-coach. We trained from eight and if we'd had a shitty game the week before, I'd keep them at it so that it was five to 10 before they got to the bar. Life revolved around how good we'd been playing . . . I really enjoyed it. We had a good club spirit. In the summers we did a lot of work raising money for tours. The camaraderie in the club was good. So I thought, well, if you're going to play and train for club rugby, you might as well go the whole hog. I was a bit disgruntled about having had my arm broken in South Africa, and not having played as well thereafter as I'd have hoped, so I could understand why a lot of rugby people thought it was time I retired. Nevertheless, I remembered something Wilson Whineray said, and that was that if you were playing and you were selected for an All Black trial team, then it was over to others to prove that they were better.

'I guess I decided to follow the Whineray line. I played and they made me captain of the All Blacks for the series against the touring British Isles. I don't think that was a good idea. Brian Lochore had retired, and while some were saying that there was no one else but me in line, that was a fallacy. There's always someone else. I think it would have been better for the team if they'd appointed Ian Kirkpatrick. You see, Colin Meads wasn't the right man. While he was a good captain for King Country, he wasn't a good captain for the All Blacks. They put the brakes on you when you're All Black captain. You're the team spokesman, you have to be . . .'

RON PALENSKI COLLECTION

The old stagers, Colin Meads (far right) and Willie John McBride (5) watch on as young bucks Gordon Brown (4) and Peter Whiting lock lineout horns in the fourth test of the 1971 series between New Zealand and the Lions.

Here Meads struggles to find the right phrase, the right tone. What he means is that as captain one has to be more discreet, more diplomatic, more dignified both on and off the field — up to a point. He preferred the freedom, and the challenge, to do the business for the team and not have to worry about the finer points. To Meads, test forward play — test rugby in general — was no place for those who had to think about more than simply giving your all physically and tactically on the field of play. Meads felt his place was in front of the forwards not in front of a microphone, or at the centre of a cacophony of pressmen. He knew he was best when at the centre of an All Black pack busting and rolling inexorably forward. 'I preferred being in the situation where the captain came up to me and said, "Piney, we've got to do something about this," and I'd go ahead and do my damnedest to comply.'

The thing was, Meads didn't mind being a servant. He took pride in being a fine and skilled and loyal servant unquestionably devoted to the All Blacks' cause. Unsurprisingly, though, Meads was pleased and proud to have been named All Black captain. But he didn't see himself as being equipped to present the required public image. On the field during the tests, Meads felt restricted. Put it this way, he says: 'When Wilson Whineray was captain, there was the odd time when he was having a bit of trouble in the front row. He'd say, "Piney, can you help us out here. Straighten this, er . . . gentleman up." So I would. But I'd be doing that for the team, not for any other reason. Once a game I might have to ask the Skip to get his head out of the road and I'd make the offender sit up. As captain you couldn't be seen to get into any sort of scrap.' Being captain meant you had a different relationship with the referee, and Colin had always seen it as his business to assist them if he felt they were being deficient.

It goes like this, ref

Meads recalls the time when he was in the audience listening to a prominent referee who said that he 'wanted to thank Colin Meads for all the help he'd given him during his career. What the referee in question didn't know was that I had to speak after him. I got up and said I'd like to thank him for thanking me for all that help, but it's like this, I've never played with a referee that doesn't need some help. I was only trying to be very helpful, to make sure he did see that knock-on.'

The great referee of Meads' time was Pat Murphy. 'Admittedly the Lions didn't like him much, but he related well to players without letting them rule him. The story I remember most vividly about Pat was when he was refereeing a game in North Auckland. There were, as I put it, a lot of wild Ngapuhi playing. It was a club game and one of the Maori fellas was getting dealt to all the time. Pat couldn't work out why he was getting such a hammering. After the third time, Pat went up to him and said that if he saw him getting dealt to again he was going to send him off. The fella spluttered, "Why, wh . . . why?" Pat replied, "Well, you must be doing something wrong." That typified how smart Pat was. Players don't go out and belt another unless he's doing something wrong, mostly. I mean, I like Richard Loe; I thought he was a very good prop and a funny man. But if a ref saw Richard getting belted, he'd probably be right to think he was up to something.

'I can remember Canterbury's Mike Fitzgibbon officiating in a shield game between King Country and Auckland. My son Glynn was playing for King Country. Now, I never told Glynn to go out and belt people. But when Sean Fitzpatrick — who would cheat a bit if he could get away with it — was in King Country's side of a ruck, Glynn belted him and sat him on his arse. Typically, Sean cried, "Did you see that?" Mike shot back, "Yes, and you deserved it." Sean was flabbergasted.'

Top: Meads had his rib cartilages torn in the opening minutes of Wanganui-King Country's match against the Lions in 1971. Here, Pat Murphy, the great referee of Meads' time, lends a hand with the strapping. Right: Meads in debate with Irish referee Ray Williams during the All Blacks' match against Scotland in 1964.

PETER BUSH

NEWS MEDIA AUCKLAND

Meads did get a great thrill occasionally captaining the All Black team during a mid-week game on tour, and that's what he thought guys like him were suited for. He realises that most rugby players would give their eye teeth to be captain of the All Blacks, but his position was that, even though he was 'terribly proud to have been appointed, you have to think about what's good for the team. Earlier on, Kel Tremain would have made a good captain, though probably not as good as BJ. 'Bunny' Tremain would have been more inclined to organise things to suit himself, as he did at Hawke's Bay where he was king of the roost.'

Commenting on Meads' role and career, Laidlaw wrote that Meads 'wanted only one thing — to be able to play for [the All Blacks] 'for as long as [he was] worthy of it, and after that to be allowed to play in lesser games for as long as [he] felt like it.' Meads felt that was 'a fair assumption' and says that he'd always promised the Waitete club that when he finished as an All Black he'd give them another couple of seasons before he retired completely. The club was always good to him and Stan and raised money so they were never out of pocket, and helped out on the farm getting the hay in and doing other essential work when they were away. So Meads played the 1973 and 1974 seasons out for Waitete. 'It's a loyalty thing,' he says. 'It's a pleasure thing as well: I enjoyed it. That's how I like to think I was a good club captain, although I admit in my last two seasons I used to cheat a bit on my road runs, and I wasn't as fit as I'd been when I was an All Black. Verna used to time me, but she didn't know that I was stopping a bit; she didn't know how far I'd gone.'

By the time the 1970s came round, Meads was the Grand Old Man of both All Black and King Country rugby. He seemed to have been around for ever. He was seen as one of the great indestructible forwards of all time. And then one night in December 1971, he crashed his Land Rover a couple of kilometres down the road from the farmhouse. Among the many injuries were broken vertebrae in his back.

Meads had been working up to 16 hours a day on the farm for the previous fortnight — shearing and wool-pressing among other things — but he had just spent the Saturday with Waitete members who were roof painting to raise funds for a club trip to the South Island. He had a couple of beers, then headed for home. A neighbour spotted the tail-lights of Meads' vehicle. He stopped and found Colin lying unconscious beside the Land Rover.

He'd been thrown out the passenger side. Sheets of skin had been torn from most of his back. It was as if he had been flayed. He woke up in hospital next morning, got out of bed, tore out the drip tubes, and fell over. After a series of X-rays doctors learned he had broken vertebrae. Meads recalls feeling very sick for days. A week later, on Christmas Eve, he was allowed to go home. He was encased in plaster from under his arms to his waist.

There was a lot of work that needed doing round the farm, crucial tasks. So family and friends — brother Stan, his father Vere, wives, children — all pitched in. Gradually, Meads became mobile enough to shift stock and to organise hired labour to crutch and shear sheep and generally help keep the farm going.

By now club training was well under way. Nationally, rugby journalists and others were speculating: would Pinetree Meads' broken back spell a bizarre, somewhat ignominious end to his great and lengthy career? To many, it wasn't that the end was nigh, it was that the end had come.

Meads had not given up all thoughts of perhaps having one final tilt at the Springboks in 1973, but the broken back seemed to have decided that for him.

Or had it? He was a cussed customer. He fretted, was impatient to have his plaster cast removed. The medical professionals would not bow to pressure from him. 'No,' they said. And no again. 'It is too soon. You will just have to wait.'

The cast was cut off on the last day of March, 1972. To Meads, life without his encasement felt strange. But he did not set out like a frisky colt for the ridgeline; he was a little apprehensive. For a few weeks he had been, a little gingerly, attending Waitete club training, presiding with the help of one or two others. He admits to having been wondering if his rugby-playing days were over, well and truly. Not so: within a week or two after having shed his cast, Meads began to move fairly freely. Sure, he felt the odd twinge but it was nothing too perturbing. He realised his 'sheer love of rugby' was still there, and felt liberated that he was looking forward to playing again. Within a month he was training with Waitete.

Meads had visited his medical specialist who had given him the okay to start back, providing he took it easy for a while. 'To be honest,' says Meads, 'the back was

Impatient patient. Meads on the farm 'recovering' from horrific injuries he suffered in the 1971 Land Rover accident.

82

very stiff and sore for a while, but I wasn't going to say much. I played a few games for Waitete and then on 17 June led King Country out at Taumarunui to play Auckland.' The locals in the King Country, including the selectors, were telling Meads that he was playing as well as he had ever played. Curly Neilsen, 13 years a King Country coach and selector, was one. Others were less enthusiastic: some said he was but a shadow of his former self. Meads disagreed. He played all King Country's games that winter of 1972. He was aware, though, that there were noises throughout the country to the effect that it was sad to see the icon battling on when he should have retired gracefully when the opportunity was there. But Colin Meads listened to his own voice; it was telling him that he was enjoying rugby, still, and that he was more than capable of playing to the standard both he and the rugby public expected of him. There was another consideration, as he explains: 'King Country was on the way down. A lot of players had retired, or had moved on — just got too bloody old — and we were struggling. We weren't the team we had been in the late 1960s. We got a few hidings, and I was the target of most teams. The trouble was,' he says ruefully, 'that I didn't have the back up that I used to have. Stan wasn't there, nor were the likes of the Bill Wordleys and Howard Paiakas. I was virtually on my own.'

It needs to be remembered that Meads was venerable, 36 years of age, and therefore old indeed, by the standards normally applied to such a physically demanding game, to be playing top-level provincial rugby, let alone contemplating another shot at test level. Soon, though, he was regularly made aware, through the media in particular, that it was time he made a dignified departure. There was an All Black tour of North America, Britain and France scheduled for the northern hemisphere winter of 1972–73; following that the Springboks were down to tour New Zealand. Going overseas in the New Zealand summer would mean that family and friends would again have to step in and keep the farm going at the most trying time of the year. Also, he was getting whispers from Fred Allen and others that the selectors weren't convinced he ought to make himself available again. According to his confidants, the All Black coach and selector, Bob Duff, thought Meads had passed his use-by date. That, and the fact that the style of play Duff preferred was at odds with Meads'. The writing was clear on the wall, Meads says he 'decided to call it quits. But I had agreed, in 1971, to give Waitete two years from the time I stopped playing for the All Blacks, so in 1973 I turned out again for my old club. I enjoyed playing just the club and sub-union football.'

As is history now, and as reports filtered home of the unhappy relations and incidents on the tour to Britain and France, speculation was rife about whether Meads' presence on tour would have been a necessary steadying influence. Would Keith Murdoch have been sent home? was one burning question. The tour went down in the books as 'ill-fated'. But Meads feels it is stretching credulity to assert that his presence alone would have prevented trouble. He has never seen himself as the ideal choice of envoy charged with bringing about peace of any kind.

When he announced his decision not to trial for the 1972–73 All Blacks, thus signalling the end of one of the most illustrious careers in the history of rugby union anywhere, he treated the decision matter-of-factly. He preferred not to dwell on it, and found the aftermath something of an anti-climax. Besides, he wasn't retiring from playing rugby at all; also, he was a rugby-for-life man, one who could not see himself as ever not being involved in the game in some way.

Then, in 1973, the Kirk Labour Government appeared to bow to pressure from some Commonwealth nations who warned that if the Springbok rugby tour of New Zealand went ahead, there would be a mass boycott of the 1974 Christchurch Commonwealth Games by many, if not most, African countries. The tour was cancelled. That meant the end of any thoughts Meads had of one final battle against his arch foes.

But Meads kept on keeping on. He did not want to stop. Age hadn't wearied him; the years hadn't condemned him. He was still respected by his peers as a rugby player. Meads liked the struggle; in a way he saw it as a challenge to one's manhood, in the sense of stoicism, toil, skill, knowledge, controlled aggression. He was prepared to go, yes, but in his own time. In that sense he was obdurate. He felt he had earned the right to decide the time and the place of his departure. But he did have to be careful, he realised, that he didn't hang around so long that he was seen as remarkable purely because of his age.

However, an opportunity came along for him to depart top-level rugby in style. On 4 August 1973, Colin Meads ran out onto Athletic Park in Wellington for the last time as a rugby player. Curiously, and not entirely appropriately, he was captain of the New Zealand Rugby Union President's Invitation XV against the All Blacks. Among those in the Meads-led side were, as vice-captain, halfback Sid Going and mercurial utility back Grahame Thorne.

Going admired Colin Meads. 'He and Stan were tremendous to me when I first got in the All Blacks, made me feel welcome. Colin stamped his authority on a game, showed leadership on the field and off. His broken arm in South Africa was devastating for us, it affected everyone's morale.' Like Meads, he thought the test against France in France in 1967 'was about as hard as it got'.

Athletic Park, 4 August 1973, was wrongly presumed to be Meads' farewell match. It may not have been billed as such, but that's how most saw it: players, administrators, public alike. They flocked along to watch their hero, who had made an impact like few others — and for longer than any other — play his last game with and against some of the great names of his era. Meads' men won the game. It was a surprise, but a pleasing one. Not a major triumph for the great crag from the King Country, but a triumph all the same.

The whole day was like both a homecoming and a departure for Colin Meads — big, bashful, overwhelmed and not entirely sure how to react. And definitely not sure of what to say.

He is said to have gone into the All Blacks' dressing room afterwards and mumbled that he was 'sorry' the All Blacks had lost. Perhaps he did say that, for Meads never found it easy to lose, especially when wearing the All Black jersey. Not that, in the fullness of time, Meads was ever to feel that he had lost out as a consequence of his involvement in rugby. Literally and

Souvenir Programme
Athletic Park
August 4th 1973

N.Z. Presidents XV

versus

New Zealand

Price 25c

NO ADMITTANCE
OFFICIALS ONLY

Colin Meads is chaired off Athletic Park by South Africa's Albie Bates and Brian Lochore after captaining the President's XV to a 35-28 win over the All Blacks.

Opposite page: Meads in white, Ian Kirkpatrick in black, lead their sides onto Athletic Park for the All Blacks-President's XV match.

figuratively, both he and rugby everywhere benefited from Meads' contributions on and off the field. On that day, if he felt more confused and humble than sad or elated, or perhaps even slightly bereft, it may have been because, while always conscious of his responsibilities to the great All Black tradition, and of the rugby public's expectations, an equally strong driving force within him had been his proud resolve to live up to his expectations of himself. Most, but not all, of the time he had.

Meads' first-class swansong actually came a week after the Athletic Park 'finale'. He was named captain of an Invitation XV to meet the All Blacks at Eden Park. This time the All Blacks came out on top, overcoming a spirited challenge from Meads' men by 22–10. When he left Eden Park that day it was with mixed feelings — pride in the knowledge of a long, illustrious career, and the powerful realisation that he had to accept once and for all that his time as an All Black was over.

The 40,000 Wellington fans cared little about the score on 4 August, 1973. They had come to pay homage to the great Pinetree.

Bryan
WILLIAMS

Meads has tremendous regard for Williams, saw him as an exceptional player, and doubts that there's ever been a better winger than the Williams he had the pleasure of watching in South Africa in 1970. For Meads, Williams was wonderful to behold and scored some astonishing tries.

For his part, Bryan Williams, a Samoan with speed, strength and marvellous elusiveness, was for a long time 'overawed' by Meads, right from the time he first met him in the tunnel at Eden Park in 1961. Williams, still a schoolboy, had played in a curtain raiser to the test match against France. 'Meeting Meads was a memorable moment, no doubt, and when I was selected to go on the tour to South Africa in 1970, I had a chance to get to know him well. I always found Colin modest and wise, especially when it came to touring and to the playing of rugby, of course.'

Williams had heard that some of the younger players — Laidlaw, Kirton and Davis among them — had felt isolated when on the long tour of the British Isles and France in 1963–64. Some All Blacks in the 1960s felt there was a bit of a clique at times, that the older hands tended to rule the roost, and Meads and his closest allies were deemed to be very much top dogs. Meads has always believed that there was little foundation for such an allegation, and feels that some younger members, and a few older ones as well, tend to be poorer tourists than others, and perhaps unduly sensitive. In Meads' view such views have more to do with temperament than the existence of so-called hierarchies. But, by 1970, Williams certainly 'didn't feel excluded'. It may have had something to do with the style of Brian Lochore, the captain, for his experience as a somewhat callow All Black on the 1963–64 tour had convinced him of the need to put more effort into reassuring and propping up younger players, and a few of those not normally in consideration for test line-ups.

To Williams, Meads emphasised that becoming an All Black was only the first step, then you had to work at being a good one, and that meant living up to high standards on and off the park. Williams saw that Meads felt it very important to 'pay homage to the history' surrounding the All Blacks. 'At the time I wasn't aware of what I know now, that not a day goes by when there's a not a reference, some way or other, to one's time as an All Black, and what being an All Black taught one.'

As for Meads' reputation for uncalled-for violence, Williams won't have it: 'I never saw him start things. He was the benchmark for locks and therefore a target. He dominated, was intimidating in that respect, just as Andy Haden was late in his career. And some of the refs were scared of Colin. He had a bit to say.'

Williams was a sensation in South Africa, and became so confident that on occasions he even side-stepped defenders over the goal-line in order to touch down closer to the posts. 'I remember playing for the Centurions after we came back in 1970. Colin was in the side. I was going in for a try and started to jink a bit behind the line when I heard this gruff voice close behind me, "Put that bloody ball down."'

Although Williams was happy to tour South Africa in 1970, because he thought the presence of non-white players in the All Blacks might open eyes to what was possible and desirable in terms of human relations, he later became concerned about the slow progress towards the removal of apartheid. In 1976 he went to South Africa and spoke to lawyers at a conference there and 'was blunt'. He certainly 'thought the 1986 Cavaliers tour ill-advised and I told people that'.

Williams saw Meads 'become shrewder, more sophisticated as he got older', and he shares Meads' concerns for the future of rugby 'in depth'. He worries about the erosion of clubs and thinks it's sad that fewer players from the smaller unions have a chance to impress sufficiently to enhance their chances of making the All Blacks today.

Meads and Bryan Williams during the 1971 test series between New Zealand and the Lions.

6.
TOUR'S END

'I was expected to play every game, and, hell, I was the scapegoat: every bugger would take to me.'

WHEN COLIN MEADS RETIRED FROM ALL BLACK RUGBY AFTER ALL THOSE EVENTFUL AND EXCITING YEARS, HE FELT A BIT DISLOCATED. 'I FOUND IT HARD TO GET AWAY FROM RUGBY ALTOGETHER. I NEVER THOUGHT A MAN COULD GO ON PLAYING RUGBY FOREVER BUT, BY THE SAME TOKEN, I NEVER STOPPED ENJOYING PLAYING THE GAME. SO I KEPT ON PLAYING FOR WAITETE UNTIL 1975.'

Meads always took as full and as enthusiastic a part in as wide a variety of Waitete club activities as possible. He always believed, and still does, that club rugby is the true heart of the game. He has often been heard to say, 'it is everything, everything that is good in rugby starts with the clubs. Waitete was good to me, I was happy, and felt a duty to return that loyalty as much as I could.' Meads may appear old-fashioned in that regard, but his commitment to club rugby and belief in its value has never wavered. 'If I'm old-fashioned, so be it. I'm not apologising.'

After the trip down south in 1973, some members got to yarning over a jug or two of beer and set their sights on the next club trip being an overseas one. One old stalwart was heard to say, 'You are getting carried away.' True, but the challenge was there, and few were prepared to back away. Two years of serious fund-raising took place and, to quote team manager Larry Boyle, 'Some 135,000 to 140,000 bales of hay later we were at the Auckland Airport awaiting boarding instructions.'

Danie Craven . . . gave Meads and Waitete the green light for the tour to South Africa in 1975.

PHOTOSPORT

As Meads recalls with pleasure and amusement, 'We in Waitete were pretty cocky as a club. We believed in taking on the best. Once or twice, members suggested we tour Australia. I wasn't keen on that and told them we'd have a better time in the South Island.'

Many members still wanted an overseas trip, however, so South Africa had been suggested. Club members were aware that Petone of Wellington and Ponsonby of Auckland had ventured west across the Tasman and then the long haul across the Indian Ocean to Africa. So it befell Meads to ring Danie Craven. The feeling in Waitete, says Meads, was that if it was good enough for the town boys to go there, 'why couldn't we go there, too?' Meads was a bit embarrassed to be ringing 'the old Doc Craven about a little country side from New Zealand, but I knew he was a bit of a fan of Colin Meads. I told him we'd have enough money to fly ourselves to Johannesburg. Can you look after us from there? He said to leave it with him and within a week or so we were contacted by the Border Union who agreed to sponsor the trip.'

By Meads' reckoning the club had to raise around $80,000 to make the trip, 'a helluva lot of hay to put in on King Country farms. But I told the club members that once this trip was over that was it for me; I was playing no more.'

So in March 1975 the party was off to South Africa, to East London to meet liaison officer Ron McEvoy and their hosts, the Border Union and Hamilton clubs. Waitete didn't have its strongest side and was startled by the intensity of the determination of their opponents. Maybe the presence of Colin Meads as captain was an added incentive, if one were ever needed to incite South African players. Larry Boyle reported, after their first game, a 0–3 loss to East London, 'South Africans as you know play the game for keeps, and we found this out very early, however the game was enjoyed and the after-match was great.' There followed losses to teams at Oudtshoorn, North Eastern Cape, a Maluti XV at Bethlehem, and an Eastern Transvaal team at Witbank. Waitete 'came right' at Pietersburg and won 68–7. Their final game was against a South Eastern Transvaal XV at Springs where, wrote Boyle, 'the boys played themselves to a standstill to win by 13–8'.

Meads was amazed by how well the team played against East London and said the result didn't make things any easier for them. 'We played too well,' he says, 'and for a club side to play as we did was unbelievable. So the next side we played brought in the monster Springbok loose forward Klippies Kritzinger, and a Springbok halfback. It was all a bit over the top.' As Meads pointed out, Waitete was obliged to give all of its squad of about 25 players games, which was fair enough but not necessarily conducive to the very best results. Not that they were concerned about that. But it made a hard tour even harder for him.

After the second match, Meads got on the phone to Danie Craven and told him that enough was enough. 'I said I'd told him we were a country club side. We wanted to stay in country districts and play country teams. Club teams, not provincial teams. They are bringing in Springboks. From there on, we played opposition that was more manageable, in the main.'

Meads remembers this tour as really tough, no picnic. And, in case anyone has missed it, he was no longer a spring chicken; he was damned near 39 years of age. If Meads enjoyed the tour, which he did, hugely, he was also slightly daunted by the expectations of him. 'I was expected to play every game, and, hell, I was the scapegoat: every bugger would take to me. Something happened to me on that trip that had never happened before: a guy head-butted me. It stunned me and sat me on my arse. So at the next lineout I said to this joker: "Are you looking for a hiding or what?"

'"Aw, no," he said, "I've just read your book. That's the sort of thing you'd do." I thought, bugger the book, and gave him a little tickle up.'

Meads hadn't realised just how keenly his advent — the return of a formidable foe and legendary hard man — was being looked forward to in the Border Union. A couple of weeks before the Waitete unsuspectings left home, Meads got a clipping from one of the papers in East London. It stated that trials were being held to pick the team to play Waitete. Meads was aghast: didn't they know Waitete was a team of club players from the rural acreages of the North Island? Admittedly, Meads says, 'we had a couple of ring-ins — including Murray Kidd from Pio Pio, who had played in the outside backs for Taranaki. But we were simply a keen bunch of club players, no more.'

This was his rugby-playing swansong. He came back and hung up his boots. The long career during which he had strode rugby fields the world over like some feared — to some pagan, to most grand and glorious — rugby god, was over.

In his book *Mud in Your Eye*, Chris Laidlaw had opined that after Colin Meads' rugby-playing days were over he would 'quietly but unforgettably vanish into the King Country to remain no more than a legend to the outer world'.

It was not to be a convincing vanishing act.

Opposite page: Meads' last 'serious' game of rugby was for Waitete on their tour of South Africa in 1975. Here he is shouldered from the field by team-mates John Lang – Verna's younger brother – and Bill Symonds after the hard-fought 13-8 win over a South Eastern Transvaal XV at Springs.

PART TWO

After the Lord Meads show

In a great many cases, today's rugby players are imposing and daunting physical specimens. In the main they are a good deal bigger than those of Meads' day. One might say that, nowadays, there are very few small men alive and kicking vigorously in the elite ranks of the game. It wasn't just better food and nutrition, and evolution's inexorable march, that brought about this state of affairs; it was THE GYMNASIUM and its vast array of quirky-looking, muscle-toning machinery.

Colin Meads is on record as having expressed misgivings about the extent to which some players appeared to have become obsessed by weight training. His view of such training is that 'within moderation it's okay'. Having said that, he sits back and states slowly, 'I'd never been to a proper gymnasium in my life until I was manager of the All Blacks. Little Mehrts took me along . . . and he's a real character. It was at the World Cup in 1995. The team had had a light training run and then were told there'd be a gym workout in the afternoon, for those who felt like it. Nine or ten of the guys decided to go down to the gym. So the masseur, Donny Cameron, persuaded me to go along and have a look. Donny gets on the treadmill and is running along going nowhere, as you do. I thought, Huh, I can do that, so I hopped on beside him. Then up comes Mehrts: "Hey, no good there. Come over here. Have a go on this." I said, "What's so good about this one?" Mehrts gave a wiggle, shifted his angle, flexed. "Mirrors," he said. By keeping an eye on the mirrors, he said, you could observe some rather good-looking persons going through their routines elsewhere. "It's much better here than way over there running by yourself and staring into nowhere," he said.

Opposite page: 'Little Mehrts' showed Meads all the right moves when it came to gymnasium training.

PHOTOSPORT

'Ever since, when I talk about gyms and the All Blacks, I say, "I don't mind gymnasiums, but I'm dead against those bloody mirrors."'

Meads is well aware that he can easily be dismissed as a fossil; as an old rugby diehard out of touch with today's rugged, pressure-cooker realities; as someone pining for the past. He admits that sometimes he plays this role, merely to entertain by meeting certain expectations. When accused of being something of an antique, he hastens to assure people that there have been refinements and improvements to rugby in all manner of ways since he retired from the game, and that many of the changes 'had to happen. And have been for the good.' But there is no way he is going to agree with those who claim that the best players of yesteryear wouldn't have been able to cut it today. 'We were fit,' he growls. Top rugby, he insists, was rugged then. It was hard, uncompromising. There was no namby-pambying.

Colin and Stan Meads did do some gym work in their off-season — from October to Christmas — with a local trainer, Scotty Thompson. They did this for two or three years. Scotty was a 'just a little guy' that Colin used to play footie with when they were youngsters. 'He was into weight-lifting and was good at it. He asked me, "Do you want to be made strong, or do you want to be pretty boys?" You will know the answer to that. He'd make us warm up properly and then get into it: three lifts with one weight, then an increase. We enjoyed it at the time. But once proper training for rugby started we stopped the weights.'

As has often been recorded, the Meads brothers felt running and hard physical work, then actual rugby practice itself, were more than adequate. Colin is aware, though, that for many, farming today isn't nearly as physical as it was. Few now carry the posts out and dig the holes with a spade the way Stan and Colin Meads did. So, with some reservations, he concedes that, in the context of modern life, there is a place for gymnasiums in the lives of today's rugby players.

———◄○►———

7.
CHAIRMAN COLIN

'I used to say that all sports people after they retired should do more to help charitable and welfare organisations in the community. I used to think about how lucky I'd been, playing for the All Blacks for 15 years. Frankly, I got a lot of pride out of doing something for a less fortunate group of people, and hoped that in some small way my example might encourage other sportsmen to do the same.'

COLIN MAY HAVE HUNG UP HIS BOOTS IN 1975, BUT HE DIDN'T RETREAT TO A LIFE OUT OF THE PUBLIC VIEW. HE MAY HAVE CONTEMPLATED IT, BUT PEOPLE DIDN'T LET IT HAPPEN.

'I'd always had a stream of visitors — people wanting me to go to training sessions, wanting to talk about my career, wanting me to open this function or that. One day, I got a visit from some people belonging to the South Auckland branch of the IHC Society. The branch had a wide territory, from Huntly down to Taumarunui and across to Turangi, so I believe. Once a year they used to get me to go to the IHC centre in Hamilton for a fund-raising gala day. I wasn't the only rugby player who attended; often the Clarke boys — Ian and Don — or Rex Pickering would be there. A mix of so-called dignitaries, or celebrities, sporting people among them. We'd do anything they wanted us to do, sell raffle tickets, chat to people, and so on.

'I got approached by a charming lady — we are all suckers when a charming lady's involved — Maureen Tilley. She and the branch chairman, Tom Hickmont, and Don Tait, came down to see me on the farm. They had a cuppa and after an hour or so's discussion I was virtually confirmed as the chairman of a new King Country sub-branch of the South Auckland IHC. That meant attending meetings here, meetings there.

'I said that I needed a way out of rugby for a while, that I was too committed to rugby and associated activities generally. For example, I can remember being down in Southland doing some work promoting Nissan vehicles and I was taken to a club near Gore. We went along to a club social evening the night before one of their matches and a lot of beer was being drunk. The team hadn't won a game for two years, so I was told, and I thought maybe this is one of the reasons why. They had quite a good pack, so between 10 and 11 at night I gave them a team talk on how to win a game. I said, "I'm told you've got a reasonable halfback, so get your best kicker and put him at first five-eighth and just kick every bloody thing." Next day the promotional team moved on to Dunedin and I got a telegram saying, "We won."

'I told the IHC that my commitments were, if anything, even heavier than when I was playing (and I had promised Verna I'd get out of rugby for a couple of years and spend more time with her and the family). No one on either side of our family had had a previous involvement in IHC. I said to Verna, after I'd signed up, "Well, that was the biggest con job I've ever had done on me."

'Rugby clubs all over the Thames Valley and the Waikato were asking me to come and take their sides for training runs. IHC seemed like a worthy alternative and, initially, less time-consuming. It soon proved to be otherwise. I became chairman of the King Country branch — a laugh really, for I knew nothing about organisations, running meetings and that sort of thing. All I'd done was play and coach rugby. I made a bit of a fool of myself at the first meetings I went to, calling the IHC the Crippled Children's Society for instance. I think some of them wondered what the hell they had here.

'It was certainly a far different scene from what I'd been accustomed to. Here was me dealing with the parents of disadvantaged children, and all of us in the organisation were worried about what might occur when we moved on. Who would replace us? It was obvious that, understandably, quite a few parents were primarily concerned about their youngsters, so within a year I was involved with regional fund-raising, then chairman of the national fund-raising committee. I came up with a few ideas — like I'd get a top horse trainer and we'd go and buy a yearling and then have a nationwide raffle for the thoroughbred. Included in the prize was a year's training for the horse with a top trainer. It was a successful raffle the first year, but thereafter not so much. Some of the older ladies in the IHC wondered who this Colin Meads was, were saying he's into gambling and horses, is selling raffles in pubs and all the wrong places. Nevertheless, we made around $100,000 the first year, but it dwindled over the next three or four years, so when the profits dropped to about $50,000 nationally it wasn't really worthwhile doing any longer.

'I was on the IHC when the IHC Calf Scheme was started. Mick Murphy from Blenheim was really the one who had the idea in the first place. Most dairy farmers get a request to see if they are prepared to rear a calf for the IHC, and the calves are sold off after three or four months as weaners. Some rear a bull calf. The King Country branch regularly sells 300 to 400 calves. The Waikato branch maybe 700

Meads encourages farmers to donate a calf to the IHC Calf Scheme, a fund-raising project which raised over $1 million in 2001-2002. Meads donates hours of his time travelling the country meeting farmers, attending fundraisers and building the profile of IHC and the scheme.

PHOTO COURTESY IHC

to 800. Income raised helps fund IHC's residential, vocational and family services. In 2001, 4700 farmers donated 5400 calves, raising over $1 million for IHC. Wrightson took over sponsorship of the scheme in 1987 and I'm the patron. In 1984, 770 calves were donated, raising $110,000, so you can see how it has grown.

'I spent a lot of time between about 1975 and 1984 in IHC administration. And from the early 1980s I'd gone back to a fairly extensive involvement in rugby — I'd been King Country's selector/coach from 1976 to 1981. Then from 1982–85 I was a North Island selector, and New Zealand Colts selector in 1985. There's only so much a man can fit in.

'I actually enjoyed my work with IHC — although I was disappointed when some in IHC spoke out against my going on the Cavaliers tour. I think I'd proved my concerns for people in less fortunate circumstances. You actually mix with a lot of disadvantaged kids and others. They have their dances — no inhibitions, they enjoy themselves, and I often thought, how bloody lucky we were. A lot of the kids

Photo courtesy IHC

and so on would come and hug or cuddle me, and I started taking some of them to rugby, down to the footy club on Saturday afternoons. We brought one lad up here from a home in Levin where he'd been for years. He was always down at the Waitete club in Te Kuiti and really enjoyed it. The club members looked after him, ran him home. He became one of us.

'I made statements back then when asked why I got involved with IHC. I used to say that all sports people after they retired should do more to help charitable and welfare organisations in the community. I used to think about how lucky I'd been, playing for the All Blacks for 15 years. Frankly, I got a lot of pride out of doing something for a less fortunate group of people, and hoped that in some small way my example might encourage other sportsmen to do the same.

'As far as I know, no other ex-sportsman got involved to the extent I did — although I have tremendous admiration for Murray Halberg's work — although many certainly turned up for one-off events with some regularity. Nowadays, in the professional era, more players are conscious of the need to contribute some of their time to various groups.

'I tend to support the placing of intellectually handicapped people in the wider community, provided they are carefully controlled and aren't a threat to other people. It's the borderline cases that cause most trouble, especially when they find

Colin presents a cheque to Jim and Pauline Hedley, winners of one of the IHC National Calf Scheme awards. Also present are Dick Chamberlain (Livestock Manager, Wrightsons Wairarapa), and Jim and Pauline's daughter Meg.

they can't properly fend for themselves.

'I used to do a lot of fund-raising talks for IHC and all the proceeds went to the organisation. I tended to specify that donations should go to the King Country branch. Money was put aside, a Colin Meads Trust set up, and when it built up to a reasonable amount, 10 acres was purchased just outside Te Kuiti and it was called Pinetree Farm. A few calves are brought in there once a year prior to being sold, and I go in and sort them out.

'Eventually, I thought I'd done my dash in IHC and tried to ease out. A Community Trust was started in Hamilton and I was the IHC rep on it for four to five years. I was invited to join it and ended up chairman for a time. In many ways I was in opposition for a time, opposition in terms of competing for funds and placing people in houses. In some ways the trust was better off and possibly more sophisticated than IHC. To all intents and purposes the Trust was a branch of the regional health board.

'There were some serious arguments about finances, legal matters and the whole way things were managed and run. In the end, it got too much for me. I got frustrated going to see the chairman of the Hospital Board, having meetings about which staff members were going about things the right way and which weren't. It wasn't Colin Meads. At times I'd sit in meetings and swear to myself, thinking there used to be other ways of fixing these things. The Trust had about eight or nine houses round Hamilton and the legal side, the number of lawyers involved, often exasperated me. It looked to me as if half the time petty points-scoring was behind a lot of it — one-upmanship is another way of putting it — and life's too short. Funds would dry up in some areas. It was reliant solely on government funding. There weren't nationwide fund-raising efforts every year like there was in the IHC. We were dealing with bureaucrats all the time . . . egos clashing, it wasn't my cup of tea.

'A group of us in Te Kuiti would decide to visit hotels. We would go to Rotorua, about two hours away, and Colin Meads would go in and ask to see the managers. I'd say we were from the IHC, would you mind if we sold raffle tickets to raise funds? Almost without exception we were told that was fine. Mainly we got a good reception, but occasionally things turned hostile. I'd intervene and say no one had to buy a ticket, but when I explained our purpose most of the objectors ended up buying a ticket anyway. Overall we did better in the working-class bars, if one can use that term today.

'I remember we were in a shady-looking sort of a bar once; a group of ladies and fellas were sitting around a table laughing and blowing smoke back and forth. I didn't have a clue what was going on — later I was told they were smoking marijuana. The people with me said, "Cripes, it was obvious, the place reeked of marijuana." Not to me. I said I didn't know what marijuana smelled like. It may be true that marijuana is grown all over the King Country, but I'm unaware of it.

'Most of my rugby associates applauded my involvement with IHC but not many were willing to get involved themselves. "Better you than me," was their position.

'Quite a lot of guys I played rugby with took up golf when they stopped playing. They would meet on Sunday mornings. I never got involved in that. I was too busy with a big farm and with IHC and rugby coaching and selecting.

'I bought more land, then some more, and had a huge debt. It's not something I want to talk about now. But I loved the compulsory golf days when away with the All Blacks and thought it would be fun to play golf when at home — trouble was

PHOTOSPORT

Meads took to lawn bowls
after his retirement, but
found the sport became
too time consuming . . .
'I do like to win'.

I was scared to take it up because of the time involved and, being me, I'd have wanted to get better at it. Mind you, I'd have been hopeless. I'd have got frustrated . . . I'd say, "I'll whack this ball a mile", and it would trickle a few yards. I'd have been outside here, playing golf in the paddock, practising. Same with bowls. I've played a bit of that and got quite keen on it. Then I thought, God, I'm never home now. I'd be ducking in to the bowling club at one in the afternoon to have a roll up on my own, just to see if I could get better — when no bugger's watching me. I do like to win.

'I never had a chance to try tennis and get keen on that like Wilson Whineray and Brian Lochore did. But I did play and enjoy table tennis while at school, and I was the tenny quoits champion. I loved anything like that, and we — Stan and I — were always at school, at Te Kuiti High, very early. We used to catch the bus here at 7.30 in the morning, were there by eight and had the best part of an hour to kill.'

8.
COACH COLIN

'We were in an era where the coach was the boss. They [the players] seemed to have come through a period where they were in joint control; they had a big input into training. Fred Allen would seek our advice, but we had no input into how to put it into practice.'

WHEN MEADS FINALLY GAVE UP PLAYING ALL RUGBY IN 1975, HIS WIFE VERNA RECALLS THAT HE HAD PROMISED HER A COUPLE OF YEARS AWAY FROM RUGBY ALTOGETHER. 'IT NEVER HAPPENED,' SHE SAYS. 'ONE YEAR AT MOST,' IS HER GENEROUS ALLOWANCE.

Meads nods, is clearly a bit sheepish about it all. He was like a big kid lured irresistibly back to the cookie jar. From 1976 he was King Country selector-coach. Typically, Meads does not overrate his abilities in that position. Compared, he says, with the long-serving Curly Neilsen, 'who really was a good selector, Colin Meads wasn't. Colin Meads used to see a young kid playing for his club and think he had a bit of potential, so I'd give him a try. I made a few blues; some of my picks didn't come off. I got criticised for that, rightly. I always liked giving underdogs a go. Not all that clever really. King Country's like most unions in that nearly all the best players come from five or six clubs, but I was prone to go and look for a find elsewhere.'

Meads finds humour in this. He likes the idea of accepting infallibility for the challenges that offers. Now and then too he remembers picking a winner. 'I put Kevin Boroevich in the King Country front row when he was 17. Kevin played for my club, Waitete. His father was a wild man. Kevin was the youngest, I think, of five boys and his father used to make them scrap.

'I think I must have been a ruthless coach. I remember Kevin's first game in 1978. It was against Auckland and Brad Johnstone, the All Black prop, was playing for them. I said to Kevin — it was the wrong thing to say and I freely admit it — that if Brad so much as blinked an eye, whack him. Brad had a reputation for not being overly robust and being all talk and not much action. So here's 17-year-old Kevin Boroevich of King Country belting an All Black prop. Someone said to Brad after the game that Kevin was only 17, and Brad is said to have replied that he hadn't realised that. If he had he may have reacted differently.'

If Johnstone found Boroevich a bit scary, Meads is not surprised for he saw him as 'a wild bugger, as a young fella', and Meads didn't try to discourage or reign him in. The King Country side was on the decline, and Meads lamented a lack of real hard men, but nevertheless they had some good games.

Meads is still on the board of the King Country union, although it is much streamlined nowadays. In the 1970s he remembers every club having a delegate and there would be well over 20 at union meetings. 'They would argue all night. Now we've gone all modern with a board and then a council of clubs. The clubs run the rugby, but the board controls the finances. The game's not the same, and I still think we were better off under the old system. Unions like Auckland and Otago, for example, are different. They have the sort of money we in King Country don't.

Fiery Fred's coaching regime

Meads says, 'When I was coaching, I often thought of Fred Allen. He wouldn't live in today's coaching environment — after two or three days many of them would piss off. Or he'd have sent them home. I'm not saying Fred's methods were wrong, far from it, but we — he and I — were of a different era. It was funny the way Fred would tell me, in front of the others, two or three days before a test, that he was going to get into me. He'd say that if he got into me it "would make the young fellas feel good". After it happened I can recall saying to him, "Jesus, you didn't have to be that rough on me." He'd have called me "a big prick; I've seen the way you've been playing, running round trying to get all the plums now, playing like a fairy", that sort of thing. He could motivate you, Fred could. There was that instance where I yawned in a talk of Fred's and he

saw me and said, "Am I boring you, you big prick? There's a bus leaving in 10 minutes if I am."

'Fred often used me and Kel Tremain as a means of showing the young ones that he had no favourites. He'd often have a few drinks on the Thursday or Friday night before a home test, and would end up in our room where we discussed what had been happening and how the team's preparation was going. Fred was straight and I liked that. But I will admit that when he first came along I had grave doubts about him and his methods. We — the All Blacks — used to be pretty dour, forward-oriented. Backs were a necessary evil. Their first responsibility was to tackle and keep the opposition out. In the forwards we used to have a saying, "We'll get 60 per cent of the ball so don't you so-and-sos waste it.

I'm a bit disillusioned by today's systems of management.'

It is not only today's union organisation and management processes that Meads finds disillusioning. Coaching methods are a far cry from his early rugby days.

Fred Allen reckoned Meads was a fine reader of the play. That is something that's both instinctive and learned, in Meads' view. One has to meld thought and aggression and skill — any one is not enough by itself. 'Know the game well, that's the first thing,' says Meads. That calls for observance, application, astuteness. Experience helps of course, but some are slower learners than others. Then there's the opposition; and here Meads' eyes light up, as if his innate rugby shrewdness as much as the cultivation of it, and memories, come flooding back. 'It would be good to play today,' he says, the old itch returning, 'and be able to sit down and watch all those videos of your opposition. We never had that. We often played against teams that had good backs and that made us scared of them getting too much ball, and running us forwards all over the place. So we were quite defensive-minded in that regard, which meant we were keen to catch up with them as quick as we could. Instinct is a part of that, but I think your instinct and ability to take the short cuts comes into play more when you've got the ball. That's when the really talented players shine. Often you have to take a gamble and go for the short cut to where you feel the play's heading, only to find someone drops a pass and you're out of the play for a bit. But that's the chance you take. You have to take those risks; a player's more value to his team if he's on-hand when a team-mate's caught. So there is an art in reading the game, and possibly it's an instinct some have and others don't.'

Meads looks out of the corner of his eye and there's a flicker of a wink when he says, drily, 'But the older you get, the more cunning you get. The young enthusiast

Keep it in front of us, we don't want to be running back."

'Where the game has changed now is that we struggle to get 50 per cent of the ball. For a time we had a simple policy: when in doubt give it to big, strong Ian MacRae at second five-eighth, get him to take it up and we'd zero in on him. We loved it. Then along came Fred and changed it all. He said, "You big pricks are going to change with it and if you don't you're out."

'Fred was a back but he concentrated on the forwards, spent more time with us than with the backs. I often think that coaches who've been backs tend to think that they know all about back play, so they concentrate on the other, just to make sure they're up to speed. Look at Laurie Mains, a fullback who's the best forward coach in the country.

'Fred convinced us that there was a better way to play the game, and our backs were getting better too.'

Fred Allen, says Meads, wouldn't live in today's coaching environment . . . 'he and I were of a different era'.

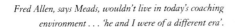

— the headless chook rushing everywhere — is entertaining to watch, but much of it is wasted effort.'

In the early 1980s, Meads enjoyed his term as a North Island selector. There was always the chance, as a selector, that one would stumble on a previously unheard of player, and Meads admits he had to be careful not to get carried away in that regard. He enjoyed going to after-match functions and having a few beers with locals who tried 'to pump their fellas up', and questioned him as to whether he was going to include so-and-so. 'I never gave anything away,' says Meads, and told them, 'you'll have to wait and see.' He wasn't intending to be mischievous, it was more that he didn't want to disillusion people. He would discuss aspects of a game with some of the players, though, and enjoyed being around players of a younger generation.

One of the first North-South games Meads went to in his capacity as a selector was held in Wanganui. Frank Ryan was in charge of coaching the North side which, as Meads recalls, included big names like forwards Andy Haden, Gary Knight and Murray Mexted. Training was nearly over when Ryan asked Meads to take the forwards. 'I asked them what they were going to do in this situation, or that, and every time the chorus was, "We've got that covered." I said, "Well, they've got Jock Ross in the lineouts so obviously they're going to drive all day on you, so you'll need a bit of depth there," and so on. Graham Mourie was there too. And whatever I said, Mourie or Haden would reply, "It's all right, we've spoken about that, it's all fixed." I thought, that's interesting. Then I asked what they would do if they regularly threw it to a tall Canterbury prop, who was good, and who stood at two in the lineout. I was trying to suss out what the South might do. "Aw, no, we've got that covered."'

Okay, thought Meads, a trace of amusement showing, there were some top players in the North side, but were they touched with a glow of the know-all? Meads knew too that as the game was being played in Wanganui, a lot of King Country supporters would turn up, and they would be interested in seeing how Colin Meads' North Island forwards went.

'Well,' with more than a touch of delight on his face and in his voice, he says, 'we got dorked. The South Island didn't expect to win. I had spoken to Billy Bush and others who were out on the Friday night having a few beers. They took us to the cleaners up front. Later, about 10 that night, in a sarcastic sort of a way I took great delight in saying to a few of the North Island forwards, "Ah, but you'd have had that covered, wouldn't you?" The response was talk of it having been "one of those games that just get away on you". I told them that it's all about attitude, and that, "You pricks thought you were going to win. It's true, play 'em again tomorrow and you'd beat them, but tomorrow's too bloody late. It's attitude on the day, and you fellas were just too bloody cocky."'

Even the talented and the august need to be reminded at times of salutary lessons. The sub-text of Meads' remarks on that occasion highlighted how, in his day, great players not only led but were willing to be led. It may be that Haden and those of his ability and standing marked a change whereby the players assumed, and expected, to have greater influence, a time when they attempted to manage the selectors, coaches and managers. Perhaps they saw themselves as leading moves away from a more narrowly focused past into a more multi-dimensional future that was soon to be touted as 'the modern game'. Meads says that, 'We were in an era

By his own admission, Meads never really made a good fist of coaching. Here he lays down the law to King Country.

where the coach was the boss. They seemed to have come through a period where they were in joint control; they had a big input into training. Fred Allen would seek our advice, but we had no input into how to put it into practice.'

None of this should be construed as meaning that Meads was anti-Haden, one occasionally seen as oracular and sharply adamant. 'Andy had a lot of great points about him, and he was a good footballer. When he was "on" in a test match, he was one of the best locks around. Andy's the flamboyant guy; he would try and rile officials. He'd speak up about the temperature of the lemonade or beer in the dressing room. The point he was out to make was that jobs should be done properly, whereas in our day we tended not to complain and just live with things. Andy changed many things in rugby. He changed things even though he didn't get bouquets for it.'

Meads is sure that in the 1980s the players didn't have the same attitude that he and his ilk did to the inter-island game. 'For us, it was always regarded as the final All Black trial. Next to test rugby, that was the hardest rugby I ever played. That attitude certainly wasn't there when I was selecting and coaching the North side.'

The inter-island games were always a highlight for Meads. Through them he met the likes of South Island counterparts, Neville Goodwin of Mid-Canterbury and Alistair 'Spud' Tait of Southland, and they became good friends. 'I always thought it a tragedy that they pulled the plug on North-South games. A main reason was that North had won it four or five years in a row and it had served its usefulness. Hah, if you played it now, with all the All Blacks that come from down south . . . how the wheels turn.'

9.
A CAVALIER APPROACH

*'To be honest, I hadn't thought much
at all about possible repercussions. Me
being naive again, I suppose. I just
loved going to South Africa, loved
playing against them, and we'd never
beaten them in a series over there.
That used to brown me off, to be
quite honest. I could see this as a
chance to beat them.'*

COLIN MEADS HAS BEEN STEADFAST IN HIS VIEW THAT FOR HIM POLITICS AND SPORT DON'T MIX. HE PREFERS TO KEEP THEM SEPARATE. IN FACT, HE'S NEVER BEEN VERY INTERESTED IN POLITICS OF ANY KIND. BUT HE REALISES THAT MANY PEOPLE ARE, AND THAT POLITICS, POLITICIANS AND POLITICKING OFTEN DECIDE WHAT HAPPENS.

To Meads, politics and deviousness have tended to seem like one and the same, which is why he's 'tried to stay out of it'. Meads says that in all the time he's been involved in rugby, remarkably few people have ever tried to draw him into lobbying and scheming. He thinks they sensed early on that he liked to 'keep things simple, didn't like red tape, just never felt comfortable with lobbying and the like'. Nevertheless, he wouldn't go along entirely with the view that he is and was merely a simple country boy, an unsophisticated soul — for many in rugby and outside it say Colin Meads is shrewder, smarter than he makes out — but he has always said and believed that frequently he's been 'a bit naive'.

Even now he says that he was unaware of the extent of the anger many players felt when the All Blacks' scheduled 1985 tour of South Africa was called off. Nor was he fully aware of who the prime movers were behind the so-called 'rebel' Cavaliers' tour of South Africa in April–May 1986.

The proposed 1985 tour and the subsequent shenanigans all related back to the ructions caused by the 1981 Springbok tour of New Zealand. Two Auckland lawyers challenged the NZRFU's decision to accept South Africa's invitation for the All Blacks to tour in 1985 and successfully applied for a High Court injunction barring the players' departure. The tour was cancelled only five days before the players were to depart. Meads was a supporter of the 1981 tour. He was always pro-rugby, pro-sporting contacts with South Africa while being anti-apartheid. He has never seen any contradiction in that. He accepted that some saw tours as morally wrong, but didn't think they had the right to impose their moral interpretations on others. He has never seen sporting contacts with South Africa as implying support for the apartheid system, and, if anything, believes such contact was to the good in that the likely spin-off was to undermine rather than preserve the system of racial segregation.

When the rugby fraternity and the players who had been selected by the NZRFU to tour South Africa were told that they couldn't go as All Blacks, but would have to travel as 'individuals', that was like a red rag to a number of single-minded rugby-playing bulls. There was an intention to proceed with a private tour but that got called off on the eve of their departure when legal action was threatened.

The ensuing events are cloaked in references to mystery and intrigue. Just who was involved in organising the highly contentious Cavaliers' tour to South Africa, and who got paid what and by whom, remains unclear. Most players and officials simply clammed up.

Thirty players made the 1986 trip but only one, the Waikato back Bill Osborne, had been to South Africa before as an All Black. But 28 of the 30 players originally named to tour by the All Black selectors in 1985 were in the Cavaliers' party, plus halfback Andrew Donald and winger Bernie Fraser. The captain was Andy Dalton. Ian Kirkpatrick was manager and Colin Meads the coach, both men having previously toured South Africa as All Blacks. Neither had played in a team that had beaten South Africa in a test series in the republic. It was something they would dearly have loved to have done.

The party didn't leave together. Some players went via International Rugby Board (IRB) centennial matches in Britain, others had been invited to carnival matches in South Africa. Words such as clandestine and subterfuge were bandied about. In the eyes of rugby's controlling bodies the players had no official standing. Cries that they'd been 'bought', paid colossal sums, and were party to changing the whole nature of rugby internationally forever, and so on, jagged about. Traitors said some; principled and courageous individuals said others; pathetic and ill-advised said many. The South Africans regarded the four games against the Springboks as 'tests' against the All Blacks; the New Zealand union, clearly and vociferously, did not. The pressures on the players were enormous. But they gutsed it out bravely in the face of considerable provocation on the field and off. The refereeing was not what any visiting side would have wished.

By the time they returned to New Zealand, the Cavaliers were hardly courtly in

Coach Meads, captain Andy Dalton and manager Ian Kirkpatrick look grim-faced at the launch of the Cavaliers' tour at the Johannesburg home of South African rugby supremo, Dr Louis Luyt.

the eyes of many both within and without rugby. Many said, 'I hope it doesn't come to this ever again. They slunk off and they slunk back.' And yet many others too said defiantly, 'Good on them for not buckling under to the wishes and deeds of moralistic busybodies.' It was hard, though, to suppress feelings that the sour notes lingered longer, that the melodies were too often discordant.

At the time, Meads' great friend Brian Lochore was in his second year as All Black coach. He was also a selector as were Tiny Hill and Meads himself. Unbeknown to them, the two feisty All Black Andys, Dalton and Haden, businessman Winston McDonald, and another former All Black captain Ian Kirkpatrick, had some months previously met in Hong Kong to begin organising what came to be known as the Cavaliers' tour. Also involved was South African rugby titan Louis Luyt, chairman of the Transvaal Rugby Union at the time, a man eventually seen by some as All Black rugby's bête noire. Others at the meeting were Luyt's solicitor Mervyn Ley, Robert Denton who managed Ellis Park in Johannesburg, and former Springbok captain Johan Claassen of the Volkskas Bank, who agreed to finance the tour. The tour, Haden has relentlessly argued, took place not for money, but because the players wanted to pit themselves against South Africa at rugby and were unwavering in their belief that that was their entitlement. Rather similar to Meads' position, actually.

Haden wanted Kirkpatrick along as manager and Kirkpatrick approached Lochore and asked him if he would be coach. Lochore had no hesitation in saying no thanks; as convenor of selectors and All Black coach he could not possibly go on an unauthorised tour.

Lochore was in England for the IRB's centenary celebrations and the players who were about to head to South Africa — Dalton, Haden and Mexted among them — told him where they were going. When Lochore got back to New Zealand, Colin Meads rang him and told him he was about to fly to South Africa and be coach of the Cavaliers. Lochore made no effort to dissuade Meads, said it

WESSEL OOSTHUIZEN

Meads in South Africa with the Cavaliers.

was his decision solely. 'He didn't approve or disapprove,' says Meads. At that point it was impossible for either players or selectors to look ahead with any certainty to the upcoming All Black tests against France and Australia, then the October–November tour to France. As for the first World Cup to be played in Australia and New Zealand in 1987, planning just had to continue.

Meads was at home on the farm in the King Country when Andy Haden had rung him and asked if he would go to South Africa as coach of the Cavaliers. He thought about it, quickly, and his old desire to be part of a group of New Zealand players who would beat the South Africans in a test series in their stronghold came surging back. He agreed to go because he 'always thought we did so much good by going there in 1960 and 1970. I thought tours were working, were helping break down apartheid, because it was so much better when I went back in 1970.

'It was noticeable of course that the blacks weren't all that drawn to playing rugby; they were soccer players mainly. That was possibly because they had poor, stony surfaces — badly prepared grounds to play on.'

Meads thought that as he had become a national selector it would be a good idea that someone like him was on hand in South Africa to watch 30 of New Zealand's top players in action. He told Lochore that, and thought that fact alone was enough to justify his going along. The extent of Meads' distance from behind-the-scenes activity in New Zealand rugby can be seen when he recalls telling Lochore that the tour was 'all hush hush, don't say anything', only to have Lochore say that he had known about it for some time.

At this stage Meads didn't know which members of the NZRFU knew about the tour, if any of them knew of his decision to go, and which, if any, privately supported the tour. None got in touch with him prior to his departure. Some players left from various parts of New Zealand, met and assembled in Sydney, and flew on from there. They went away, says Meads, under some sort of peculiar party name — 'Goat Breeders or something.' With a sigh, Meads says, 'To be honest, I hadn't thought much at all about possible repercussions. Me being naive again, I suppose. I just loved going to South Africa, loved playing against them, and we'd never beaten them in a series over there. That used to brown me off, to be quite honest. I could see this as a chance to beat them.

'I was probably less well aware of it then, but when I look back I realise that in many ways Colin Meads wasn't a good coach. Colin Meads saw rugby as a game that you played this way; it was pretty straightforward to me. I wasn't a schemer, wasn't good at devising tactics on how to beat such and such a side. In some ways, Fred Allen had indoctrinated me. We'd done so well under him and his methods and strategy.

'But by now I'd been away from playing and coaching top-level rugby for several years — except for a few one-off efforts with the North Island team. The players were different.

'In my role as coach of the Cavaliers, one of the differences was that in my day the coach was the boss. Possibly a bit more dictatorial, not that there's anything wrong with that. By 1986, players' lifestyles and expectations were different. Attitudes had changed. The likes of Haden, Mexted, Stu Wilson and so on questioned. They'd ask, "Why should we do it this way, why not that way?" I found, even though I'd coached King Country for a while, and had taken the North Island team, that I always thought the players thought they knew more than I did.

'Some of those North Island players were in the Cavaliers. I tended to take the training like Fred Allen did. He was ruthless at training and he made the backs do a lot more running than they were used to. They hated it. They never said anything at the time but afterwards would say he'd trained them "like marathon runners. That's not what back play's all about", and so on. I can remember doing similar sort of stuff with the Cavaliers. I heard Bill Osborne say, "Jesus, I've never trained like that. I'm stuffed, stiff and sore. I'll play ratshit, I won't be right for Saturday." Then he actually played a pretty good game and I sidled up to him and said, "You played pretty well today, Bill."

'"Yeah, I felt pretty good."

'"Might have something to do with the training, Bill?"

'No answer. I realised that in order to be a good coach you had to be more of a diplomat. Like Brian Lochore was. This team needed a bit of both, a Grizz Wyllie on the one hand, a Lochore on the other. It's a big ask. I was trying to be both hard and nice. I didn't seem to get the right mix.

'If we had had John Kirwan, I think we would have won the series. John was in his prime. Unfortunately he was in Italy. David Kirk pulled out, although he wasn't such a loss. We had David Loveridge, and he was a tremendous halfback. When he got belted that cost us.

'Andy Dalton getting his jaw broken almost straight away, by a king hit from Burger Geldenhuys from Northern Transvaal in the second match, was a great loss too. Not so much for his on-field leadership, but certainly for his all-round ability.

That included not being provoked and doing silly things like Hika Reid was unable to resist doing at times.

'I was impressed and a bit bemused by how organised the players were. They had a committee for this and a committee for that. Nothing like in my day. They had so much gear given to them. They had team sessions at the start of the tour where each player was asked and would have to state what he wanted from it, why he was there . . . We had none of that in my day. We didn't have to stand up in front of everyone and say why we were there . . . crikey, I had no doubts about why I was in the All Blacks, say, it was obvious. We all knew why we were in the team and what we had to do. Most of us felt the same. In the Cavaliers the one who impressed me there was Mark 'Cowboy' Shaw. He got up and said, "Stuff all this bullshit, there's no good talking about it. We want action." There'd be this talk stuff before every test on the Cavaliers tour. It wasn't my style. I'm still not sure if that's the right sort of motivation.

'Nowadays there are debriefings. I always said the debriefing came at the next training run when Fred Allen got hold of us. It amounts to the same thing.

'Of course one discusses team strategies. That's what you do during pre-match training. When I travel around New Zealand these days I sometimes discuss the make-up of the All Black team. We used to have two managers — two too many at times, I sometimes thought — but now they have 12 or 13 people; psychoanalysts; forward, back, kicking and throwing-in coaches; bio-mechanists and physical trainers . . . on and on. I say they're possibly confusing the players with too much information. It is necessary to think things through carefully, to train and prepare properly, but perhaps we've gone a bit too far and instead of being focused, the players are actually preoccupied with too many different things.

'On the tour I developed a lot of respect for Jock Hobbs. When Andy Dalton was injured, Haden took over, then Hobbs. We'd discuss whether to take the opposition on up front, or run the ball, and this was where Colin Meads wasn't a good coach. I'd say we should do it this way and a lot of them would disagree with me. It was hard to teach Andy Haden or Murray Mexted anything. Andy was a good player, and when it came to lineouts perhaps I wasn't strong enough. I was a bit of a schemer in lineouts, if I could get away with it . . . everyone was in my day. You never saw photos of me six feet up in the air. I always used to say that it's the guy who ends up with the ball who is the good player and it stops there.'

Meads may have underestimated the regard in which Haden held him. In *Lock, Stock and Barrel*, he writes that he found 'Pinetree Meads was a cunning, clever tactician'. But Meads' self-doubt was strong. 'Kirky, the manager, was younger than me and maybe he should have been the coach, but he's not the sort of guy who wanted to be coach. So I was it.

'The nature of rugby is such that you have to take the opposition on in the forwards and gain some ascendancy there if you're to have a better-than-even chance of winning a game. Get clean ball and drive with it is still a sound, basic tactic. I got sick of hearing about "good" and "bad" ball, and I have never liked the terms. There's no bad ball, it's what you do with it was my way of thinking. I was a great believer that you had to do everything going forward. If you're not, come back and resurrect things, then go again. I may have been inclined to try to get our blokes to run the ball too much.

'It was an odd mix of a team. The contrasts were sharp. Wayne Smith and Grant Fox at first five, and 'Buck' Shelford and Murray Mexted at number eight

Wessel Oosthuizen

for example. It wasn't a long tour — four tests, separated by matches against the Junior Springboks, Northern Transvaal, Orange Free State, Transvaal, Western Province, Natal, Barbarians and Western Transvaal — 12 matches all told. I wish we'd had more games apart from the tests. There was a test side and a Wednesday side, nevertheless I think we had a big part in the development of Shelford, Steve McDowell and Fox. We tended to play Fox as a goal-kicker when playing Kieran Crowley at fullback, and when Robbie Deans was there to kick we had Wayne Smith at first five.

Grant Fox sets the Cavaliers backline away in 'test' action from 1986. Other Cavaliers in the frame are, from left: Andy Haden, Murray Pierce, Mark Shaw and Gary Knight.

'I didn't greatly enjoy the tour. I had a crook knee which prevented me running around and I actually had an operation on it during the tour. I had a piece of cartilage removed that was giving me hell. Mind you, I'd got the impression from some of the players that I wasn't really needed anyway. Andy Haden, the team's Minister of Lurks and Perks, and Andy Dalton were dominant figures — Haden's a pretty strong personality.

'Of course, the team was full of tough, good guys — the likes of Gary Knight for instance — and I used to say to myself, "I'll get into some of these fellas in team talks." After we'd lost the first test in Cape Town (15–21) I let them know I wasn't very happy. But I remembered how Grizz Wyllie once fooled a side that arrived at training thinking it was in for a hard run. He put some beers on instead and when they'd had a few, tongues started to wag and he got the truth out of them. Compared to my day these guys got free this, free that. I could have sat around after matches and spent a couple of hours finishing off the half to three-quarter full cans if I'd wanted to.

WESSEL OOSTHUIZEN

Giant South African lock Louis Moolman climbs above the Cavaliers' lineout men.

'I thought, "Here's my chance. You've just been beaten in a test." So I arranged with ex-Springbok Dougie Hopwood to have plenty of beer and a decent-sized room at the Seapoint Hotel where we were staying. I wanted to have a real heart-to-heart. "Don't tell anyone, just tee it up with the manager." The beer was no trouble — Dougie worked for a brewery. The players were wearing training gear and I got them in, sat them down and told them how spoilt they were. I said, "You have all these court sessions where you pretend to skull your beer. In my day, if you were told to drink your beer, you did. I don't care whether you drink beer, coke, lemonade, or anything, but if the judge says drink, you drink. None of this sipping and leaving the rest. That's how you're playing your rugby, you're cheating. Not putting the effort in. I could sit around after a match and get myself blind drunk just drinking you fellas' left-overs." I gave them a real talking to. "You be clear what you want to drink and drink it. In our day we used to get Sid Going drunk on orange juice or lemonade."

'So we had a court session to end all court sessions, and after a while all the truth came out about Haden and one or two others. Accusations about others trying to take over and run the show. "Pinetree doesn't coach the team, you do," and so on. There wasn't anything bitter or nasty about it, but it confirmed what I felt, which was that they were of a different era, and I wasn't really strong enough to take full control. That may sound odd coming from Pinetree Meads, but that's the way it was. Many of the guys knew more about what was happening on the field than I did. But we did win the second "test".

'Winston McDonald travelled around with us and he and some of the players were often having little conferences. He'd had a lot of dealings with Louis Luyt on matters to do with the tour. So a lot went on that I didn't know much about.

'There were a lot of great fellas on the tour. Bernie Fraser was one, but he was at the end of his career. He'd largely given it away. It was very much a social trip for him. I think I should have been a bit harder on some players. I remember Andy Dalton saying, "Get into so-and-so, look at him dropping the ball" during training. There was that element in the team, and I always look back to the 1967 tour of the British Isles and France when, after a while, it became obvious that six or seven players weren't going to get any more games. Fred wasn't really going to consider them, and then little things would happen, and one or other would have to play and they weren't ready. I suppose I was a bit like that with the Cavaliers, and concentrated on the keen ones and the main guys.

'As for how much the players got paid — just what arrangements had been made there — was something I never knew. I was told I'd get as much as the players, and if that was true they didn't get as much as some of the rumours stated. I'm not going to say what I got, but it wasn't big by today's standards — a couple of test matches' worth.'

Most of the players clung to the line that they didn't go for the money and that for many, touring South Africa was a lifelong ambition. There was what they indelicately described as 'a good team fund'. David Kirk, who declined to go, said he'd been offered $100,000. Andy Haden, who ought to know since he was one of the main organisers, is reported as saying in Keith Quinn's *Legends of the All Blacks*, 'Financially, it was well worth the players going on the trip' and that he got 'exactly the same as every other player'. No one got $100,000, said Haden. 'The team fund mounted to maybe $50,000 a player, about four times what it had been on previous tours.'

Louis Luyt said that Dr Danie Craven and the South African Rugby Union were right behind the tour and sanctioned it. They, like Luyt, saw it as a full-strength All Black team. Luyt, always emphatic as a cannon going off, said to Keith Quinn that, apart from the absent David Kirk and John Kirwan, New Zealand's best arrived. 'They were a tremendous side. That was New Zealand.'

It is undeniable that this Cavaliers team tried extremely hard. They had many skilled, hardened, greatly talented and determined players. They had some fine young talents. The tour wasn't a long one, but it was arduous physically. There were some vicious incidents on the field and the refereeing infuriated, and, at times, virtually enraged the Cavaliers players and management.

There was no TV coverage of their games shown live back in New Zealand. And while many rugby supporters approved of their going, there was also a greater amount of opprobrium than usual directed towards them from people who were traditionally contemptuous of New Zealand rugby's obsession with titanic contests with the Springboks. If the tour did little harm to rugby in New Zealand in the long run, there were few who saw it as doing much good. For Colin Meads it was another lost opportunity to beat the Boks in a series of 'test' matches in the republic. He felt the players to do it were there and that, had they been given a panel of referees to choose from, as in their view they'd been promised, the results would have been different.

There were a number of unseemly incidents on the field that cost the Cavaliers dearly. The most affecting were, probably, the punch that broke Andy Dalton's jaw in the second game on tour, and the late hit on Dave Loveridge in the third 'test'. He was knocked out and took no further part in the tour. Andy Dalton said after the last 'test', when the penalty count went against the Cavaliers 21–7, that they felt cruelly let down by the referee Ken Rowlands of Wales. Dalton said the Cavaliers were given a choice from a panel comprising Ken Rowlands of Wales, Ken Rowlands, Wales, and Ken Rowlands (Wales).

The last 'test', played at Ellis Park in Johannesburg, was won by South Africa 24–10. Journalists Doug Laing and Kip Brook, who covered the tour for NZPA, reported these remarks from a dispirited Colin Meads:

> 'It was an awful irony to go there this time with a referee from a neutral country and find him actually worse.
> 'The team played so well in that final match — so well that given a fair run they had the beating of the Springboks. To win that match meant everything to the players and to me.
> 'Ken Rowlands' efforts were not even subtle.'

Meads got so upset watching the game that he left his seat before the end and went elsewhere and watched the final few minutes on television.

The Cavaliers didn't return to New Zealand as a group. Some stayed on and had a holiday in Durban, others went elsewhere. Meads, though, high-tailed it out of the place and was on a plane back to New Zealand the day after the loss at Ellis Park. He got into Auckland on the Tuesday morning. Unbeknown to Meads there had been grumblings back in New Zealand about his absence. Irresponsible, said some; insensitive said others. The temerity of the man. There was a move to have him punished. A number of NZRFU councillors were believed to be waiting to call him to account, grill him, and sack him; send Pinetree back to his King Country rural enclave in disgrace. It was true, but Meads had other ideas.

Cavaliers' record

The Cavaliers lost the 'test' series 3–1. They went down in the first by 21–15 in Cape Town, won the second 19–18 in Durban, lost the third 33–18 in Pretoria, and the last in Jo'burg, 24–10. In these matches the Cavaliers were highly competitive only to fade in the latter stages. There was the suggestion that this was in part because Meads worked the team too hard at training. Meads does not accept there's truth in that at all.

They won seven of their eight other matches on tour, two by one point only, but those results still reflected well on the team.

10.
FALLEN IDOL

'I felt a number — what proportion I don't know — wanted to sack me there and then. But Wally Bain had reminded them of what they might be in for if they did, so they didn't. They seemed to be implying that I could remain as selector but don't bother to reapply next year. That's virtually what happened.'

WHEN BIG BAD COLIN ARRIVED IN AUCKLAND AND BOOKED INTO HIS HOTEL THE PRESS AND TELEVISION WERE WAITING. HE HADN'T EXPECTED THAT. HE SAYS, 'I WAS PUT THROUGH THE WRINGER, TOLD I WAS GOING TO HAVE TO APPEAR BEFORE THE NZRFU WHERE CES BLAZEY HAD RETIRED AND RUSS THOMAS WAS THE NEW CHAIRMAN.' AS IT HAPPENED, THAT MAY NOT HAVE BEEN A BAD THING.

Meads, in his usual somewhat naive, also resolute way, had been so preoccupied with his job as coach of the Cavaliers in South Africa that he had been unaware of the extent of the clanging back home. (It wasn't till later that he learned that the local police sergeant had called on his wife Verna and had given her his private phone number just in case there was trouble on the farm.) In New Zealand rumours were flying about like litter. Indignation and outrage in some quarters,

118

Cavaliers captain Andy Dalton was greeted by protestors at Auckland airport on his return from the tour.

'good on the bastards' approval in others. The 'rebels', Meads and Kirkpatrick as well as the players, should be banned from rugby for life. That was the most extreme position. Some councillors were said to be so incensed that they were pushing to have Meads censured and sacked from his selector's job. Pinetree was going to be felled this time, no doubt about it.

Blazey had been at an International Rugby Board (IRB) meeting in London when Andy Haden and other players — there for festival matches — told him of their impending tour with the Cavaliers. He was also told that other All Blacks were already in South Africa, awaiting the arrival of those from London. Meads believes Blazey had retorted, 'Well, they'll be home before I will be.' South Africa's Mr Rugby, Danie Craven, when quizzed pretended to be unaware of what was

PHOTOSPORT

Former NZRFU
chairman Ces Blazey,
who threatened Meads
with 'revocation of his
appointment' in the wake
of the Cavaliers' tour.

going on. But the IRB wasn't going to move against a team of individuals; they handed the problem back to the NZRFU.

The Cavaliers slogged their way round South Africa while the panjandrums — in the eyes of some — on the NZRFU debated what to do about the recalcitrants overseas. Eventually, on 15 May, chairman Blazey sent Meads this message:

ATTN: C.E. MEADS, ESQ.

DEAR MR MEADS,

RE: YOUR APPOINTMENT AS A NEW ZEALAND SELECTOR

ON 4 OCTOBER 1985 YOU WERE APPOINTED BY THE COUNCIL TO BE A MEMBER OF THE NEW ZEALAND SELECTION PANEL FOR THE TERM OF ONE YEAR. IN MAKING THE APPOINTMENT THE COUNCIL ANTICIPATED THAT YOU WOULD BE IN NEW ZEALAND AT REASONABLE TIMES THROUGHOUT YOUR TERM OF OFFICE AND, IN PARTICULAR, YOU WOULD BE HERE TO ASSESS PLAYERS DURING APRIL AND MAY WITH A VIEW TO MAKING SELECTIONS FOR THE VARIOUS NZRFU FIXTURES, INCLUDING TRIALS, IN JUNE AND SUBSEQUENT MONTHS.

YOU HAVE BEEN OUT OF NEW ZEALAND SINCE EARLY APRIL AND ARE NOT EXPECTED TO RETURN UNTIL EARLY JUNE. AS A RESULT, YOU HAVE BEEN ABSENT FROM CERTAIN MATCHES ALLOCATED TO YOU BY THE CONVENOR, MR LOCHORE. YOU HAVE NOT BEEN IN A POSITION TO ASSESS THE CURRENT FORM OF A NUMBER OF PLAYERS WHO HAVE BEEN OR WILL BE NOMINATED FOR SELECTION. THIS HAS PLACED AN UNFAIR ADDITIONAL BURDEN ON YOUR FELLOW SELECTORS.

THE COUNCIL IS MOST CONCERNED ABOUT THIS HIGHLY UNSATISFACTORY SITUATION AND INTENDS TO REVIEW YOUR APPOINTMENT AT ITS MEETING ON FRIDAY 16 MAY NEXT. AMONG THE OPTIONS OPEN TO THE COUNCIL IS THE REVOCATION OF YOUR APPOINTMENT FORTHWITH.

YOU ARE INVITED TO COMMUNICATE YOUR VIEWS ON THIS MATTER TO THE COUNCIL EITHER BY TELEPHONE OR BY CABLE OR TELEX. ANY REPRESENTATIONS YOU MAKE WILL BE GIVEN SERIOUS CONSIDERATION BY THE COUNCIL.

YOURS SINCERELY

C.A. BLAZEY

CHAIRMAN
15/5/86

Some saw this telex from Blazey as rash and heavy-handed. And preposterous too, given that it seemed that the union was intending to go ahead and review Meads' position in his absence. Where was the evidence of a willingness on the union's part to comply with the rules of natural justice?

In response to the Blazey bombshell, Meads replied:

When offered the position as coach of the 30 players I thought it important that a New Zealand selector be involved to assess the form of the players. I discussed the matter with Mr Lochore and told him of my intentions. He agreed that it would be of benefit to have first-hand knowledge of the top 30 players. I didn't think I had to inform anyone else.

One who was watching the matter unfold in New Zealand was Meads' friend and solicitor Wallace Bain, a partner in a law practice in Te Kuiti. Meads says, 'Wally was on the King Country rugby union and was a bit of a rugby nut. He had been pretty good at defending and getting players off when they were up for misdemeanours.'

Bain was deeply concerned and thought it time 'we as his solicitors intervened. We rang Colin in South Africa and he was quite astounded at what was going on in New Zealand.' Bain says that 'it appeared the Union were going to take [Meads' response to Blazey's telex] as his reply and deal with him in his absence.'

'At that point we stepped in and reminded them of the rules of natural justice and that there could be no hearing or consideration of anything without a detailed opportunity to discuss matters with Colin.' Bain says that they wrote to the NZRFU chairman on 16 May 'pointing this out and the necessity for proper notice'.

After speaking to Meads on 16 May, Bain got in touch with the NZRFU and asked that on behalf of Meads the following be added to his initial response to Blazey's telex:

> I have now had the opportunity to discuss the telex with my solicitor. I hadn't appreciated it was a possibility that the Union would be dealing with my continuation as selector in a final way today. I very much would like the opportunity to make representations to the Union before any decision is made to take action against me with respect to my position as a New Zealand selector.
>
> I would like the Union to appreciate that I believe I am very much fulfilling my role as a New Zealand selector faced with the fact that the top 30 players were going to South Africa.

On 27 May, Meads' solicitors wrote another letter to the NZRFU. Bain was worried about the way they seemed to be 'trying to keep the matter low key and informal and were wanting Colin to come and "have a chat" with them. On the other hand, they were really proposing to have this as some form of hearing so that Colin could put his case and they were going to reconsider his position as a selector.' Meads' solicitors told the union they couldn't do that and that they, his solicitors, 'would need to be an intimate part' of whatever they decided to do.

Bain says, 'It appeared there was nothing in the NZRFU rules or the IRB rules or anything concerning having to be in the country the entire time you were a selector and so on. In other words they were attempting to define rules to meet this particular circumstance retrospectively and then apply them.'

Around this time E.J.H. Morton, the President of Meads' Waitete club, sent a letter expressing the club's support for Meads to the NZRFU.

NZRFU councillors rang Bain at home at night and 'put various propositions' to him. 'One suggested that Brian Lochore was going to pull out next year and so Colin would then step up and they wanted him to resign just for this year and assured me he would be picked again next year.'

Another councillor rang Bain wanting Meads to resign and then said 'they would get Lochore to use him anyway'.

Then, says Bain, a member of the rugby union's staff suggested to Meads that he go along to the meeting on his own, without a lawyer, 'and send his written views first. Colin of course was worried that they were going to pull the wool over his eyes.'

Meads was now aware that a lot had been going on behind the scenes as well as in the open. But he still had difficulty in understanding why there was such a furore. Difficulty because of his attitude to rugby, to relations between people generally, and to rugby people in particular. To him it all seemed 'over the top'.

Bain, however, given his knowledge of Meads, of the law, and of the manoeuvrings of people gained from his legal experience, saw only too clearly that Meads and his future in rugby were under serious threat. After all, he recalled receiving a phone call from the NZRFU's solicitor who said that, 'they had administrative reasons that they could dismiss him [Meads] for betrayal and breach of trust and he could kiss goodbye his future involvement in rugby.' Bain also got a call from the union's lawyers saying that 'they had four press statements prepared [for] they had no idea which way the Council was going to go' at the hearing.

What Meads didn't know prior to returning home was that the councillors had virtually agreed to suspend the Cavaliers players for two games when they returned. That meant Lochore and his co-selectors needed to pick a fresh, scarily inexperienced team to play tests against France and Australia. That left the council with the thorny question, says Meads, of 'what to do with Colin Meads.'

The media reception — it seemed like a barrage to Meads — had left him at a loss. 'I wasn't sure what to do, so next morning I rang Ron Don, the Auckland councillor, and said, "What shall I do? I've got to appear before the Rugby Union on June the 9th. There's this game on in Dunedin that I ought to look at. Normally I'd be ringing up and saying I was coming . . ."'

'Ron said, "You just carry on as though nothing's happened."'

'So I got on the blower and said I'd be arriving in Dunedin to watch Maori hopefuls play a Prince of Wales Cup match and would they have a car to pick me up. [For the record, Northern Maori beat Southern Maori, 24–3 on 5 June.] I was embarrassed and so were a lot of others. I don't think they thought I'd turn up. And although I've never spoken to Brian about it, I don't think he and Tiny Hill thought I'd turn up either. But there were trial teams to pick and I took full part in that. But I was never asked to say anything to the players we selected and I felt there was a bit of the cold shoulder there.

'I have to say, though, that our selection panel was the most ridiculous ever chosen by the NZRFU. Lochore, Meads, Hill: all forwards, and virtually all tight forwards at that.'

Around this time Meads admitted that he'd wanted to be an All Black selector from the time he had stopped playing. 'It had taken a long, long time. I thought, if they disqualified me now, I would not go through the process again.'

This was typical Meads signalling that he had no stomach for politicking, for lobbying. 'Either I'm wanted, or I'm not,' that has always been his attitude. Says Meads, 'When I got home to Te Kuiti, Wally Bain and I had a meeting and he advised me on what to say — and not to say — to the council.'

As Meads and Bain understood it, the council would be asking Meads for an explanation and then requesting that he answer questions from them. Then they would retire and decide what they were going to do and announce their decision that day.

Says Meads, 'Wally Bain advised me that if asked to justify my actions I needed to convince the councillors that in my view my going on the tour was in the best interests of New Zealand rugby, and that I genuinely believed I'd done all I thought I had to do by contacting Brian. Also that I'd have breached confidences if I had notified the Union in advance, and that more harm than good would come to New Zealand rugby if they dropped me as a selector.

'Wally briefed me and gave me notes, in case I had to use them. He said I should point out that I had had the advantage over the other selectors in having seen the players in a "test" series, and that had to mean I could make "a very significant contribution in selecting future teams" because I knew the form of the players. I knew who were looking at retiring, who weren't up to test rugby, and which positions needed to be looked at very closely in order to find replacements. In this respect I had an advantage over the selectors who had remained in New Zealand. Contrary to what some had thought, going on the tour had given me the chance to make a greater contribution to the development of New Zealand rugby.

'Another thing that Wally pointed out was that it was "important to stress that any previous schedule or understanding as to who was watching particular games in New Zealand for the purposes of selecting trial teams and North and South Island teams became an entirely different situation once it became clear that New Zealand's top 30 players were going to be playing overseas. The earlier programme pre-supposed that all players would be in New Zealand playing in New Zealand."'

Meads says that both he and Wally Bain agreed that if necessary he could also explain that he, Meads, hadn't anticipated that his involvement might be seen as in effect an involvement by the NZRFU, because he didn't consider himself to be an 'official' as such. Says Meads, 'I was prepared to say that with hindsight such a view was probably wrong and that I regretted the difficulties it caused, et cetera . . .'

Colin Meads went to Wellington and trundled up to the offices of the NZRFU. The media were in full attendance — for what? Rugby's equivalent of the OK Corral? The traffic didn't actually stop in nearby Lambton Quay, no gallows had been erected either, but there certainly was simmering curiosity and apprehension from the lofty heights to the scuffed grass roots of New Zealand rugby.

Meads was invited into rugby's Star Chamber. He says, 'I appeared before them, many of whom I knew well, friends, and you could see after a while that they were having difficulty. They'd ask me a few questions, send me out of the room, get me back in again, and so on.

'I felt a number — what proportion I don't know — wanted to sack me there and then. But Wally Bain had reminded them of what they might be in for if they did, so they didn't. They seemed to be implying that I could remain as selector but don't bother to reapply next year. That's virtually what happened. For the World Cup, as co-selectors Brian Lochore was given Alex "Grizz" Wyllie, noted for his great run with Canterbury, and John Hart.

'Around this time, two or three councillors said to me that I needn't bother putting my name forward again as I wouldn't get picked. My response was to say that that was all the more reason why I should put my name forward and make them drop me. I wasn't going to make it easy for them.'

Meads was given the message not to re-apply for his position as All Black selector in 1987. The 'chosen three' were, from left: John Hart, Alex Wyllie and Brian Lochore.

And what of Brian Lochore's role in all of this? He says that at no time during the Cavaliers tour, or after, did the chairman or any members of the rugby union's council approach him and discuss the tour itself, or Meads' presence on it. And nor was he aware that Meads had been advised not to stand for re-appointment as a selector.

And the upshot of Meads' appearance in front of the NZRFU Council? The council recognised Meads' 'valuable contribution to the game over a long period', and 'severely reprimanded' him.

Before Meads was dragged before the Head Boys of New Zealand rugby, the news media had reported Ian Kirkpatrick as saying he would be very upset — if not furious — if the council sacked Meads. Andy Dalton expressed similar sentiments. Yes, Dalton had a couple of regrets regarding the tour. He wasn't sorry to have gone, but he regretted he 'didn't duck in time' to avoid the punch that broke his jaw at the start of the tour.

Meads was grateful to Kirkpatrick and Dalton for backing him up, and to rugby union councillors who sympathised with him. He had stood unsuccessfully for an All Black selector's post four times before his appointment in 1986, and he didn't want to be dumped without actually having played any part in selecting even one All Black side. That would be a farce. Fortunately, says Meads, 'It wasn't as if I had no support on the NZRFU. Ivan Vodanovich and Ron Don would usually back me up. Russ Thomas, taking over from Ces Blazey, was in an awkward position, but Russ was a real rugby person and I always felt he was on my side. But some of the councillors were sure I'd done the wrong thing, and a few were anti rugby tours of South Africa. But I can honestly say that I never met a rugby official or player who was pro-apartheid.

'I recall when I first went to South Africa in 1960 that one of the biggest problems we faced as a touring rugby team was how to stay impartial in relation to the friction between the English and the Afrikaners. We often heard references to "those Boer bastards". Obviously there was a real hatred there as far as some were concerned, but by the time we returned in 1970 much of that seemed to have gone. The tension then seemed more a straight black–white thing.'

Meads remains somewhat perplexed by the intensity of some people's views on political, moral and ethical questions, and thinks his views may date back to the nature of his upbringing. As children, and as farmers, the Meads family knew what it was like to have to work hard and struggle. In many ways, and for many years, they were underdogs. When he first arrived at school in Te Kuiti, having arrived in the district on his seventh birthday, he'd come from a 'little school with 20 or 30 kids in all. In Te Kuiti I was plonked in a class with 40 kids. That was a nightmare for me. In the main, apart from two others for a short time, Stan and I were the only white kids on the bus, the others were all Maori. As a little kid I used to get a few hidings too. Not that I ever held it against anyone. And sometimes, Colin Meads had a victory. There was a quite a big Maori settlement locally and a busy marae. When I was about 10 or 11 I had a bit of a scrap with one of the Maori kids and the next morning one of the Maori fellas dragged me off the bus and booted my arse. Then it snowballed and my old man was down there having his say. There was a bit of strife in those days. But we had to learn to get on and grow up together. I made some good friends there. Koro Wetere, the former MP for instance. I lease his farm these days.

'In South Africa we used to get quite a kick out of blacks coming up and telling us how much they were on our side.' To a degree, then, he saw himself and the All Blacks as representing what the underdogs could do when they set their mind on the pursuit of excellence.

To this day, Meads doesn't believe he was wrong to have gone on the tour, but given all that happened there and afterwards, he was lukewarm about it. He thinks that a few players regretted it, felt it didn't do their image much good. 'I have a feeling that Jock Hobbs has sometimes wondered whether it was the wise thing to have done. Jock is a good guy. I regard his dumping from the NZRFU's board in 1996 as one of the saddest things to have happened to anyone in New Zealand rugby.'

Another who went up in his estimation after the tour was the new chairman, Russell Thomas. He told Meads that 'working out what to do about me was the hardest thing he had to deal with in rugby. Two or three years on he was quite happy to come and talk to me about it. I found Russ open — some weren't like that.

'And as for anti-tour groups, no one like Trevor Richards or John Minto ever approached me. But I do remember during the 1981 Springbok tour of New Zealand saying to the press that I'd like to invite Minto down to the front bar of the Te Kuiti Hotel to have a drink with all of my friends and see what they think of it all. Around that time I said to a gang fella who used to shear for us, "If Minto happened to come, I'd want a bit of support." And he said, "Aw, Christ, we'll run that [impolite word] out of town."'

Meads laughs about it all today. He admits he couldn't quite understand the extent of the opposition to South African rugby tours and was amazed by the emotional heat surrounding the issue. To him it's long been plain that Maori were divided on the issue and still are. He was thrilled to, at last, take so-called non-whites on tour to South Africa in 1970. 'It was a great breakthrough and I was

FOTOPRESS

Russ Thomas, who told Meads that working out what to do with him was the hardest thing he had to deal with in rugby.

pleased to see how well they were treated. Everyone in the party was pleased about that and wouldn't have had it any other way. So I saw sporting contact as working.'

Personally, the Cavaliers tour cost Meads and his family quite a bit. Farming was depressed, and his son Glynn, who farmed with him, was overseas. Their stock numbers were high. Meads told the rugby union councillors that he had made arrangements as best he could 'at considerable personal expense to myself and my family and I believe that the sacrifice in that regard was being made in the best interests of Rugby Union Football in New Zealand'.

Meads was upset in the sense that he'd been looking forward to continuing in New Zealand rugby at the highest level, but he was determined to continue to work in and for rugby. 'After the Cavaliers tour I concluded that I was never going to be a successful coach at top level. I didn't think that I'd been all that good with King Country, really. But I did enjoy being North Island selector and coach in the early '80s. I liked giving these prima donnas teamtalks, in a sardonic sort of way, and I enjoyed catching up with many of the players and having a few beers with them afterwards. It's satisfying being around talented young people.

'A good few of that sort were on the Cavaliers tour. But there was also a contrasting group in which Andy Haden and Murray Mexted were prominent. You had to hand it to the likes of Andy — he was getting old in the tooth — for he was smart and worked to improve the lot of the players in all sorts of ways. As Minister of Lurks and Perks he had a fair few schemes going. 'At one point we were based in Johannesburg and travelled back and forth for a few games from there. We used the same bus company and one of the members of the company wanted a photo of the team standing outside his bus. Perfectly legitimate I thought. Ian Kirkpatrick and I were approached and I said it would be fine and if he got a photographer along we'd do it before we drove off. I told the guys that a photographer had arrived and the guy wanted a picture of us in front of his bus. Well, along comes Murray Mexted, another in the Haden mould, and says, "Hey, who arranged this?" Either me or Kirky said we had. "Wait on," said Mexted, "that's Lurks and Perks. We say what happens there." I said, "No you don't, we said they could have the photo." Well, the team had a little meeting about whether they'd pose or not. They wanted to know what was in it for them. That, more than anything, brought home to me how rugby had changed since my time. We were, I suppose, really amateurish in that way. I would never have thought of anything like that. I just wasn't up with the play there, and I probably still wasn't when I became manager with Laurie Mains' team for the World Cup in 1995.

'I still tended to be in the King Country chairman mould where if the boys got 10 dollars for a game they were lucky.'

When it is suggested to Meads that he may, also, have been thinking that some of the lurks and perks stuff was to a degree a distraction from the principal purpose, playing rugby well and successfully, he says that he often thought about that. But in the end he saw how the players performed — 'I watched how Zinzan Brooke and Sean Fitzpatrick played and I concluded that it couldn't be doing them much harm in that respect.

'But I was amused to watch the growth of player power, how they had a dress committee and they required the rugby union to meet with them and be told what they wanted for the tour. I couldn't help compare that with my day when we got a pair of grey slacks, a tie and a blazer and were grateful for it. Of course, Haden and Mexted and co were into that sort of stuff well before the Cavaliers tour.'

Meads recalls that Haden copped a lot of adverse comment around this time but he isn't a Haden knocker. He sees Haden as one who 'did a lot for rugby and for rugby players', as one who drove the train travelling down tracks towards open professionalism a bit faster than it would otherwise have gone. Meads thinks it wrong to impugn him for that. 'There was money being paid to players from their provinces before the Cavaliers came along. There was a lot of underhand stuff going on that I never knew about. I'd heard of Auckland clubs paying players, but I didn't really want to know. On the other hand, I was scared that the end result might be that King Country would lose all its players to Auckland.'

To those outside the main provincial centres, Auckland and its environs especially was like a giant amoeba, steadily enveloping all. 'And that's what's happened,' says Meads a trifle ruefully, 'if you're good enough you don't stay in King Country.' One hears the same lament from those in the Manawatu, in Nelson, in Central Otago.

To those who knew Meads best, and thought he was a stoical, decent bloke, he had come out of the Cavaliers affair and its aftermath with his dignity intact. He remained, in large part, the 'sincerely simple man' that Chris Laidlaw had referred to in his book *Mud in Your Eye*. But not a push-over.

Birth of the
'Baby Blacks'

Lochore, Hill and Meads still had to select All Black test teams to play against France at Lancaster Park in Christchurch, then Australia at Athletic Park, Wellington. The New Zealand union had decided to invoke a residency rule that had seen little use and declared the Cavaliers players ineligible for the French test. Then, as further punishment, they were suspended for the next international, so that ruled them out of consideration for the match at Athletic Park.

The union then insisted the Cavaliers supply affidavits swearing they had not been paid while on tour in South Africa. This became the issue, really, not the fact that they had gone. The wriggling that ensued, the semantics engaged in, and the union's perceived schoolmasterly behaviour tilted sympathy back towards many of the Cavaliers' so-called recalcitrants. The public mood changed — more and more started to say, 'Come on, get real, enough's enough. Is all this in the interests of New Zealand rugby, especially with the World Cup looming in 1987?'

Some were saying that the new All Blacks would be dog tucker. They were fresh-faced, nervous. Novitiates. Not all were, of course. There was John Kirwan and David Kirk, appointed captain. There was the prop Kevin Boroevich, now of Wellington but schooled in the King Country under Pinetree's gimlet eye. 'He was a hard nut,' says Meads, 'a real fiery bugger.' The team selected was as follows: Greg Cooper, John Kirwan, Terry Wright, Joe Stanley, Arthur Stone, Frano Botica, David Kirk. Those were the backs. In the forwards were

Mike Brewer, Mark Brooke-Cowden, Brett Harvey, Andy Earl, Gordon Macpherson, Kevin Boroevich, Sean Fitzpatrick, Brian McGrattan.

Looked at then, and now, that's no bad team. There were some mighty good rugby players in it. Honest rugby players, and many with flair. No wonder some of them didn't much like the label 'Baby Blacks'. Many were brawny and not given to being mucked about. They showed that New Zealand rugby had some depth. And if the French thought they were going to have an easy time they were mistaken. The fact that a Frenchwoman, Dominic Prieur, one of those responsible for sinking the Rainbow Warrior in Auckland Harbour the year before, was in jail in Christchurch, was a reminder to them that the French were not awfully popular at the time.

The All Blacks won. There was jubilation. The Cavaliers, presumably, smiled and gritted their teeth simultaneously. They would not have enjoyed the noises of a few who reckoned New Zealand didn't need them.

Oops: Australia won the match at Athletic Park by one point. Lochore wondered if the players had been looking a bit far ahead, might have been 'looking beyond the match against Australia to when the Cavaliers would again be available'.

With the Cavaliers players eligible again for the second test against Australia at Dunedin, the selectors made 10 changes. They kept Cooper, Kirwan, Stanley, Botica and Kirk. When Wayne Shelford broke a bone in his hand, Brewer was brought back. Meads denies the selectors panicked after the loss in Wellington, says they picked what they

FOTOPRESS

David Kirk leads New Zealand out for the first test of the 1986 series against Australia at Athletic Park. With the Cavaliers under a two-match suspension, Kirk's 'Baby Blacks' lost by a solitary point.

thought was the best team. New Zealand won the test by one point. Derek Bevan, the Welsh referee, devastated the Australians when he declined to award No. 8 Steve Tuynman a try that would almost certainly have meant a win for the Wallabies.

The Cavaliers-dominated team went to Auckland for the final test. Rumours were rife about a split between some of the Cavaliers players and the rest. Lochore, as reported by Ron Palenski in *Lochore: An Authorised Biography*, confirms that, 'By Auckland, there was more feeling than I thought', and, 'Some players had their own agendas'. Lochore

didn't know until later just how angry some of the Cavaliers players were with David Kirk, didn't realise the hostility he had to bear. He says, 'If I had been aware, I'd have done something about it.'

Whatever, the All Blacks lost. Lochore said, 'It was lost because we tried to play an expansive game and made too many mistakes while the Wallabies played it cautiously.' He still doesn't think 'the Cavaliers-Baby Blacks business had any effect on the field. Not at all.'

Meads is not sure. He had input into the team selections but wasn't required to say anything to them.

11.
COUNCILLOR OR COUNSELLOR?

'I snapped, asked why we couldn't just change the word — put another in that we all understood. I don't know what the word was, but it was a big one. They were arguing about the laws of rugby — commas here, question marks there, a full stop there. Colin Meads couldn't come to grips with that sort of thing.'

BY THE TIME MEADS WAS ELECTED TO THE COUNCIL OF THE NZRFU IN 1992, HE HAD SERVED FOR SO LONG IN VARIOUS CAPACITIES ON THE KING COUNTRY UNION THAT HE WASN'T UNDER ANY ILLUSIONS AS TO WHAT HE MIGHT MANAGE TO ACHIEVE. SLIGHT GAINS HERE, A FEW IMPROVEMENTS THERE, AND NO MIRACLES WAS HIS ASSESSMENT OF WHAT WOULD EVENTUATE.

Meads would not have stood for the council if it had not been for Ivan Vodanovich, a former King Country, Wellington and All Black representative. Vodanovich had been All Black coach at one point in Meads' career, had asked Meads to stand for council on two previous occasions, and they had affinities in outlook. In 1992,

NZ RUGBY MUSEUM

finally, Meads allowed the King Country union to nominate him. He thinks he forgot to tell his wife, Verna, and she ticked him off. His reply was, 'Don't worry about it, you never get on the first time you stand.' Ah.

Vodanovich had assured Meads that 'it wasn't a big job. We have all these sub-committees but the new fellas never get on them. You might get on one sub-committee but that's all, so that might mean one extra meeting over and above the monthly council meeting.'

Famous last words, again. Meads recalls that he was on as many as five sub-committees from the outset. 'Hell, it was a huge job.' He was on the coaching committee, on refereeing appointments, a rep on the Rugby Foundation, and others. From an outsider's point of view, Meads was always fully employed on council matters for the NZRFU. In his last year, 1996, before the council was discontinued and a smaller Board created, Meads was on the Boston Steering Committee, liaison to the Rugby Foundation, Maori Rugby Board, Players' Liaison Committee, and the Rugby World Cup Committee. He was also what is known as a 'Buddy Councillor' to the East Coast and Bay of Plenty regions. If a union thought its concerns were not being aired and heard, it was meant to go to its buddy on the council and get him to raise issues.

Occasionally, when sitting around the table in the council chambers, Meads admits to thinking, 'What the hell am I doing here? They were talking way above my head.' He sometimes became perplexed and irritated by the length and tone of the debate on rules and regulations generally. Once, he recalls councillors arguing for over half an hour about the meaning of one word. 'I snapped, asked why we couldn't just change the word — put another in that we all understood. I don't know what the word was, but it was a big one. They were arguing about the laws

Meads joined his great friend and All Black team-mate Kel Tremain on the council of the NZRFU in 1992. The memory, however, is a bitter-sweet one for Meads. Tremain died only a few months after this photo was taken. Here, Tremain and Meads pose with union chairman Eddie Tonks (centre).

of rugby — commas here, question marks there, a full stop there. Colin Meads couldn't come to grips with that sort of thing.'

It also irked Meads to find that a councillor wasn't allowed to mention his own union in discussion except indirectly. 'We could say, "The union that I am associated with", but not mention our own union directly. It struck me as hypocritical. Of course guys were going to try to further the interests of their own unions at times. It was expected of them back home. So, while I was sometimes disillusioned, I still enjoyed the company of John Sturgeon, Mattie Blackburn and Dave Galvin among others. There was a group of us that came from small unions — Richard Crawshaw and Tim Gresson were others — and we got the impression that those from Auckland and Canterbury, Otago too, were seeking ascendancy. Wellington didn't seem quite so interested in pushing their own barrow. One result was that the councillors from the smaller unions tended to be supportive of each other and we had real influence. At times the big unions may have resented the fact that we didn't vote according to their wishes. I never worried about that.'

It was important to Meads that he be a voice for small unions. Now, since the replacement of the council with a trimmed-down board, he is worried that the needs of smaller unions have been seen as less of a priority.

Meads disliked all the lobbying for votes that went on before the AGM and the election of councillors of the NZRFU. Lobbying relating to remits didn't appeal to him either. Either a proposal made sense or it did not, that was the King Country way.

Meads was startled by the manoeuvrings that took place at his first meeting of the NZRFU's council. Virtually their first task was to elect a chairman. It was, thought Meads, like being in the midst of a collection of over-active conspirators. 'We were read stuff about rules of procedure and so on, and mention was made that unless a councillor indicated otherwise, it would be taken that he was available for all positions. We were all handed a piece of paper. Here I was thinking that some bugger will say he doesn't want to be chairman. I was waiting for a lead. No bugger said a word. I waited, then when it was clear the meeting was about to proceed, I said, "Just one minute; I want to make it perfectly clear . . . I thought someone would say they didn't want to be chairman. Well, I don't want to be chairman."'

One year, before the election of officers, Meads was approached by several people who wanted to know who he intended to vote for as chairman. He told them he didn't know, meaning that it was his decision. Lobbying remained an anathema to him, in the main. He saw voting for members on council as similar to voting for MPs and political parties, a private affair. Which suggests that Meads never belonged to factions. His response to that is that he didn't, by and large, although it could be said that 'Perhaps I was part of a faction for minor unions, and I was always pro-active for Maori rugby. Not that I wanted to be, but if I was put on a Maori board I saw it as my job to go in to bat for Maori.'

In 1990, prior to Meads' election to the council, long-serving NZRFU chairman Russ Thomas was swept away on the wash of a wave that had time for a change written on it. 'There was a general feeling,' says Meads, 'that Eddie Tonks would be a better front-person for upcoming jubilee celebrations, would be a better modern-day administrator generally. Some saw Eddie as being better able to negotiate business deals with hard-nosed sponsors.'

Tonks himself was later 'ousted', as Meads puts it, by Richie Guy. There was a feeling that Tonks had got too involved in the internal politics of rugby — in the selection process for instance. Meads thought that although Tonks never said so in public, 'You didn't have to be a Rhodes Scholar to know that he was a John Hart supporter. That was his right and I had no problem with that. Circumstances evolved so that when I became manager, and liked what I saw, I backed Mains. So there were two camps within the council, one for Mains, one for Hart. Of course, there were a number of councillors who didn't openly say which man they were for, but unlike on a number of other issues, where many wouldn't have known where I stood, because I was Laurie Mains' manager, it was clear who I favoured. I saw it as my duty to support Laurie. Unless a manager supports his coach, and vice versa, a team won't succeed. I couldn't see how I could be manager and not display that sort of loyalty. I don't think John Hart could see that. Once he rang me about it. I broke my pattern re lobbying and lobbied for Laurie in a big way. From then on, the Hart faction saw me as an enemy. I shrugged and just got on with my job.'

It may have been forgotten that Meads had had no part in Mains' appointment as All Black coach in the first place, for he was not on the NZRFU council then. When it came time, in late 1995, for the appointment of an All Black coach to follow Mains, Meads was no longer on the committee that made recommendations and interviewed candidates. He had been roundly ticked off by councillors for having done a poll of the players and asked for their preference while they were on tour in France. Meads won't repent there; all he had done, he explained, was enquire and then offer to let councillors know what the players thought — if councillors were interested. If they weren't, so be it. 'The ones who were most outspoken were the members of the Hart faction.'

It may be that Meads' action, in asking the players' opinion on who should be the next coach, was misunderstood. He doesn't believe players should influence the selection of management, he merely thinks that it can help to know their views and that in some cases it may be important to be mindful of them.

Meads was surprised by the heat. He felt that when he was a North Island selector, in the early 1980s, he had 'got on well with John Hart'. Then, when he was a New Zealand selector for that one year in 1986, after they had picked their first team — not the 'Baby Blacks', the one that included Cavaliers who had served their suspension — Meads recalls 'Hart was quoted in the media as saying that our choices were typical of what could be expected from us. I was a bit surprised and disappointed, for I used to seek his advice when selecting North Island teams. I suppose his remarks, about lack of imagination et cetera, were directed at all of us, but it certainly didn't help me since I was under the gun regarding the Cavaliers tour.'

What did Meads think of Hart's abilities as a coach? 'I thought he was a great coach when he had the Auckland team. Over time, though, he appeared to become the overall manager of everything. I think he would have been better off sitting back and confining himself to the coaching role. He inherited a great team, it played very well for a couple of years and then the wheels started to fall off. He couldn't get them back on again. But I knew that Hart was going to get the job because the chairman of the coaching selection committee, Mattie Blackburn, told me.'

So, yet again, Meads had been left out of the lobbying loop. Perhaps it was because he had come to be seen, in most cases, as unwilling to take part in machinations — because he was, possibly, incorruptible — but also because it was known that he felt obliged to support Ross Cooper, who had been Mains' assistant on the tour of Italy and France. Meads had previously told the council that he thought it was best that the coach who took a team to the World Cup should stay on another year. So he had put that to members of the incoming board. It wasn't well received. He thinks that Mains would have carried on for another year if more enthusiasm had been shown.

Tonks knew about the challenge to his chairmanship in 1995 and must have decided that, upon enquiry, that he didn't have the votes needed to stay in the job, so he pulled out altogether, announced he wasn't standing for re-election to the council.

Meads says he doesn't know how one can ever be sure of who is going to vote for whom, or for what. He recalls councillors saying, before a meeting, that they were in favour of a remit, and then finding on the day that it was defeated. 'My impression over time was that there must be a lot of bullshitters around here.'

Richie Guy had told Tonks that he, Guy, had the votes needed to win the vote. Tonks believed him, but the question that puzzled Meads was, how did Guy know. 'I asked Richie that,' says Meads, 'because no one ever asked me who I was going to vote for. Maybe Richie assumed that he had my vote. But assumptions are dangerous. I was disappointed. Eddie pulled out, decided not to stand again, and I compared that with the times when I'd been told by various people that I need not bother to stand for a position because I wouldn't get it. My response was always the same: all the more reason why I should stand. A classic example was all the Powers That Be telling me in 1986 not to stand for reappointment as a New Zealand selector. "You won't get it," they said. Pulling out is not Colin Meads' way. Let the democratic process take its course. I always said that no matter what happened I wasn't going to run away from rugby; I'll still be around King Country.'

And what would have happened if Tonks had stood against Guy? Says Meads, 'I don't know, but it wasn't a foregone conclusion. I still think that if it had come to a vote he may have got back in. I think Eddie panicked.'

The NZRFU council of 1993. Meads is standing fifth from right.

Meads has always seen himself as a 'players' man' and looked to satisfy their needs. He worked hard on the Maori Rugby Board with Mattie Blackburn and attended a great many Maori rugby fixtures. Warren Alcock, for a time a member

MEADS FAMILY

of the Maori Southern Region committee, feels that Meads worked hard to try to persuade the NZRFU to come up with more fixtures for Maori, and funding for Maori regional tournaments. He felt that, 'If Colin hadn't been on our board we'd have made little or no progress with the NZRFU.'

In Noel McQuilkin's view, Meads was a staunch advocate while on the NZRFU council, and in other places, for the smaller unions, and especially for Maori rugby. 'When he was on the Maori rugby sub-committee on the New Zealand union he seemed to go to all the Maori districts, all their games.'

John Dowling of Otago never had any doubts about Meads' value on council. To him he represented commonsense rugby values, the voice of grass roots rugby. And, Dowling said, Meads had a better idea than most of what effect law changes would have on the playing of the game, and whether they were even workable. The difficulty there, though, is that submissions on law changes are routed through the International Rugby Board and the IRB decides.

Meads remembers Tane Norton, the former All Black hooker, and a man for whom he has a lot of time, proposing that at the moment a scrum engages there should only be five players from each side on it. To Meads that made a lot of sense. He says that pressure from the flankers can create difficulties for a prop. 'I took it that Tane was saying that with five players only on the initial contact, if the pressure's too great, the hit is too hard, a prop can get out of it without breaking his spine. All the referee would have to do, once the scrum had settled, was tell the rest to join. I thought it was a tremendously good idea but it has never been accepted.'

Meads thought it important that councillors keep up a hands-on involvement with rugby at all levels. That meant that he was in favour of councillors making themselves available to manage national trial teams of all ages. He was also keen on attendance at coaching clinics over several days that were often held at the Police College in Trentham. He enjoyed that because it gave him first-hand knowledge of what was happening. He did not enjoy discussions on technicalities in relation to laws, nor was he comfortable with dealings regarding distribution of financial resources.

Nowadays NZRFU board members, as far as Meads can see, have little involvement with the grass roots of rugby. Not in the way that councillors used to. To him that is a pity. Also, while he thinks business expertise is important, the jury is out on how good a job our business-oriented appointees have been doing. There was a feeling, no doubt, says Meads, that Richie Guy was not seen as the man to negotiate with the Rupert Murdochs of the world.

Colin Meads would have been happy to be a member of the New Zealand union's sexy new Board in 1996 but knew that, since two members only were to be drawn from rugby's Northern Region, he stood little or no chance of being elected. Why? 'Because both the chairman, Richie Guy, and the vice-chairman, Rob Fisher, were standing. The press came to me afterwards and asked me if I was upset. I said I wasn't, that I knew that it would happen. I said that I was terribly upset that Jock Hobbs had missed out as a Central Region rep.'

Despite reservations, Meads thinks his time on the NZRFU council was worthwhile. He hopes he did some good. And he thinks the national administration's performance in the years since has been a mix of the good and the not-so-good. But, as always, he has no intentions of running away from rugby. He says, 'I would never do that.'

12.
MANAGER MEADS

'I thought I had a bit to offer as a manager of the All Blacks in the sense of a "been there, done that" sort of thing. I'd seen many a manager when a player, and many a style of manager.'

COLIN MEADS HAD NEVER HAD ANY DOUBTS ABOUT HIS ABILITIES AS A RUGBY PLAYER, AND HE KNEW NO ONE HAD QUESTIONED THE INTENSITY OF HIS COMMITMENT TO THE ALL BLACK CAUSE. HE KNEW TOO THAT HE HAD MADE A PRETTY GOOD FIST OF HIS WORK FOR HIS KING COUNTRY UNION — AS A PLAYER, COACH, SELECTOR AND ADMINISTRATOR. MEADS, BY 1994, RANKED AS THE ALMIGHTY BIG CHIEF, COOK AND BOTTLE WASHER OF NEW ZEALAND RUGBY.

He had also come to believe that as a coach of players of international standard, he was so-so. So what new challenge was there for him in New Zealand rugby? There was one thing: manager of the All Blacks. Meads thought that would be an interesting, diverting job; and he thought he could do it well.

In 1993, during his time as a NZRFU councillor, Meads became aware that Laurie Mains, the All Black coach, was dissatisfied with the service he had been getting from his All Black manager, Neil Gray. It wasn't that Mains disliked Gray, it was simply that Gray seemed unable to persuade the rugby union's council to meet many of Mains' requests. As he saw it, the councillors weren't being as helpful as they ought to be in helping the All Blacks in their lead-up to the 1995 World

Cup. Mains had become incensed at times that Gray was unable to gain successful outcomes to his requests.

Meads, an old stager indeed, had more than a few inklings of this when he went up to Mains in Invercargill during celebrations to mark the 200th game between Otago and Southland. What, Meads enquired, was the problem? Was it a big problem? They talked. Meads said that most people knew that it was important for the manager and coach of the All Blacks to gel. 'I could tell Laurie wasn't happy with some of the members of the council. He felt that his views either weren't being aired properly or, if they were, weren't being sympathetically received.'

Councillor Meads was not sure exactly where the problem lay, or whether it was as bad as Mains believed. But he was keen to assist. He did not know Laurie Mains well, although he had played with him in 1971, Meads' last year as an All Black, when Laurie took over at fullback from Fergie McCormick. In subsequent years, he encountered Mains at meetings — 'we called them the Wool Sale meetings' — when representatives from all the New Zealand unions turned up to sort out the fixtures lists for the next season. 'Laurie was very much an Otago man, and if something didn't suit Otago, you heard from him.'

So Meads knew Mains was forthright when he approached him. 'I thought I had a bit to offer as a manager of the All Blacks in the sense of a "been there, done that" sort of thing. I'd seen many a manager when a player, and many a style of manager. A lot of them were good guys, but some were there as a reward for service on the NZRFU council. I had seen the lot, from Bill Craddock of Buller in my early days as an All Black — when one of the jobs of the young guys was to look after Bill — to one such as the strong and tough former All Black reserve prop, Tom Pearce. Tom was a great orator and I admired a lot of things about his approach to life. So I had had thoughts about putting my name forward for the manager's job, but I wasn't going to do it before first seeing what Laurie thought

Christchurch, 26 June, 1994. A forgettable result, but still a noteworthy occasion. Jonah Lomu (middle row, third from right) played his first match for New Zealand and Colin Meads (front row, second from left) took over as manager. The French side, however, rather spoiled the party, beating the All Blacks 22–8 in the first test.

138

about that. Laurie appeared to jump at the idea.'

So far so good. Then Meads thought some more. Unless he made his intentions clear to the other councillors, he thought he wouldn't have much of a chance of being appointed. Even then, given his observations of council practice, he thought it unlikely he would be given the job straight away.

At the next council meeting, Meads saw Neil Gray and told him he was thinking of putting his name forward for the manager's job. Gray stood again too. Meads says he did not lobby for the position. Lobbying went on at times, for selectors' positions among others, but it was never Meads' style. He thought that 'if you have to lobby for something, you are doing a job for the wrong reasons. I used to lobby for other people, but not for myself.'

Meads didn't expect to be appointed. In fact, he hadn't mentioned the possibility to Verna. 'I think one morning, just before I was leaving to go down to Wellington for a rugby union council meeting, I said to Verna that a new All Black manager was going to be appointed and, although I'd put my name in, I knew I wouldn't get it. The wives were coming down later that day for a social function, and when Verna arrived I told her I had got the job after all. She wasn't terribly impressed. I think she thought that I was going to be away again just as much as I had been when I was a player, which was true.'

Meads took over as manager for the All Blacks' home tests against France and South Africa in 1994, including the infamous match at Athletic Park in Wellington

C'est la vie. The 1994 home test series against France has been lost and manager Meads, in company with coach Laurie Mains and captain Sean Fitzpatrick, face the media.

PETER BUSH

in which the Springbok prop Johan le Roux nibbled Sean Fitzpatrick's ear and caused a quake which almost brought down the Millard Stand.

One addition to the All Black sanctum from Meads' days was a strange new creature called a media liaison officer, in the shape of one Ric Salizzo. Yes, Meads was sceptical of the need for such a beast. Salizzo, who had been attached to the All Blacks from 1992, remembers Meads telling the players that when he first made the All Blacks, he had been told never to trust the media, and not to say a word to them. Meads said that his policy was to look away and keep moving. However, these were different times, and if, in their wisdom, the rugby union had decided that a media person — in this case Mr Salizzo — was necessary, then they should get used to him.

Salizzo admits to having a short fuse, at times. And after he had got into a fiery exchange with a press photographer, Meads kept a close eye on him. 'At Athletic Park, he actually stopped me going out through the tunnel at one point because he thought there was a danger I might make an inappropriate outburst. Colin held me back, said, "No, you're not going out there, you're too fiery."'

In many ways, Meads was a revelation to Salizzo. The legendary Pinetree appeared to amble about, but his casual air was counterbalanced by an eagle eye. Says Salizzo, 'He seemed to know when to take control and when not. His authority was never questioned.'

About a month or so before the World Cup squad was announced, Meads recalls meeting with Mains and some of the All Blacks' sponsors in Wellington. He arrived half an hour after most of the others, sat down and listened as Mains and a brewery representative discussed filming a video on the Tuesday or Wednesday before a test. 'I spoke up, said that as manager I wanted to ensure that we got the best performance possible out of the All Black team. I said I wasn't talking about the coaching side, just that the first thing a team should be concerned about when it assembles before a test is their first training session. In this regard I always referred to the prop Jazz Muller. He worried himself sick about the first training session — it was always a hard one, and it sorted out who was fit and who wasn't. We were all a bit in awe on the first day we assembled. I was never worried about the fitness side, but others were. Laurie said that a way around that was to assemble a day earlier. I said I didn't give a damn when they assembled, but the first training run should be the ultimate thing. I said, "You go out and do a coaching video and the backs will be flipping it here, flipping it there . . . take one, take two . . . they'll be joking and laughing . . . that'll be a great build up for the test, won't it?" I said, "You're not going to do it. Assemble some other time and do it then."'

The impression Meads was left with was that Mains was more than a little surprised. 'He came to me after and said that no All Black manager had been that insistent before. I said that it was my job to see that the team's preparation was such that nothing interfered with its chances of playing well.'

Laurie Mains agreed with that. He said that he was under a bit of pressure from the NZRFU to provide the union with a coaching video. Meads sympathised, to a degree. However, he pointed out that the union was the first to complain when the All Blacks lost or didn't play well. Meads is glad he took a stand from the beginning. From then on he feels he and Mains got on very well, and their disagreements were few and far between and never major.

For a time, Meads was open-mouthed when seeing just how much gear the

Opposite page:
All Blacks coach Laurie
Mains at training with
props Craig Dowd and
Olo Brown.

PHOTOSPORT

*Meads' first managerial
assignment was with the
All Blacks for the series
against France in 1994.*

All Blacks were given. 'I'd go into my room and there would be bags of the stuff. I was getting track suits, shoes . . . they even wanted to know what size rugby boots I took. I laughed: why does the damned manager have to get football boots? I'm not going to have to play. I was from an era when a player was tickled pink to get his blazer and a pair of grey slacks and that was about it. I got boots the size that my son Glynn wore, came home and gave a lot of the stuff to him.'

Early on, Mains and Meads sorted out their areas of responsibility. Mains decided when and where and how training took place. Meads kept right away from that. He said to Mains that they, not the union's councillors, would make the decisions as to where they stayed and how they functioned as a unit. Meads decided too that he would have a major say in which hotels they stayed in. 'I am a great believer in rugby hotels,' says Meads, 'and I know that wasn't a popular decision with some of the players.' He is not so keen on the ultra-modern, sumptuous and somewhat impersonal modern hotels. He preferred places where a separate part of the dining room could be set aside for the players to have their meals together, and where they could develop closer relationships with staff.

Old rivals. Meads with Springboks manager Jannie Engelbrecht during the 1994 series between New Zealand and South Africa. The two men had opposed each other on the playing fields in 1965.

PHOTOSPORT

Meads had a few words each day about what the programme was, but tried to be as unobtrusive as possible. He felt Mains shouldn't have to pay out of his own pocket if he wanted to take the captain or one or two senior players off for a couple of drinks, or a meal, to discuss how things were going and plan, so he slipped him some money now and then to meet such expenses. 'I thought it better that he shouted rather than it be seen to be coming from me. After all he was the coach, I was just the manager.' This was something new and a welcome bonus for Mains.

When Meads was an All Black he had been impressed by Charlie Saxton. 'He was the best manager of my playing days. Charlie and Fred Allen had a great relationship. Charlie was the boss of his area, and he would often come along and sit down beside you in a lounge and ask what you thought of something. Then, I'm sure, he'd have a word to Fred and report whatever he thought was useful. I often used to think of Charlie, although he was a very different sort of animal to me. I would encourage the guys to meet in the team room and have a couple of beers between six and seven, say, before we went to dinner. A few ideas got bandied around and a few problems aired. We even compared my era with today — it was good.

'I never foisted my views on Laurie regarding selections even though I didn't always agree with them. It's not the manager's place. But there were a few times, on a bus for instance, when he would ask me for an opinion and I would give it. We're all selectors, that's what I've found. Even the lady in the dairy in Te Kuiti. But when I was with Charlie and Fred, even though Charlie had his views, it was always Fred's team.'

LAURIE
MAINS

Otago's Laurie Mains, one of a handful of former All Blacks who also became an All Black coach, is another sometimes spoken of as having similar characteristics and qualities to Meads. By that one means he is seen as resolute, sometimes severe, uncompromising, intensely committed to a belief in what the All Black jersey stands for. No short cuts in preparation off the field, discipline in the execution of game plans and skills on it, and no quarter given. Hard but fair.

Mains admires Meads, and is another who saw him as a 'colossus'. Mains and Meads played for the All Blacks against the Lions in 1971 and Mains was struck by the lock's 'mana, mental strength and focus. He was absolutely unequivocal about his rugby in whatever he did; he was one of a select few who made All Black rugby what it is. Colin would do what the All Blacks wanted him to do. An icon, definitely.'

Mains is known to work players hard, both physically and mentally. No shirkers is a Mains mantra. So it's significant to hear him say that 'No one trains now as Colin trained. Colin could have played in any era: he was mobile, skilled, tough.' Mains leans towards me as if to assert that the unusual significance of such an assessment cannot be overemphasised. Mains nods his approval when recounting the tales of Meads and his brother Stan running miles back and forth from their father's farm, cutting scrub, shearing, digging holes for fenceposts, and so on. To Mains, a supporter of what he calls 'specialised gym training', there is definitely a place for the sort of all round physical work the Meads boys did, and he is in favour of 'aerobic running over rough country' as a help in building stamina and agility. Such running works a greater range of muscle groups and in some ways better simulates the changes of direction and physical adjustments required in the course of playing a game.

Mains barely knew Meads when he played with him in the early 1970s. But his interest in renewing and developing their association was seeded in Invercargill early in the 1990s when they were both guest speakers after the 200th match between Otago and Southland. Mains was looking for a more compatible manager, preferably one who had more first-hand experience of the requirements of upholding the great All Black tradition.

To Mains, Meads seemed like a man who would share and understand his burning wish to lift All Black standards and to instil more pride in the jersey. In Mains' view this had slipped a little and in Meads he saw someone who was an exemplar of an All Black who had been resolute, unswerving, reliable. A player who had the mental and physical presence and strength to go unfazed into the international cauldrons of top rugby. Unsophisticated perhaps, but streetwise in so far as rugby was concerned.

Speak loudly and carry a big stick . . . Laurie Mains has an attentive audience on the beach in Sicily, 1995. Behind Mains are, from left: Michael Jones, Craig Dowd, Meads, Sean Fitzpatrick (partially obscured) and Eric Rush.

Meads offered himself to the NZRFU as All Black manager and was appointed. Mains was soon able to confirm his instincts, finding Meads unobtrusively fitted into the manager's role. He was, says, Mains, 'logical, forthright without being heavy-handed, receptive, approachable. I had no grumbles from the players about Colin Meads. He backed me up on the need for discipline. He had a good understanding of team tactics and the techniques required at top level. And if he disagreed with me as coach he didn't voice it in front of the players.'

It was not that Meads was indifferent, phlegmatic or deferential. He simply didn't believe in making a fuss about all manner of matters and risk becoming pedantic and possibly petty. Meads dislikes focusing on trivialities, prefers to concentrate on the big picture. On the surface, in more recent times, Meads can appear somewhat benign, docile, but when his patience goes his annoyance will not be deflected or denied. Mains vividly recalls being 'stiffened up by Colin after we had lost the first test against France at Toulouse in 1995. I realised then that he'd come to the end of his tether and was not going to stand by and witness another, to one of his perspective, feeble effort from the All Blacks.'

Meads was affronted by the way the All Blacks caved in. To him their performance was shameful, cringe-making.

While Mains was aware that Meads had his views on team tactics and patterns, and on the merits of individual players, 'he never tried to force his selections on me. That said, Colin's no saint. He can be grumpy and he dislikes pretentiousness and dishonesty. And it's no secret that he was not a fan of John Hart's approach to running a team. I doubt that he and the likes of Rob Fisher would have been soul-mates either.'

Both Mains and Meads convey the impression that while they saw the need to adapt and adopt new methods, and that attempting to stand in the way of many of the changes to the game in recent years would be like trying to pee into a fresh and blustery wind, they were in accord in believing that 'one forgets the pre-professional era of rugby at one's peril'. They also appeared to agree that while it is hard for any one person alone 'to stay abreast of all the changes that have gone towards the modern game, it is stupid to ignore the fact that the basics are the same as they've always been'.

As a duo they have observed the way the rugby league influence has made for what Mains calls 'vastly different defence patterns', and that today's forwards play more loosely and 'cover big areas'. Mains thinks that Australia's influence on law changes and refereeing forced a movement away from more traditional driving forward play. However, Mains feels that more recently there have been readjustments, signs that the pendulum may be swinging back, and any movement towards a return to the driving play will help New Zealand.

13.

IN SICKNESS AND
IN WEALTH

'Kronfeld blamed the chicken on the tables at Thursday's lunch. I blame the milk. Maybe he was right, and it was the chicken burgers. Jeff Wilson had had two chicken burgers. Laurie was convinced that the British bookmakers were behind it.'

MAINS FOUND 1995 A VERY STRESSFUL TIME WHEN, AS ALL BLACK COACH, HE BUILT HIS TEAM TOWARDS THE WORLD CUP. HE DID NOT WANT PLAYERS CHOSEN FOR THE ALL BLACKS TO PLAY IN A 'FRIENDLY' MATCH BETWEEN NORTH HARBOUR AND AUCKLAND ON VIRTUALLY THE DAY BEFORE THE ALL BLACK SQUAD WAS DUE TO ASSEMBLE.

He had hoped, for example, that the Auckland coach, Graham Henry, would not require certain All Blacks to play in that match. They did, and a number of All Blacks who turned out were injured and were 'half-crocked', as Meads puts it, when they reported for duty with the national side. Meads recalls having a meeting with Brad Meurant of North Harbour and Henry prior to this match. 'In my view, it was a match of no consequence,' says Meads, 'but Henry wouldn't have a bar of any moves to pull the All Blacks out. I remember Laurie saying words to the effect that, did they want the All Blacks to win, or were they only interested in their own neck of the woods? To me he had a good point.'

As Meads remembers it, Henry's position was that Mains had a job to do, he had a job to do, and his was to pick his best players in the interests of developing the Auckland team. He thinks that North Harbour was more willing to release the likes of Bunce, Little, Jones and Osborne, but Auckland was very anti. Meads took the matter to the NZRFU without success. In most cases he was able to get the council to agree to go along with requests from Mains, but not this time.

Nevertheless, as Meads is quick to say, he and Mains gelled. Any spats were minor and didn't last long. They had some entertaining times socially. Before the World Cup in South Africa, Meads persuaded the secretary (renamed Chief Executive Officer) of the NZRFU, George Verry, to let him have a credit card which he could use to pay for incidentals, including entertainment and a few 'treats' for players and management. 'Not too often, just now and then. Laurie and a few others said that previous managers hadn't been able to do that.' When in South Africa, the All Blacks had an effervescent and capable liaison officer, who worked for Stellenbosch Wines. Occasionally, when Meads felt there was a need to shout a few players and others a treat, they would get their liaison man to arrange a venue; and when asked who was to pay, Meads answered, 'This will be on George.' The handy credit card had become a benefactor named after Verry, the NZRFU's CEO.

Mains was driven by a fierce dedication to All Black rugby, which was one reason why, says Meads, 'He sometimes had a short fuse when it came to anything that interfered with training.' As an example, Meads recalls that at one point during the World Cup, the team was training at school grounds in Johannesburg, a few hundred yards from their hotel. 'Walking distance,' says Meads. 'There was a big crowd of spectators and some were encroaching on the field. Things weren't going right and he got very frustrated and wild. For some reason he decided it was my fault that the crowd had got too close. Usually it was poor old Ric Salizzo who got the blame. This time he flew into me. I gulped and said I'd see him back at the hotel — there were people in earshot — and all I said after that was, "Don't you ever do that again. We can have our disagreements, but not in public." Laurie accepted that. But boy, did he give Ric what-for at times. Ric was a good guy. He had played a bit of rugby, and now and then, if they wanted a spare forward to lock the scrum at training, he'd go in and do it. Or if they needed someone to hold a tackle bag, he'd do that, and the guys would give him hell, bowl him over.'

Meads says that Laurie could get a 'bit paranoid. If he was having a secret training run, all the time he'd be watching to see if we were being spied upon. I used to think back to Fred Allen's days. Fred never had secret training runs. He never believed in them. The bigger the crowd, the harder the training run, that was Fred's policy. We used to go and look at the size of the crowd and that told us what we were in for. I remember going out one day in France and there were six or seven thousand waiting. Jazz Muller came out and almost fell down. "Geez," he said, dismay on his face. "We're in big trouble now, we'll be training all day."

'But Laurie was all for secret sessions. We were having this training under lights at the Sydney Football Stadium. Laurie was looking everywhere. I got as far away as possible. He'd see a light in a box somewhere and think, "There's someone up

Media liaison man Ric
Salizzo — 'he usually got
the blame' — and Laurie
Mains in 1995.

Meads and Brian Lochore — great friends and New Zealand team-mates — were reunited for the 1995 World Cup campaign.

there watching us." And he'd sing out, "Ric, this was meant to be private . . ." Laurie got a bit carried away about that, but it showed how important it was to him that the All Blacks' plans not be upset.'

Mains liked players to admit they had played poorly, had made mistakes, and was not averse to giving a few 'a bollocking' at times, says Meads. 'He was careful, though, as to who he picked on. He would give it to Robin Brooke, say, or Olo Brown, I think because he knew they could take it. And probably because he felt it important to show that the older players weren't immune from criticism. If they dropped a ball in a lineout, he'd say that wasn't good enough. "Don't you want to play in the test? Keep your mind on the job. If you don't want to play, I won't pick you. Let me know." He did it well. He'd get to training the next morning and say, "By the way, Robin, you haven't told me yet." He was less likely to go for younger guys like Jeff Wilson.'

'No stone unturned' was a phrase that fitted Mains and his approach to the 1995 World Cup campaign. His intense, relentless preparation — some said meticulous to the point of pedantry — brought to mind Meads' own single-minded and ruthless ways as a player, then selector/coach. Meads not only accepted the need for a hard line, no quarter-asked-or-given style, he believed it was necessary if you were to succeed at the highest level of rugby. No namby-pamby stuff: both Meads and Mains were in total accord there.

To Mains' mind, and Meads agreed, the pre-World Cup training camps for front-line All Black candidates were essential. They could well represent the key to a successful tournament. Mains was just as consumed by the desire to win in South Africa as Meads had ever been. Speak the word 'Springboks' to Meads and a lust for victory over them was so strong it almost made him shudder. Mains appeared to be much the same.

The first camp was in Queenstown, a familiarisation camp as much as anything, in late 1994. Partners — that dinky, all-purpose, PC-term — attended some of it, the gathering was that cosy. Discussions centred round the style of play to adopt in the coming months, and Mains wanted to get a line on personalities and the degree of their commitment.

'Somewhere along the line,' Meads says, 'I asked Laurie, "Would you like another trial?"' The Otorohanga club in the King Country wanted to put on a special match to mark their centenary in 1995. Meads suggested the squad travel down from Hamilton, where they had been training and played a match against a Harlequins XV on 16 April, stay the night at the Waitomo Caves, then play a game at Otorohanga next day. 'Laurie jumped at the chance. He hadn't sorted the team out finally — he was unhappy, for instance, with the way Jon Preston was playing and hadn't made up his mind on a second halfback. He wanted to have another look at Ant Strachan. Because we were going to play King Country, he asked me to tee it up so that two or three ring-ins got to play for them, and Ant was one.

Meads makes a point to coach Laurie Mains (left) and his assistant, Earle Kirton, during a break away from the rigours of the Queenstown World Cup training camp.

That's how he got in; the King Country forwards played pretty well and Ant, a noisy character behind the scrum, kept them going.'

A number of matters were arranged during the lead-up period that Meads had nothing to do with. Mains did. A case in point was the flash black Fords that were provided for the use of some, not all, of the players in the All Black squad. Meads thinks there were 'about 21 of them. I had no say in who got them. In fact, it was such dangerous ground to get into that I was happy to stay out of it.'

One of the new initiatives developed around this time was the All Blacks Club, basically a means of providing more perks for leading players. Mains was on this committee, which was chaired by Rob Fisher. Others on it were Richard Crawshaw, Malcolm Dick, Eion Edgar, Richie Guy, Sean Fitzpatrick, George Verry and Kevin Roberts, the marketing guru.

Meads was intrigued. 'Laurie seemed to know a lot about the personal circumstances of many of the players. Say, for instance, that Shane Howarth had just got the use of a new car through work, he would deem that Howarth didn't get one of the Fords. Laurie had it all sussed. But in Queenstown the decisions on who got cars and who didn't caused a few rumbles. I said, "This is not for me," and stayed right out of it. Some time after this, it was suggested that Colin Meads and Earle Kirton — one of the selectors — should have a car too. Whether they were additional cars, or not, I don't know. But the fact that Earle and I had cars got back to the New Zealand council, and a few players and others had complained. The press got hold of the story; photographs appeared of Earle's Ford alongside a couple of his own cars outside his place . . . Well, next thing the council told me to hand my car back. So I did."'

Verna well remembers taking the car back to the Ford dealers in Otorohanga and telling the manager there that 'under no circumstances does Colin want it back. I think the manager there was hopping mad about the whole episode,' she says.

Before this, Brian Lochore had been added to the management team. It was thought that he would be better at talking to the media, among other things. Meads smiles: 'It was felt that Colin Meads was too abrupt; or didn't like the press that much. Brian was seen as more of a diplomat.'

The fitness — the lack of it — of a few players was a concern at the first two camps. Mark Cooksley was given three weeks, Meads recalls, to rectify it. He didn't and was dropped from contention for the World Cup team. Meads thought that the car he had been required to return had gone to Cooksley, so he said to Lochore: 'I've got a little job for you, will you go and tell Mark he won't be wanted any more, and also could he leave the keys of the car behind. I thought BJ would have said to me, "You dirty so-and-so," but he didn't. He said he supposed he'd have to go and do it.'

One can joke with Meads about the size of the All Black management team leading up to and during the 1995 World Cup, and since for that matter. Hasn't Meads been known to scoff, mildly and wryly, about the numbers of administrators and advisers and experts generally that seem to guard the All Blacks like a squadron of fighters accompanying a presidential jet? Compare all this to what pertained in his day. After all, in 1995, there were Mains and Lochore and Meads and Salizzo; assistant coaches Kirton and Ross Cooper; doctor Mike Bowen, physiotherapists Barry Donaldson and Chris McCullough, masseur Donny Cameron, and fitness consultant Martin Toomey.

Says Meads, whose gestures accept a degree of guilt: 'I was against the media

officer, but I was wrong there. I hadn't realised how big the press contingent had become.' And Mains could justify them all, said they were doing a good and essential job. 'Then we got a request from some of the players: they wanted a masseur. The Otago boys had a great relationship with Donny Cameron and I liked him. So getting the NZRFU to take him along was one victory I had there. I said we needed one of our own. Some guys say they can't play without a masseur. Donny was the hardest-working guy along. Some players just have to have a massage; I think it's in their psyche and you can't get rid of it.'

Colin and Verna about to brave the rapids during a whitewater rafting excursion, Queenstown, 1994.

Richie Guy and John Sturgeon were among a few councillors who half-seriously told Meads that he 'wouldn't be able to control everyone, there's so many of them. You need another manager to manage the management. I can laugh about it now. I go round criticising the set-up which got up to 12, I think. The right number was the number we had. It was a good group; we got on well together.'

The final camps were, according to flanker Josh Kronfeld, not for the faint-hearted. In his book *On the Loose*, Kronfeld wrote that along the way they had been so hard that a few of the guys 'fell over, including a former international or two'. He wrote:

> We'd spend a whole morning doing heavy physical confrontation work among the forwards — to put it bluntly, bashing the shit out of each other . . . Live drills are commonplace but this was pretty brutal stuff . . . Half the guys were in tackle suits and pads, yet it was still tough work. I had a double mouthguard so I could bite into it and look after my jaw. We worked all day.

Josh Kronfeld (with ball) and Simon Culhane during one of Laurie Mains' legendary training runs prior to the 1995 World Cup.

Kronfeld, one of the fitter players, found some of the fitness work comprised 'exhausting combinations'. Overall, he said, 'it sure tested us and Laurie found out exactly who had the bottle and who didn't . . . this camp provided conclusive evidence. There were a lot of shattered boys at the end of it all.'

What did Meads think of the team selected for the World Cup? 'There are always some who are unlucky, but I think the mix was about right. Stephen Bachop was pretty upset that he missed out as a five-eighth. But Simon Culhane was a good player and a very good kicker. I thought we had an excellent bunch of guys.'

Meads went off to South Africa for a couple of weeks in advance of the team to check out hotels, among other things. He found it a 'big waste of time' because after he'd been there and returned to New Zealand, the South Africans did a deal with a hotel chain and changed all the arrangements. He went back again for a meeting of managers. The All Blacks were to be based in Johannesburg and Bloemfontein, because their pool games were to take place there. Ireland and the All Blacks were in Johannesburg, Wales and Japan in Bloemfontein. Noel Murphy, whom Meads had played against, and whom he describes as 'quite a character', was the Irish manager. Murphy said to Meads that two hotels were set aside for the teams in Johannesburg and that the All Blacks would get the better of the two, 'because they always get what they want'.

'Murphy said to me, "That's the best one, you have it." I had to laugh.'

Laurie Mains had Meads 'schooled up on what he wanted me to arrange. Some expert had told us that for every hour's time difference between New Zealand and South Africa — they were 12 hours behind us — we needed a day to acclimatise. That meant 12 days there before we played our first match against Ireland on 27 May. This was Colin Meads after getting it from on high. I stood up at the

155

Photosport

manager's meeting and said that I had it from the top man in New Zealand that we needed a day for every hour's time difference. Four hours difference between London and South Africa — four days for the English, 12 for us. To my amazement a lot of people agreed with me. I think we were there about 13 days before, and it was too long.'

The team wanted to play, not train. They were frustrated. They drove to Sun City, about four hours, and trained there. Had a round of golf, came back to Johannesburg. Nine or 10 days beforehand would have been ample, says Meads.

He sometimes wonders whether training sessions have not become too complicated nowadays, though he accepts that one has to take notice of new ideas and more sophisticated and/or structured ideas and training regimes. But he still likes the simpler approach of Fred Allen. 'You weren't allowed to kick a ball until you'd done four laps of the park,' says Meads. Do that and you wouldn't pull muscles was Allen's view, and Meads shared it. Today, the players do lots of exercises in a group, and grids. 'We never had grids in my day,' Meads says. 'Pass to your right, pass to your left. Once you get into it, it's too easy. You're only running, at most, 10 yards. Then you go to the back of the line. Someone drops the ball and the coach balls them out.'

The All Blacks put 100 points on Japan in their third pool match of the 1995 World Cup. Here, captain for the day, Paul Henderson, attacks with Kevin Schuler in support.

Many of the practice routines have been introduced for 'the fun element' to lessen the likelihood of boredom. Meads' response is a long, considered 'Yee-ah. I can never remember being bored with Fred Allen. Nervous was more like it. But everybody's different. If you went and spoke to Billy Davis, one of the backs I played with, he'd say he used to get pissed off with Fred's training. Too much running, sprinting from the back to the front, and so on. I used to give it everything. Fred would tell us we'd keep going until everybody sprinted. "Including you, Billy Davis. You're meant to be quick. You're running like an old carthorse."

'Looking at it now, there's a balance between the modern way and the old way. I think they've got too far away from doing the hard yards. Laurie Mains, though, he made the players do a lot of hard running, and lots of down and ups, especially in his camps. It was brutal stuff. And Fred used to give us a real hard workout two days before a test.'

During the 1995 World Cup, Meads believes the All Blacks consistently played the best rugby he's seen. Ireland, as they always do, 'took to us from the start, but by the end of the game we were so superior. We were superior to everyone we played against up to the final.

'The game against England — the semi-final at Newlands in Cape Town — was a dream game. In your wildest dreams you couldn't see how a team could play that well,' says Meads, and it was a game he can't forget. Kronfeld wrote that the match 'was a climax to a whole week of anxiety and a colossal determination to kick England's arse'.

Meads again: 'Half an hour or so before matches the managers were required to go to the referee. He drew marbles with numbers on them and the players whose

The Big Four —
Lochore, Fitzpatrick,
Mains and Meads —
during a press conference
after the All Blacks' World
Cup quarter-final win
against Scotland in
Pretoria, 1995.

PHOTOSPORT

numbers came up — two from each side — had to take a urine test, which was witnessed by both managers.

'On this occasion, Mehrts (Andrew Mehrtens), came to me and said that he wanted to talk to the referee. I said he couldn't do that. He said he had a plan and he wanted to explain it to the ref. He said to me, "You couldn't explain it. You're a dumb forward." This was Mehrts in his prime, the cheeky little bugger. He kept on at me: "I've got to talk to the referee, otherwise he'll get in the road. We've got a cunning move."

'I sighed and thought, okay. So I said to the referee, Irishman Steve Hilditch, "Our little guy who kicks off, he wants to have a word to you. He's got something he's worried about and he wants you to be aware of it. He'll be brief." So I went to Mehrts and said, "Right-o, Mehrts, be quick."

'Mehrts said to the referee, "Well, we've got a plan, and we couldn't tell you before now because it's top secret and you'd have told every other bastard. I'm going to run in this way, with the forwards lined out here, and then I'm going to swivel and kick it the other way, and I'm telling you this now so you won't be in the road when I change direction. I want you to know so you won't stuff the move up."

'I said, "Come on, Mehrts, you can't talk like that". He ignored me, and said to the referee, "Jonah's going to catch it and he'll score."'

Meads said he laughed and thought that he'd heard all that palaver before. It never happens the way you want it to. Shortly after, he left to look for BJ Lochore. He and BJ had a ritual which was to watch the game with all 'the dignitaries in the chairman's box. It was one of our superstitions. I said to BJ, "We'd better hurry. The kick-off's going to be one of the biggest balls-ups of all time." As it turned out, Mehrts' kick-off didn't go exactly to plan. Will Carling actually knocked the ball on, but Jonah was still able to score probably his most famous try from the scrum that followed.'

The All Blacks won 45–29. The scoreline for England was inflated owing to a couple of soft, late tries. To all intents and purposes the game was won by the All Blacks in the first 20 minutes of the match.

The mood in the All Black camp was one of optimism, but not complacency. The men in black were overwhelming favourites to beat South Africa in the final to be played in Johannesburg on Saturday, 24 June. The general view was that New Zealand was the best team in the tournament. It seemed that all the rigorous training, and the speed, endurance and skill with which the team had been executing its plans, would bear fruit. But it all turned to custard on the Thursday before the final at Ellis Park. Meads' memory tells him that 'about 28 members of a party of 36 were hit by food poisoning'. Some of the players were not simply sick — convulsions, high temperatures, vomiting — they were stricken. A few, once in bed, couldn't get out for 24 hours or more.

Were they deliberately poisoned, or were they just unlucky to have eaten contaminated chicken — or some other food — at a buffet lunch on the Thursday? Did someone spike their drinks? It seems no one will ever know.

Some of the players keeled over on the Thursday afternoon. They were put to bed and isolated on a different floor of the team's hotel. Meads and other members of the management planned to go out for dinner that night and take players who were not included in the squad for the final along with them. 'George' would be paying. By the time Meads and Mains and Lochore were ready to go out, 'Six or

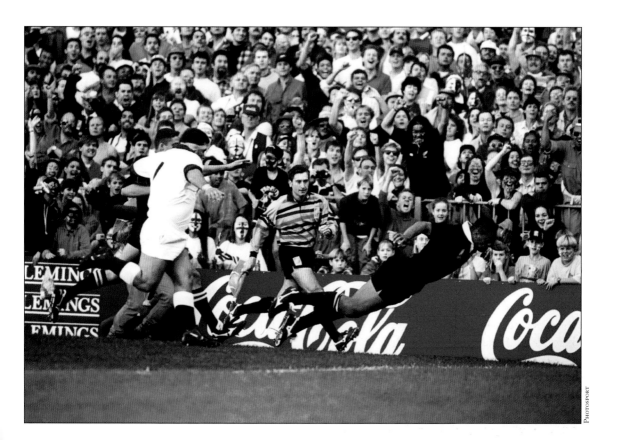

Photosport

Jonah Lomu scores the sensational opening try against England in the semi-final of the 1995 World Cup at Cape Town.

seven of the boys were down, including Jeff Wilson and Mehrts. We were already running out of room in the "sick bay" we had set up. Then the hotel management said they needed the rooms we had the sick guys in so we had to shove everyone back where they'd come from.

'Some of the players went off to a movie and many of them started to feel crook too. Laurie did too, and I wasn't feeling too flash either. The day, now the evening, had really turned sour. Laurie was worrying, and when Laurie's like that he can be a pain. Everything was wrong where we were: the food never came quickly enough; it wasn't cooked properly. We had set out to have some fun and to make a really good night of it. We were all back in the hotel before 11.'

It had turned into the beginnings of a lengthy, chronic nightmare for Mains and Meads and virtually everyone associated with the team. The only ones who didn't get sick, so far as the team's fitness consultant Martin Toomey could see, ironically perhaps, 'were a few of the bros who had ducked away to McDonald's instead of eating the food in the area specially set aside for us'.

By now the players and management were highly alarmed. Many were greatly distressed. Calamity reigned. Meads remembers Richard Loe panicking and not game to try to get into the hotel and up to his room. 'He ducked out of a taxi and into the rose garden opposite and was sick there. What a sight that was, Loey in the rose garden. Meanwhile Laurie was rushing hither and thither, wanting a doctor. If the doctor wasn't there within 30 seconds he was too slow for Laurie. Five minutes went by before Loey was relocated. It wasn't funny at the time, but in retrospect it was a real pantomime.'

All Black managers are provided with a voluminous handbook, A4 size and mighty thick, in which there is instruction and advice on protocols and everything else. But Meads rarely if ever looked at it and, without bothering to check, he assumed the NZRFU manager's guide wouldn't be of much use in helping cope with the near-farcical events unfolding that day. 'At this point, I didn't know what the hell to do any more, so I headed to the House Bar. By now there were eight or nine guys down. I'd said there would be a meeting in my room at eight in the morning. I was feeling rotten and I went to bed. About one-thirty or two in the morning I got out of bed, just, and tried to get up and totter to the bathroom. I crashed on the floor. I was like a cow with the staggers. I rang the doctor's room but he'd moved to another. I apologised to the person there, then rang him again with the same result. "I'm sorry," I cried, "but I want the bloody doctor." Eventually I found him, but I was no good.'

The plan for the Friday morning had been to go to Ellis Park, walk through a few moves on the ground, check out the dressing room . . . familiarisation. Meads said he just couldn't go. He and Mains decided that they would not tell the media, or anyone outside the party, of their situation. They saw it as dire. Some of the players went along to the ground, others stayed behind. Brian Lochore was feeling okay, so he looked after the players who did go to Ellis Park.

Some players began to improve late on the Friday, but none were 100 per cent by the Saturday, finals day. And as far as Meads was concerned, they badly missed the regular pre-match build-up — 'no cup of tea and a few sandwiches together in the afternoon,' says Meads, shaking his head. To his mind that was deplorable. Some of the players were more debilitated than others. In his view, the players who had vomited, recovered more quickly. 'Kronfeld blamed the chicken on the tables at Thursday's lunch. I blame the milk. Maybe he was right, and it was the chicken burgers. Jeff Wilson had had two chicken burgers. Laurie was convinced that the British bookmakers were behind it.'

Ten of the 15 players who started the game for the All Blacks had been sick on the Thursday and Friday beforehand. Within a few minutes of the kick-off in the final, both Meads and BJ looked at each other. They were concerned by what they were seeing. It was a lethargy they had not seen in any of the preceding games. The South Africans were wired, and Meads remembers the highly excitable James Small 'tracking Jonah wherever he went'. At fulltime the score was 12-all and Meads turned to BJ and said, 'We're right now. We've come this far, I think we'll do it.'

As far as Meads knew, the All Blacks had decided to stick to the style they had played throughout the tournament. 'We thought that our backs were better at running the ball than anyone else's. We knew they were defensive-minded, but Bunce would lay the ball off to others, and Os [Glen Osborne] was playing brilliantly at fullback. There was an intention to use Jonah on the blind side . . . I thought it made sense.'

However, in retrospect, Meads realised that the disruptions in the days before the game were so severe that the on-field disruptiveness of the South Africans gravely compounded the All Blacks' problems. 'Mehrtens wasn't right, and Wilson had to come off early. It turned out to be a disaster.'

Meads felt for Fitzpatrick especially. 'Fitzy was extremely frustrated that day because he hadn't got sick beforehand. He may even have thought that some of them weren't as bad as they made out. During the game, Dowdy [Craig Dowd] went down. Mike Brewer did his ankle. Something went terribly wrong there. I think he'd had a painkiller and he wasn't walking properly because he couldn't feel his foot . . . something like that.'

Joel Stransky kicked a dropped goal in extra time and the South Africans won 15–12. Afterwards the mood was terrible. As manager, Meads remembers 'disbelief and despair' among the players. It was ruinous having to attend press conferences and to be saying that 'players had been down with food poisoning or the flu. No one would believe us. I was a little annoyed with some of the New Zealand media who were sceptical. I got the feeling they didn't quite believe us either. We thought that beforehand, on balance, it had been better to hide the fact that so many were sick. From certain quarters there was more than a hint that we were poor losers.'

Some of the players were reluctant to go along to the tournament dinner afterwards. Meads had told them that, 'Win, lose or draw they would attend and wear the bow ties they'd been given. There was a bit of rebellion about that. Some of the guys tried to make out they had lost theirs. But I was awake to that, and had put a few extras away in my kit, so when we got there I pulled them out.'

Andrew Mehrtens does his best to charge down Joel Stransky's dropped goal attempt in the 1995 World Cup final at Johannesburg.

The All Blacks arrived at the dinner and had a few drinks with the French and reps from other countries. Everyone was waiting for the South Africans to turn up. Meads says that it was the best part of two hours before they deigned to grace the gathering with their presence. No one was impressed. 'The mood was not good,'

PHOTOSPORT

says Meads. It deteriorated further when South Africa's Big Cheese, Louis Luyt, gave a speech which was seen as boastful and offensive by turns. He presented the Welsh referee Derek Bevan with a gold watch, reward for South Africa deeming him the best referee of the tournament. This didn't endear Luyt to anyone, especially the French who felt Bevan had denied them a win in their semi-final against South Africa. Luyt further incensed many by saying that this World Cup was the true World Cup, and that the previous ones hadn't been because South Africa was absent. If South Africa had been there, he implied, they would have won those too.'

Fulltime in the 1995 World Cup final . . . 'Afterwards the mood was terrible,' says Meads.

Mike Brewer was livid. He asked Meads if he could have a word to Luyt. Meads said, 'Yeah, go for your life'. And that came from one who had always seen Luyt mainly as a friend rather than foe. In his book, Brewer says that Luyt 'shouted' at him, told him he 'was a typical New Zealander, who couldn't take losing', and that he 'was a pig'. The rugby writer and former Lion, Andy Irvine, reported that when Luyt was asked if Brewer and he had had 'a conversation or a confrontation', he replied, 'It depends on how you interpret "Big Afrikaner Bastard".'

Meanwhile, the French had walked out, and the Brits were audibly derisive. What should have been, and could have been, a gracious and generous-spirited evening turned into something of a boorish farce. Or as Meads remembers it, 'A complete and utter shambles. As for the French, knowing them,' says Meads, 'they probably had other things planned for that night anyway. Most of us, including BJ and me, left before the desserts came along. We'd had enough.'

Back at their hotel, Lochore and Meads and one or two others had a couple of beers and said things like, it's not the end of the world or life goes on, and all that stuff. Then they went to bed, quite early.

Meads quickly decided that there was nothing to be gained from protracted post-mortems. His view was similar to that of the team's fitness trainer, Martin Toomey, who had been with them from the time the All Blacks squad had begun preparing for the World Cup nearly a year before, in mid-1994. Toomey thought the team had done everything it could have done at the World Cup and before. 'The players were strong physically, they had good speed, and they played up to their potential.' Toomey saw the team as well managed and well coached, and felt their 'biggest advantage over their opponents was their endurance'.

In the morning, Meads says, 'We had the court session to end all court sessions. It even went so far as to involve punching the guy beside you. The guys were pretty kind to BJ and me, not so kind to Laurie, and a bit hard on Mike Bowen, the doctor. There were all sorts of rules, and one was to stay close to your seat. If you got caught in the middle of the room you got tackled and roughed up. At one point, Doc Bowen got tipped over in the middle of the floor and knocked about. Later, one member of the hotel staff reported one of the All Blacks lying in the hall outside his room. It was Mike Brewer. He had flaked there. We just told him to open the door of Mike's room, drag him inside, and leave him there.

'The session was meant to help everyone get over the loss, and by and large it worked.'

After the tournament, the disappointing thing for management and players was that they came home — after having been seen by almost every other nation, and most of the media, as clearly the best-performed, most exciting team at the tournament — wondering, how had they lost after all the work they had put in? If only that bout of food poisoning hadn't scythed through the team in the 48 hours prior to the final . . .

South African rugby boss Louis Luyt (above) and Mike Brewer had a heated exchange at the official dinner after the 1995 World Cup final.

Now, they had to regroup and get ready to play against Australia. Two tests for the Bledisloe Cup, both before the end of July. They had also to confront an organisation that appeared, in so far as Meads and most NZRFU administrators were concerned, as unethical and immoral as Mephistopheles: the predatory World Rugby Corporation (WRC). As far as the NZRFU was concerned, the WRC, a front for the media magnate Kerry Packer's bid to scupper the other Australian magnate Rupert Murdoch's media sporting plans, was out to capture the bodies of most of New Zealand's finest rugby players, and to destroy the soul of rugby itself.

It's a win. Meads looks on as Mike Brewer embraces Andrew Mehrtens after the All Blacks' convincing win over Australia at Sydney in the second test of the 1995 Bledisloe Cup series. It was after this match that the real fight for control of world rugby began.

The odd thing was that Colin Meads knew little or nothing about the WRC and its scheme, but some of his All Blacks certainly did.

Meads found it very odd when he learned that just about everybody knew something about the ogreish WRC before he did. He didn't hear about it until the day after the World Cup final. No one with any WRC connections, nor any of the players being targeted, was likely to have wanted to let Meads in on the proposals being developed. After all, he was a rugby union councillor as well as manager of the All Blacks. He, surely, would be an opponent of the WRC. Meads remained in the dark for weeks. But when the team got to Sydney for the second Bledisloe Cup test in late July, he noticed that many players were avoiding Brian Lochore — whom the NZRFU had asked to look into just what this mysterious WRC was, and who it had approached, and so on — like the plague. 'When compared to most of the others, in many respects I was still in the dark at the time we got to Sydney.'

Meads just couldn't conceive how it would be possible to dismantle international rugby as he knew it, and had seen it for 40 years and more, and replace it with, what? If he thought about it at all, it seemed like a dog's breakfast of a proposal to him, a mish-mash of Fido, Tux and a few mutton bones chucked in for the animals to chomp on. One of the reasons Meads found the rumours of a cataclysmic change in the nature of rugby competition worldwide to be far-fetched, thus unlikely, was that he couldn't believe that rugby people as he knew them would put money first, the game second. Meads wasn't in any way averse to players being well recompensed, but only so long as the essence of the game of rugby as a game was not badly tarnished. So at this point he was amused more than outraged by the rumours flying about. In a speech in Sydney on the eve of the 100th test between Australia and New Zealand on 29 July 1995, he told the audience that all these new professional teams that these mysterious backroom boys were supposedly trying to sign up were going to need experienced managers. He said, 'I'm starting to get brassed off. How come no one's asked me?' He admits to making light of the WRC. 'I was flippant: for example, I said that I'd been sitting there with the Australian manager and he didn't seem to know much about the whole affair either, so that must mean that we weren't thought very highly of as managers. The strange thing was, some took my comments as being pro the WRC. I got back to my hotel to find that Ross Turnbull, one of the prime negotiators and planners behind the WRC, had sent me a fax thanking me for my support.'

While Meads had clearly been kept outside the loop when it came to the developing battle for the future of rugby as it was known to young and old, that was far from the case with a number of those whom he held in the highest regard. Brian Lochore and Jock Hobbs, for instance. They were in Sydney to deliver a letter to the All Blacks detailing the NZRFU's offer meant to counter the WRC. When the test was over, Lochore handed every All Black a letter that ended with a plea presumably intended to prick the conscience and tug the heart-strings of them all. It read:

> We are conscious of our duty towards you and the other 150,000 rugby players currently playing in New Zealand. We are also conscious that we must act responsibly so that all New Zealand rugby, including All Black rugby, continues to be strong, and your sons have the same opportunity to wear the Silver Fern that you have had.
>
> Yours faithfully,
> Brian Lochore, Jock Hobbs, Rob Fisher.

The penny dropped well and truly, thunk, when All Black loose forward Mike Brewer came to Meads and told him solemnly that this test would be the last time many of the players would run on the field together. Some would be retiring, some would not be picked again, others would be playing elsewhere. Brewer told Meads that he 'got a little pub jacked up so the players could have a final few beers together'. Meads recalls Brewer mentioning that the pub was run by a New Zealander, and that he asked Meads to exclude the Australian liaison officer and one or two other local officials. As long as they got away from the ground fairly quickly, there would be a couple of hours before they were due to attend the 100th anniversary dinner. Brewer said the meeting would be held at a venue only 10 minutes' drive away. It would be their last time to 'really be together', said Brewer.

'I asked Brewer if he wanted me to do anything and he said that wouldn't be

Four men who played significant parts in the battle against the World Rugby Corporation. Clockwise from top: Rob Fisher, Brian Lochore, Jock Hobbs and Richie Guy.

necessary. After the game we got in a bus and away we went. We drove and we drove. I started to get agitated. Where is this damned place? I said, "You told me it was 10 minutes away." Laurie Mains then told me they were going to a meeting with negotiators for the WRC. Although I didn't find this out until later — partly because I didn't want to know — we were going to meet Brian Powers, who was deputed to act on behalf of the media mogul, Kerry Packer. Laurie said Powers lived in a flash house in the suburb of Vaucluse. I was furious, but I bit my tongue. The bus stopped, all the players trooped into this mansion, and we waited. I wasn't sure what to do. Young Anton Oliver, who had been dragged in as a reserve hooker when Norm Hewitt was injured, went in too and then got told bluntly by Fitzy that he was not needed, so he played basketball with some kids. Laurie knew I was ropable and, after going into the house for a while, came out and got back on the bus with me.'

Meads sat there quietly steaming, feeling rather like an old Hereford cut from the mob and driven into a yard by himself. Masseur Donny Cameron had, naively, wandered into the palatial residence only to be told to buzz off immediately, so he returned to the bus and joined Meads and All Black Marc Ellis, all of them feeling bemused. Ellis was soon to switch to league, so he was superfluous to requirements as far as the WRC poachers were concerned.

To cap it all, they had driven into a dead-end street and it took the best part of 15 minutes to turn the bus round. Ric Salizzo stood outside in the cul-de-sac, shouting and directing the driver. This was after he had been sent in to the meeting to remove Doc Bowen and physiotherapist Barry Donaldson, who had been sitting at the back of the room so inconspicuously that the ever-alert Fitzy can't have noticed them. Salizzo says he made so much noise in the street, and attracted so much attention from residents, that it must have been a case of 'so much for the so-called secret meeting'. The fiasco regarding the near-entrapment of their bus just made Meads more grizzly. The players said they would be half an hour and were away nearly three times that. The party was late for the dinner. Meads thought he had been conned.

Meads wasn't, therefore, able to shed much light on the developing events for those acting for the NZFRU, and Jock Hobbs in particular. But now that the test was over, he took more of an interest. The dinner for 600 people at Sydney's Hordern Pavilion was not an especially congenial affair. The tensions between the pro- and anti-WRC camps were obvious. A lot of emotional rucking went on. At one point a video was shown highlighting great moments from the 100 tests between the Wallabies and the All Blacks. Then Bruce Hayman of the Australian Rugby Football Union spoke emotively: 'You can't replace 100 [sic] years of fierce rivalry and national pride with created teams that lack support and purpose, and which are motivated only by the dollar.' It was clear from the response that there were deep and passionate divisions within the room.

Meads talked with Mains and others and realised that they knew a great deal more than he had thought. Mains said that John Hart and Andy Haden were two of many interested in being involved in the WRC's scheme, and that he was seriously considering getting involved too. 'I laughed and said to Laurie, "You and John Hart?" He replied that it was a money thing, that one had to be in it, that it was going to take off.'

Soon after the team returned to New Zealand, Meads recalls Mains ringing him and saying that he and others felt all the players should be brought together in Wellington for discussions with the likes of Jock Hobbs, Richard Crawshaw and Rob Fisher of the NZRFU. One of the stronger memories Meads has of this meeting is the way some players referred to having been offered contracts to switch to rugby league as a means of persuading the NZRFU to increase the size of offers to them to remain with the NZRFU.

'There was a bit of a joke going round regarding Richard Loe. It was said he was the only player willing to accept the NZRFU's initial offer because no one would believe him when he said he had a league offer.' Meads chuckles when saying this, for he has always regarded Loe as a good player and an amusing character. And he is careful to say that when it comes to the WRC saga, much is and was hearsay. 'I make light of it now, because it all turned out for the best, by and large, in the end, although it was dramatic for those most closely involved, and it was a close-run thing for a while. When Josh Kronfeld and Jeff Wilson agreed to sign with the NZRFU that certainly opened the gates and others quickly followed.'

Meads first got to know Jock Hobbs when he took over as captain of the Cavaliers in the course of their contentious tour of South Africa in 1986. In 1995, Hobbs, then a member of the NZRFU Council, took over as the union's chief negotiator in the battle to defeat the predatory WRC. No one should underestimate the debt New Zealand rugby owes to Hobbs, says Meads. To him, Hobbs was 'a quality person', and 'a saviour of New Zealand rugby'. When Hobbs was sidelined, then failed to be appointed to the revamped national body in 1996 — a streamlined board which replaced the old council in line with the recommendations of the Boston Report into rugby in New Zealand — Meads was one of a number who thought it shameful and a missed opportunity. 'Some of the players saw Hobbs as a bit of a Scrooge acting for the NZRFU. At the same time, some on the union were grumping about him being a spendthrift. I'm sure, in light of subsequent events, the irony of that was not lost on Jock,' says Meads. 'Put it this way,' says Meads, 'some of the guys that beat Jock for his job wouldn't blow smoke up his proverbial.'

Meads is quite scornful of the way the New Zealand administration has grown like Topsy. 'My guess is that there are four times as many people there today.' It may be, though, that there is just so much more to do. Nevertheless, he says, 'I remember councillors in my day would go along to the likes of under-19 tournaments, say, and observe and help out in all manner of ways. Now no board member goes near those sorts of activities — or very, very rarely. We saw that as part of our job.'

At a rugby union council meeting not long after the WRC had been repelled, Meads remembers all the councillors being 'cleared out of the chambers. Sean Fitzpatrick had come down from Auckland to sign a deal with the union. Fitzy's a shrewd character when it comes to money, and he came up to me beforehand and said that he was going to put it to Rob Fisher and Richie Guy that the All Black captain should be given an additional amount, say 20 per cent, over and above what other leading players got. To compensate a captain for the extra pressures and responsibilities. "What do you think, and how would I do it?" he asked. I told him to go for it, he might as well get what he could, now that we were openly going down the fully professional road. I said he could take Fisher and Guy aside — there was a small room next to the chambers — and have a word there. Fitzy said he wasn't sure that he would be the captain when John Hart took over as coach, but

THE DOMINION

Was there ever a more precious signature for New Zealand rugby? Sean Fitzpatrick signs up with the NZRFU, thus ending the WRC threat. Looking on are Rob Fisher and Richie Guy.

he wanted the union to set up a precedent of giving the captain extra. Fitzy told me that Richie Guy wasn't keen, initially said that the union couldn't agree to that. So he told Fisher and Guy that if that was the case, he'd have to reconsider his decision to sign with the union. All the media were there waiting for him to sign. He was being seen as a kind of saviour of New Zealand rugby. It only took Guy and Fisher a few moments to change their view. I tell the story that it only took Fitzy five minutes to make himself an extra 50 grand.'

Fitzpatrick signed and all was well with the New Zealand rugby world. The so-called greatest threat ever to the game of rugby football in New Zealand had been vanquished. The players had garnered unprecedented spoils, but just what, if anything, the NZRFU had gained was not yet clear. All round it was, perhaps, a case of, never such innocence again. A photo in Wellington's *Dominion* newspaper showed a satisfied-looking, boyishly charming Fitzpatrick signing a contract, and seated alongside him are Rob Fisher, looking a little coy and, possibly, rueful, and a chummy-jovial Richie Guy.

ANTON
OLIVER

Anton Oliver's view of Meads is that he must have been a great player because almost everyone who saw him play says so. Oliver himself shares many of Meads' attitudes towards rugby. For one, he believes as Meads did in hard work and working his other forwards hard. That earns him respect and a reputation as a formidable opponent. And when former All Black assistant coach Tony Gilbert said of Oliver that he is 'the best in his position in the world. He leads from the front, gives strong direction,' he could easily have been talking of a lock of a former era, the Colin Meads of old.

Oliver's ethos is similar to that of Meads', he simply and eagerly wants to continue to play rugby for the All Blacks. He'll do the business, for the team's sake, for rugby's sake, irrespective of who's in charge.

Oliver's whole demeanour, from his powerfully muscled frame to his chiselled countenance — the reason why many of his team-mates call him 'Hatchet' or 'Hatch' — spells resolve. The man himself would say he hopes he has true grit and loads of determination. He's the sort of rugby player popular with rugby traditionalists from the heartlands, from Tuatapere to Taumarunui, because he 'does the hard yards, pulls his weight'.

An example. In a pub in Central Otago a craggy, slightly grizzled bloke with calloused hands said to me, 'I like that Oliver. He doesn't back off. He's a no-bullshit rugby player.'

But none of that has shaken his belief in traditional, no-nonsense, no-frills rugby culture. He likes a set-up where senior players are seen as exemplars and mentors.

Says Oliver of Meads: 'I admire him for his longevity and unwavering conviction to give his all for the All Blacks.' And when he says, 'I just want to remain an All Black. Anything else would be a bonus,' it could just as easily be Meads speaking.

14.
CIAO AND AU REVOIR

"'Don't start that with me," I said. "Can we charter a plane? Answer me." I was told, after humming and haaing, that we could charter a plane that seemed a bit like an old DC3. I said, "Come on. Is it safe? These are high-class players.'"

IT WAS GRATIFYING FOR MEADS TO HAVE SEEN HOW WELL THE ALL BLACKS BOUNCED BACK AFTER THEIR DESOLATING EXPERIENCE IN THE LAST DAYS OF THE WORLD CUP IN SOUTH AFRICA. TWO WINS AGAINST AUSTRALIA AND POSSESSION OF THE BLEDISLOE CUP WAS AN INDICATION THAT THIS WAS A GOOD ALL BLACK SIDE.

It had the heart and soul that Meads admired and required of men who wore the black jersey. The team played 'terribly well, were super-confident against Australia,' says Meads. It surprised him a little given the loss in South Africa and the cloak and dagger stuff associated with the WRC kerfuffling. He was looking forward eagerly, as he has always done, to touring France. As Jeff Wilson, still a callow though hugely talented youngster in many ways, was to observe to his amazement, 'When Colin Meads is on tour with the All Blacks, he's the main attraction.' To which one could add, and especially in France. Wilson is not the first player in the past 30 years to have noticed and been astonished by that.

Meads recalls that Mains wanted 30 players to go on the tour of Italy and France. 'I wasn't 100 per cent in agreement with Laurie on the need for that, and the new chairman of the NZRFU, Richie Guy, was dead against it. He had been manager of the All Blacks when there was a squad of 30 players, and he was heard to say that half of them do nothing, a few get injured and they are just a nuisance. In the end, we were allowed 26, then that got increased to 28. Getting the extra two resulted from a bit of skulduggery. Tabai Matson, a big mid-fielder, came courtesy of a company he was representing over there. Then, because Fitzy was out for a game, at least, at the start of the tour, he saw a chance to get Mark 'Bull' Allen along. I had to explain to Richie that Olo Brown could act as the spare hooker, had experience at throwing the ball in, so that meant there was room for Bull. Richard Loe was recovering from an injury but he would be right in a week. I had to do some sweet talking.'

Before the NZRFU council meeting, at which Meads was bound to put Laurie Mains' request for a touring party of 30 players, he did something that always discomforted him: he engaged in a bit of lobbying. 'I rang Laurie before I went in to the meeting and said to him, "I'll try hard, but I don't think we're going to win this one; the vibes I'm getting aren't good." So I put the case and found that the blokes I'd lobbied didn't agree with me. It went to the vote and I lost 18 to one. I thought, what a great job I've done.'

Meads wasn't cut up about it. He found it amusing. Laurie Mains would have had to take a couple of deep breaths and grit his teeth before accepting it, Meads thinks. 'But it did show that some councillors put their personal liking for people aside when it came to making decisions,' says Meads. 'Some of those guys — John Sturgeon, Richie Guy and John Dowling, for instance — were friends of Laurie's. Well, maybe Dowling stuck up for Laurie. I'm not sure of that. Anyway, I rang Laurie and told him the result: only one in favour, and that was me. Deep down I wasn't really, but I wasn't going to say that.'

The touring party was a mix of the old and the new. Some might say, given the complement that included Loe, Lomu, Blackadder, the Brooke brothers, Fitzpatrick, Michael and Ian Jones, Hewitt, Rush, Bunce, Little and Ieremia, it was a case of the Big, the Bad, and the Ugly.

New faces included Todd Blackadder, Taine Randell and Justin Marshall. Carlos Spencer was brought in as a replacement.

A few older hands had cried enough, or said No thanks. Mike Brewer was off to Ireland; Graeme Bachop and Kevin Schuler returned to Japan. Ant Strachan was going there too.

Meads didn't know what to expect of Italy. He had never been there for rugby purposes. And he found it hard to believe that a people so fond of pasta could ever hope to turn out a seriously good rugby team. The All Blacks flew to London and then on to Rome where they were, on arrival, exhausted. A short stop in Rome and then they were airborne again, to Sicily. They had been warned to be careful — the place was run, they were told, by the Mafia.

Former All Black fullback Don Clarke's brother, Doug, got in touch with Meads and said that a daughter and some friends were going to be in Sicily and were keen to go to the game. Did Meads have access to a few tickets? Yes, he did. 'Leave it to me.' Famous last words.

Meads asked the team's liaison officer for their quota of complimentary tickets. A day went by; no tickets. Come the morning of the match, still no tickets. Meads had to 'line the fella up. Come on, we want our tickets. Some of us have friends and family arriving. I've promised some people tickets myself.' Meads tried hard to avoid giving the man the impression that he would have to consider strangling him with strings of pasta.

Eventually, the liaison officer told Meads that there weren't any tickets. He didn't have any. How, then, did people get into the ground? That's what Meads wanted to know. Did everyone pay at the gate? The answer was: No, no one paid. It was free.

Action from the All Blacks' encounter with Italy A at Catania — a match apparently funded by the Mafia. Pictured here, from left, are: Richard Fromont, Mark Allen, Frank Bunce, Todd Blackadder and Alama Ieremia.

'I was mystified. I told him I wanted our friends to have seats, covered seats, so that if it rained . . . and so on. I needed to be able to tell these people where to go and what to do. In the end, it was agreed that a section of the ground would be roped off and reserved for guests of the All Blacks. Afterwards I learned that the locals had put in a successful bid to hold the game, which had originally been going to be held in Rome, and that it was funded by the Mafia. That was what we were told.'

The game, against Italy A at Catania, was won 51–21. But it was a victory at a price. Mehrtens incurred a knee ligament injury that ended his tour.

Ric Salizzo, who had played rugby in Italy in the mid-1980s, was with Meads at

PHOTOSPORT

PHOTOSPORT

the after-match function. Salizzo says an elderly man of some importance was sitting to one side, but was regularly acknowledged and clearly deferred to. Meads grabbed Salizzo and said, 'Ric, come and meet The Godfather.'

Salizzo says that Meads was a heroic figure in the eyes of many Italian rugby players. 'When I was playing club rugby in Casale in Northern Italy, one player had a large cardboard cutout of Meads on his wall.'

From Sicily the team flew to Bologna to prepare for the test against Italy. Meads had gone to Bologna several weeks before to check their accommodation and to look over training facilities and the like. He had been told that it would be okay for the team to train at the test venue on the Thursday and Friday before the game. After arriving from Sicily, the team went along to Stadio Renato Dall'ara in Bologna, got changed and then were told that they couldn't train there after all. 'It was a beautiful-looking pitch,' says Meads, 'and groundsmen were out marking it for the soccer match to be played there on the Friday.' So the All Blacks were directed through a tunnel to a soccer ground a few hundred metres away. It was bare and hard. Mains' first reaction was to spit tacks. He told Meads that they couldn't and wouldn't be training on this ground. Meads replied that six weeks ago he had been told they would be able to train at the match venue. 'All hell broke loose. Laurie got into the local officials who were standing close by. They included the chairman of the Italian rugby union.'

Despite efforts, another ground could not be found and the team had to train on the scruffy and baked soccer ground after all. It looked like a paddock in the Upper Clutha area that had been grazed for a week in summer by a mob of hungry merinos. Says Meads, 'Laurie spluttered, "Here we are, the best team in the world, the All Blacks,

While several of the 1995 All Blacks were visiting the Ferrari headquarters near Bologna, Meads was at the airport . . . trying desperately to get the All Blacks out of Italy.

PHOTOSPORT

Jeff Wilson tests out the Italian defence in 1995. The All Blacks cantered to a 70–6 victory.

having to train on a dirty, stinking bloody soccer pitch . . . full of holes and rubbish."'

Meads said he didn't see it as a major problem. All that could usefully be done was to have some lineout practice and run through a few moves. But it was clear that Mains had a contrary view and Meads kept quiet. He had noted that the players enjoyed hearing Mains get stuck into outsiders, and, in this case, Fitzy and others didn't like having to train on a poor ground. Mains' fear was that someone would break an ankle. A concession was made and the All Blacks were allowed onto the stadium ground to kick a few balls around. There was a cycle track around the ground, so the dead ball area was small, but the adjacent sections of the track were covered.

On the afternoon before the test — which the All Blacks won easily, 70–6 — some of the team went and visited the Ferrari headquarters. Meads didn't, he had an inkling. He went out to the airport to check on their travel arrangements. The party was due to fly to France the day after the test to prepare for a match on the Wednesday against the French Barbarians in Toulon. His enquiries were greeted with bewilderment. 'Staff at the airport said, "Give us some names." I tried to explain there were 30-odd of us, we were the All Black touring party. But no, they wanted some names. They had about half a dozen names, including Zinzan Brooke's, mine and Fitzy's. "Does that mean," I asked, "that you can confirm that the whole lot of us are booked to fly out of here on the Sunday morning?" They couldn't assure me. I didn't know what to do. I got onto someone in the Italian union and asked if they had booked us all on flights to France. The Italians were hedging. The guts of it was that New Zealand paid to get to Italy, and to get out; while the Italians paid for all our internal travel and accommodation. Everyone was duck-shoving. The travel agents in New Zealand had asked the Italians to make the bookings. They had made a gesture only. So I rang the French union, asked if they had made bookings for us. They said they had, but I couldn't get details. So I went back to the airport. No more progress. I thought there was little more I could do except turn up at the airport on the Sunday morning and take it from there. When we got there, there were bookings all right — for six or eight individuals only. I phoned the New Zealand union offices in Wellington and was told the bookings had been made from Italy . . . or was it France? I asked them back home if they thought they could do anything. I said, "Here we are, sitting here like burnt stumps. Do I send seven off, or what?" Then, I started thumping tables at the airport. I told them I wanted them to get us to France. The duck-shoving had to end. It was all about who paid, and to me New Zealand should pay. "Can we charter a plane?" Not sure. I was told four could go on this flight, two on another. "Don't start that with me," I said. "Can we charter a plane? Answer me." I was told, after humming and haaing, that we could charter a plane that seemed a bit like an old DC3. I said, "Come on. Is it safe? These are high-class players."'

Media man Ric Salizzo, who was seen as a protection against media incursions, remembers Meads taking a credit card out of his pocket and slapping it down on the counter. That told the airline staff exactly who was paying.

Meads continues: 'In the end, I sent Laurie and half a dozen others off on the regular flight and a bit later the rest of us went on the charter. I think most of the players thought it was a balls-up on my part. If you had seen us; the All Black team has an amazing amount of gear. Tackle bags, doctor's equipment, it's mind-boggling. There were no baggage handling staff to help us. Not enough room in the hold. Those who had gone ahead of us left all their extra stuff with us. We loaded half the gear, including luggage, into the passenger section of the plane, filled up seat spaces that we didn't require, and chugged off for France.'

Unbeknown to the Tail-end Charlies, that is, Meads and the bulk of the team, they would get to their destination ahead of Mains and his small group. The Mains plane stopped off at another town on the way.

The saga hadn't ended. The small group that included Mains got off their plane in France and waited for their luggage. Hard luck, boys. Their plane had taken off for its next destination without all their baggage being unloaded. Mains' gear had been taken on. Mains gave the French officials there to meet him verbal Exocets. The Eiffel Tower, no small distance away, shook. Meads knew how he felt and was browned off too, but it is not his practice to take it out on others.

The team got on a bus and drove for an hour to Toulon. Mostly silence on the bus. The players were used to Laurie letting off verbal bazookas at those who were insufficiently attentive and mindful of the requirements of a team of the All Blacks' abilities and eminence. Meads says that the officials in Toulon were falling over themselves to be gracious and helpful. They took him and a few others out that night. Mains wasn't interested in going. '"That Mr Mains, he very angry!" I said that they had to realise that we had had one awful day. Laurie didn't like his room, didn't like the facilities, didn't like the hotel. The missing gear arrived next morning and things quietened down.'

Meads is no linguist, so he couldn't make subtle explanations. He says Richard Loe seemed to have some French, but his own, apart from the likes of *merci* and *bonjour*, is 'mostly garbage'.

The team played well enough in its first two games, beating the Barbarians 34–19 and Languedoc-Roussillon 30–9 at Beziers. There was a distance between where the team stayed and where they played. 'Like,' says Meads, 'staying at Whangaparaoa and playing at Eden Park.' But when he had been there checking things a couple of months before he thought the players would like it. Swimming pools, a resort-style atmosphere. But when the All Blacks arrived it was the off-season. 'No one for miles,' says Meads, 'winterish. Some of the beds were no good. A few of the boys put the beds outside in the corridor and slept on mattresses on the floor. I told them they were fussy, but it wasn't the best actually.'

All the while, Josh Kronfeld, the idiosyncratic openside flanker, had been battling to recover from a severe ankle injury he had sustained in the NPC final against Auckland at Eden Park several weeks earlier. If he was to play the tests, he had to perform against Côte Basque-Landes at Bayonne on the Tuesday before the first test. Beforehand, Kronfeld stood in a hole in the tunnel under the stand and wrecked his ankle completely. A few minutes later, after Doc Bowen had given him the bad news, he was sitting in tears in a small room beside the main dressing room when Meads came in. 'I was pretty upset for Josh. I knew how much he wanted to play a test against the French. I knew how much playing for the All Blacks meant to him. I went off and got a test jersey and came back and gave it to him.'

Kronfeld knew he would have to go home. He recalls the jersey was in a paper bag, and that, 'Tree said to me, "Here, you have that. Take that home." It was Tree's way of commiserating with one of his boys.'

After Kronfeld got home and had to undergo a major ankle reconstruction, the NZRFU was unwilling to pay him for going on the tour. The union said that he hadn't been covered by insurance. But his lawyer, Warren Alcock, disputed that. He had a letter saying otherwise which he had elicited before the tour began. Alcock had a word to Meads and Lochore when they were in the south and soon after the union reversed its decision. 'I'm sure it was Meads that did it,' says Alcock. 'I showed him the letter and he said, "Right, if that's what was said, that's what should happen." Words to that effect.'

Meads recalls with a laugh that before the tour he negotiated on the players' behalf to have them all paid something like $20,000 for the tour. 'Myself, all I got was a daily allowance and reimbursement of expenses.'

Meads says that not many people 'understand that France isn't really a rugby country. Rugby teams like people around them, they don't like being isolated. That's where rugby has changed. In my day we stayed in the middle of town. In Dunedin, say, we'd stay at Wains Hotel; in Christchurch, the old Clarendon. Things changed, and the trend was to stay somewhere apart, away from shops and so on. Before tests, atmosphere builds up, and it's better for the players to become part of it. Now, in Auckland, they've gone back to the likes of the Poenamo on the North Shore instead of the more up-market hotels. I don't think they're good rugby places.'

'Some of the accommodation in France was a bit below what we wanted. I went ahead in a car to Toulouse to see that we got better rooms, and especially to see that Laurie's was all right. Some of the players who had toured a bit liked a bit of luxury, rather than going along with my views on where they should stay. I think the French had fooled me a bit by showing me a few good rooms and not the lot in some places. Little, narrow beds are no good for big fellas.'

PHOTOSPORT

The first test was to be played in Toulouse on 11 November. Lead-ups to tests in France are different, says Meads. There is a banquet on the eve of the game and a luncheon before the game. The manager is expected to attend, which means someone else has to be deputed to look after the team. Meads arrived at the ground close to kick-off time, went and had a quick word to a few in the team, and then marched around the perimeter to sit with the dignitaries. It was not a game Meads enjoyed. As he says, 'I am not a good loser. Nevertheless, I had to shake hands with all the local officials and big cheeses from the French rugby union and tell them how well they had played, and so on. They did play well, and got into us up front. To me, the Colin Meads way of looking at it was the whole team had been running a bit scared. I thought back to my day when many of our players were also a bit uncertain when playing the French — they gabble and yak away at you in a strange language. It's easy to be intimidated by the French.'

Meads was keen to get across and into the All Blacks' dressing room. For a time he couldn't; he had to spend time with a whole lot of excited French officials enjoying post-match euphoria. When he did get away and entered the team's dressing room, what did he see? 'They were all covered in ice. Ice packs here, ice packs there. The doctor's jinking this way and that — someone's got a sore shoulder, someone else has a sore leg. Ice is the modern theory carried to its

Josh Kronfeld's stance on French nuclear testing in the Pacific was clear for all to see in 1995. Meanwhile, an ankle injury ruined his chance of playing against France, but Meads was still able to present him with a test jersey.

extreme. Socks full of ice. The works. One forward, he had four ice packs on him.'

The sight of rugby players festooned in ice, as if they've just come from working outdoors in an Antarctic blizzard, has never appealed to Meads. It is not that he lacks concern — on the contrary, many speak of his compassion — it is more that he thinks a few too many in the modern game are touched by fears that tilt them towards hypochondria. So as he looked at the four-pack forward he was thinking to himself, the only place you should have that ice is on your head, that's all that's really wrong with you.

Up till this point, Meads had never interfered with the way the team played or trained or prepared or recovered after games. He saw it as Mains' area. The players were clearly upset about the game, the way they had played, the way they had allowed themselves to be dominated. Some felt traces of shame. They had let Laurie Mains down too, that was the feeling. Meads saw and sensed all that and more. That night he encouraged them to relax and have a few beers, if they wanted to, and enjoy their dinner. There was no official dinner.

Earlier in the evening, in a small bar, Zinzan Brooke and a number of other players asked Meads what happened when the All Blacks of Meads' vintage got beaten on tour. 'What would happen?' asked Brooke. Meads chuckled and said he couldn't really tell him for, 'I've never been beaten by France.' But the discussion continued for some time later that night. Meads' view was that one had to get on with training and playing as normal, and be determined to bounce back.

Eventually, Meads said it was time for him to go to bed. The team had an early start in the morning. Bags at 6.30, leaving at seven. Some of the players asked if it

Early days on the 1995 tour of Italy and France. It was after the All Blacks' first test loss at Toulouse that Meads delivered his famous salvo at the players.

PHOTOSPORT

179

would be okay if they went out for a while. Meads said it would, just as long as they knew that they would have to train seriously the next day. A group went out on the town. Some were very late getting in. A number had quaffed a fair bit of rum and/or other fire water. One of the late-night revellers was a noted noisy snorer, so before tests he was given a single room. In the morning he was missing when the players assembled to leave for the town of Nancy where they were to play a French Selection on the Tuesday. Someone was sent up to his room. No sign of him. Meads says he lined up Zinzan Brooke who had been out with the lost All Black. Brooke assured Meads that they had come back together.

The missing player had gone up in the lift to the sixth instead of the fifth floor, tried his key in the lock of room 617 instead of 517, found it wouldn't fit and then started kicking the hell out of the door. It was soon opened, says Meads, 'by a little Frenchman wearing knickers only. The All Black wanted to know what this guy was doing in his room, grabbed him, chucked him out, shut the door and went to bed. The Frenchman is left standing shivering in the corridor. He finds his way down to the lobby, tells the guy on duty that a "monster" threw him out of his room. They go up and find the monster snoring on the bed. They couldn't wake him, so they packed up the Frenchman's gear and put him in another room. But the hotel staffer on night duty didn't leave a note for the morning shift that started at six, so no one knew what had happened. No one knew there was a stray All Black in 617 rather than 517. Zinny worked it out somehow, found him, packed the monster's gear up in 517, and brought him down.'

Not for the first time, Meads was asking himself what sort of an All Black manager he was. As Ric Salizzo used to say, Colin didn't always go about things in expected ways but he got there in the end. He was mainly worried about all the press staff who were hanging around asking what the hold up was all about. He fell back on the old one about hotels and accounts, arguing about personal bills.

When the team got to Nancy, Meads realised that — the more so in retrospect — he wasn't at all happy about what he had witnessed in the test in Toulouse. They all had lunch, then Meads talked to Mains, asked if he could have a word to the team later in the afternoon. 'After you've done; just me and the players, no one else.' Mains agreed to that.

This was one of those occasions that Ric Salizzo refers to when advancing the argument that Meads is 'an incredibly talented amateur psychologist'. He remembers Meads kicking everyone else out of the dressing room one by one, starting with the Steinlager rep Tim Barry, brother of All Black Liam Barry. Tim had become virtually one of the boys. Salizzo says Meads barked that he 'didn't want any sponsors' reps in the room, things had got too slack on this damned tour', and the fact that Tim was there was his, Meads', fault as manager. Meads then kicked Salizzo out, which got rid of the media, he said; then the doctor Mike Bowen, then Laurie Mains as well.

Colin Meads had decided that he was 'going to give these jokers a Fred Allen wind-up, I really will. So it's true, I got rid of Ric, and the assistant coach Ross Cooper, and Laurie. I told them to buzz off, I just wanted the team. I said I had two things I want to talk about: one was about all the talk going on back home about who should take over as coach from Laurie, so, as a rugby union councillor, I'd be interested in your views on who the next coach should be. I said, "Just put your name on a piece of paper and another name beside it". I said it wouldn't go past me but I'd be interested. I've been told that wasn't the right thing to do, but I was genuinely interested. Later, I got some heavy criticism for that from journalists like Wynne Gray and Murray Deaker, and from some councillors. As we know, John Hart got the coach's job. Not all that many players were enthused about that, I can tell you. I think the names that popped up most often on the players' lists were Gordon Hunter, Graham Henry, Ross Cooper and John Hart. Only one player didn't put down a name, that was Olo Brown. He wrote down that he didn't care who it was, that it wasn't his job. The players certainly thought about it. A couple came back to me and said they wanted their bit of paper back because they'd changed their minds. Ross Cooper probably got most votes. I put that down to the fact that he was with them at the time. I liked Ross and got on well with him, but I think he might have been too nice a guy to be a successful All Black coach.

'The other matter I raised was their own performances individually and as a team. I gave it to them, told them they were scared of Frenchmen just because they spoke another language. I told them they were a pack of wimps. I eyed Jonah and said that there were three black wingers playing international rugby: Jonah, Chester Williams of South Africa, and Émile N'tamack of France. They're meant to be pretty good. Now the French are saying their man's the best and you, Jonah, you're number three. I called him a great big useless so-and-so. I gave them all a barrage. And to the poor fella who had had the four ice packs on, I said that when I'd got to the dressing room you could imagine how I felt after having had to sit with all the dignitaries and watch that appalling exhibition of so-called rugby, and I find you and all the others getting the doctor to fill up socks of ice so you can wrap them round yourselves and say to Laurie, "Aw, I've got a sore leg, that's why I played so poor." Sore, my arse, the only two fellas that didn't have ice on them were Zinny and Fitzy. They're the only ones with any guts, the rest of you are wimps. The only place you should have put the ice was on your head because you're scared between your ears.'

At this point, Meads started to worry that he'd been too extreme. He realises that such talk is basic, anything but eloquent, but he believes that, occasionally, a real roasting is needed and can work. He sees some of them using ice as a crutch and, possibly, an excuse for insufficient effort.

Meads said that now he had that off his chest it was time for them to get their gear and head off for training. At the ground, Mains asked if there were any injuries. There weren't, so he decided to have some scrum practice. About three-quarters of the way through the training session, Mains came over to Meads and wanted to know, 'Just what did you say to these guys? I can't believe what I've been seeing. I'm worried they're going to hurt one another.'

But Meads wasn't going to go into many details, he merely said that he'd given them 'a good rark up'. So it could be said that the team's preparation for the second test had been given a sharper edge. Media liaison man Ric Salizzo certainly thought that when, later in the week, in Paris, Mains got him to chase away about 15 television crews. Meads never tired of enjoying the way Mains used Salizzo as a sort of whipping boy, would get him running hither and thither like a ram let into a paddock full of ewes at tupping time.

But in Nancy, in the evening after Meads' now-famous ballistic verbals, Eric Rush, a non-test player, came to him and asked if he could give the Tuesday side a similar talk before their game against the French Selection. 'Hell, no,' said

Meads, 'that was just a oncer. I've interfered enough. It's not really my job.' Meads has always held Rush in high regard, sees him as a good trainer and a good team man, and was thus intrigued as to why Rush would have thought another rocket was a good idea.

Jeff Wilson vividly remembers Meads hauling the team over the coals. It came as a shock, he says, but the team accepted it because they respected him so much. 'Colin Meads defined All Black rugby,' he says. 'He accepts that the game has changed since his day but he understands it still. In France, after Toulouse, I think he was saying we were patting ourselves on the back too much, believing our own press. Basically he called us a bunch of fairies. He accused us of making the game too complicated.'

The second test was played at the Parc des Princes in Paris and resulted in an emphatic win, 37–12 to the All Blacks. 'Jonah played a boomer of a game,' says Meads, 'and he had also played very well against the French Selection on the Tuesday. Liam Barry and Justin Marshall played well on the Tuesday and they were rewarded with test places in Paris.'

Sean Fitzpatrick impressed Meads that day. 'Fitzy had an inspiring game. He was ruthless. And he was right on the borderline when it came to his "interaction" with the referee. If he hadn't been captain he would not have got away with it. I was sitting with the President of the French Federation and I was shuddering a bit. Frank Bunce had a really good game, and the new boys, Marshall and Barry, were very good. Barry had a brilliant game. Oddly, it was his first and last test. That was quite sad. Jeff Wilson hurt his shoulder in the first test and missed this match, a pity for him. I may have contributed to keeping him out because I had this view that if a player wasn't fit to play by the Wednesday before a test he shouldn't get in. Laurie went along with that.

'It was Laurie's last game as All Black coach and I was moved by the players' reaction. They paid him a great tribute. They grabbed him and hoisted him onto their shoulders and carried him off the ground. His team talk before the test had been tremendous. He spoke about loyalty, about what the jersey meant. I passed the jerseys to him and he gave them out, and told each player what he wanted from him that day. This was late in the morning before the game. The French team was a great side, so the victory was really significant.'

At the pre-match talk, Mains paid tribute to Meads' work too. It was clear to all that they had been a terrific, diverting, occasionally unpredictable, but effective team.

Though no one knew it at the time, it was Meads' last tour as All Black manager. He would have been asked to stay on, he thinks, if Ross Cooper had been appointed coach to follow Mains. That didn't happen, and although Meads put his name forward again, he was not reappointed. He wasn't surprised. Once John Hart got the job he knew that he was history. 'Hart had stood against Mains in 1994 and he knew that I was behind Laurie. I was on the coaching sub-committee of the NZRFU and we interviewed the candidates for the coach's job. The politicking surrounding that selection was intense, and it was very hard to pick which way it would go. The 1994 international season hadn't been a good one for New Zealand, but despite that I thought Laurie was on the right track and was the man to take us to the 1995 World Cup.

Watching the test in Paris was a very satisfying experience for Meads. It seemed like a fitting, rousing finale to Mains' term. It was the manner of the All Blacks'

The Brooke brothers, Robin and Zinzan, hoisted Laurie Mains onto their shoulders after the All Blacks' second test win against France in 1995. It was Mains' last match as coach and Meads' as manager.

victory, the way the players went forward with remorseless commitment and skill. This, thought Meads, was a real All Black team. This was All Black rugby at its best; no quarter asked or given. Although it is not a word he normally uses, Meads thought the All Blacks had played some scintillating rugby. What a breathtaking transformation after the pathetic — as he had told them all — effort at Toulouse the previous week. Now the press, after slating them all seven days before, were singing their praises, and rightly in his view. It had been a great swansong for Mains and Meads, two relentless, devoted, hard-nosed but fair All Black campaigners. Their departure had the dignity that went with upholding the prouder aspects of the All Black tradition.

DONNY
CAMERON

Meads' liking for the underdog, for those who eschew airs and graces, and for those who work hard and, mainly, without complaint, is behind his high regard for the Otago, Highlanders and former All Black team masseur Donny Cameron. Donny, confidant to and popular with the big majority of players, was given the title 'Aristotle of Carisbrook' by the greatly talented former All Black open-side flanker Josh Kronfeld. Josh spent hours on Cameron's table under Carisbrook's main stand, and like many players he divulged many of his innermost, more serious concerns while on the table. Masseurs can be seen as getting rid of emotional and psychological aches and pains as often as they work out the knots from sore muscles. Kronfeld saw Donny as a good man to confide in and found his shrewd common sense assuring and helpful, hence his applying the name Aristotle.

Donny Cameron did not know Meads personally before they met in his room at Carisbrook before the first test against South Africa in 1994. Cameron was working on a 'bad knock to the quad which Zinny [Zinzan Brooke] had got on the Thursday. I had to get into it — some deep tissue massage — and Zinny was squealing a bit. Colin walked in and was laughing at Zinny's antics. In the bar later that day Colin said that Donny, with the chirpiness and all, reminded him of the likes of masseurs Charlie Buckley and Larry Salmon in days gone by.

'We were in the side bar of the Shoreline Hotel after the test and Zinny and Mike Brewer came up and told Colin that I'd done a good job on them prior to the match. I got asked to go along to the next two tests against the South Africans and then, when the NZRFU wouldn't pay for me to go across for the Bledisloe match in Australia, the boys in the team did a whip around and I went along on that too.'

The next year, 1995, was World Cup time in South Africa and Meads got Cameron added to the touring party for the tournament. According to Laurie Mains, Meads had decided Donny was 'a good little bugger', was good at his job and was liked by the players. He worked hard and seldom complained. Additionally, he was an agreeable man to have a beer with, after the work was done. Always that, said Meads, not before.

Cameron says Meads was not your usual manager in the sense that he didn't believe in fussing about, wouldn't have known what airs and graces or officiousness were. 'He was,' said Donny, 'scornful of those who were happy to get an All Black jersey and not determined to go on to become an exceptional All Black.' Cameron remembers Meads' reaction to the response of one player who was very close to having been selected for the semi-final of the 1995 World Cup. The player accepted the decision and then appeared to be, as Meads put it to him, 'cruising' at training. Meads told him never to stop trying his hardest to impress, 'never to give up' no matter what the circumstances.

'You could see where Colin's own reputation came from,' says Cameron. 'He had this massive pride in All Black rugby. Both he and Mains wanted guys with big hearts. The best players would get the job under them.'

Cameron smiles and says, 'With Colin, the black jersey was everything. I'll give you a classic example. At the World Cup we were due to play Scotland. So the managers had to toss a coin to see who would play in white. One of the All Blacks said that he wouldn't mind playing in white, "for a change". Colin overheard him. "That'll be the day," he spat, "don't you ever look forward to forgoing a chance to play in the black jersey."'

Meads remembers the instance, grunts, grins: 'I lost the toss. We had to play in white.'

Cameron says Meads bristled when riled, cites a time in France late in 1995. 'He was livid after the loss in the first test at Toulouse,' says Cameron, and the way he lambasted the players after that match is now part of All Black rugby lore. 'I remember being in my massage room working on one of the boys the night before the second test in Paris. A video movie was on the TV screen and Tree walked in just as there was a scene showing a fair bit of naked flesh — it wasn't a film notable for that sort of thing at all. But Tree wasn't to know. He hit the roof, said to the players, "If I come in here ever again and see that sort of stuff on the screen, I'll throw the lot of you out the window."'

So-called blue movies have never appealed to Meads one little bit, and he's sometimes wondered about those attracted to them, 'wondered what their next move in life might be'.

Donny says the players soon realised that Colin wasn't a manager to dote on them. 'He wouldn't spoil anyone, refused to be over-protective.' Cameron approved of that, for in his view there are quite a few 'softies in rugby today. I remember Jamie Joseph was one who said that the players knew that Colin had been there and done it and they had a lot of respect for that.'

For some reason, and Donny couldn't put his finger on it exactly, Meads and the French had a rapport. 'Colin said to me, "I feel like having a few drinks tonight, Donny, what do you think?" I'd been working hard, so I said to him, "Sure, Tree, I'm a starter."'

Donny nods and looks at me as if to say, I should have known better. 'We went out and started to drink this stuff I'd not had before. It wasn't wine, or not the sort of wine I'd drunk previously.

Very smooth it was. Now Tree warned me: "Sip it quietly, Donny. Be careful, it can sneak up on you. Have a wee beer with it." I didn't take any notice. After a while I got cocky: "C'mon Tree, are we drinking or not?"

'He looked at me and his eyes twinkled as he said quietly and slowly, "Donny, you're out with Tree, you know." All of a sudden the stuff hit me. I went rigid. They carried me to a cab. I threw up in it. Not a performance to be proud of.'

In Cameron's opinion, Meads had a good and sympathetic understanding of the varied personalities among the players, from the likes of the 'complicated' Jeff Wilson to the — and he emphasises he means this kindly and without any patronising or disparaging element — 'man-child Lomu'.

But for all his respect for Meads as manager and as a person, Cameron says, 'I wouldn't like to cross Tree, no way.'

Meads, Richard Loe and Donny Cameron (standing at right) with a bunch of locals at an All Blacks training run in Italy, 1995.

PART THREE

———◀◦▶———

The modern diet

Meads is aware that he raises laughs when he says that today's players spend too much time interviewing mirrors in gyms, eat too much pasta, quaff special drinks and don't devour enough meat and vegies. But he is only partly joking. He speaks as a farmer when he asserts that meat is no good unless it has fat on it. He doesn't kill the skinniest sheep, he selects the fattest and trims the fat off it. To him, the modern generation and their mums — his daughters are no different, he says — avoid providing their offspring with cooked breakfasts. 'It's the same with the All Blacks. I have them on about all the Weet-Bix they're given. Weet-Bix are okay but you need a lot more than that — what about the eggs and bacon and tomatoes? Laurie Mains got this top dietitian to come and talk to the guys when I was manager. Initially, I took no notice; I was down the back and then I pricked my ears up. She was on about building up to a game on Saturday and she said no meat after Wednesday night. I thought, "Hell, that can't be right, surely."

'I was serious. I didn't say anything there and then but afterwards I had her on. I said, "I'll tell you what my diet used to be when I was playing, at home or on tour. With a big test down for Saturday: steak and eggs for breakfast at about eight o'clock. If we were playing at three o'clock, I'd have lunch at 12 — cold meat and mashed potatoes. I've listened to you — no butter either you say — no meat after Wednesday night. Jesus, I used to get my mashed potatoes and put a big blob of butter in, wait until it melted, stir it all up and . . ." Well, she stopped me, said, "You don't know how good a player you could have been."

'I think that Laurie thought he hadn't been getting through to the players on this one, so he'd got in wives and girlfriends so that they could be told what to feed the guys.

'The dietitian, she had her scheme which involved carbo-loading on

187

Fridays, pasta on Thursdays . . . I'd have a bit of fun by saying that if pasta was so damned good, the Italians would be the best in the world, but they're useless. "I'm a farmer," I said, "and if all you stopped eating meat from Wednesdays, all us farmers would be down the gurgler." I said that when I was on tour I played most of the time, which meant Wednesdays and Saturdays quite often, so when would I get to eat any meat at all if I followed her recommendations? I said I'd be anaemic within three weeks.

'I think they've moved away from that a bit. I'm a believer that your body tells you what you need. I've always loved my vegies and I've become very fond of cabbage. I say to Verna, "Not the raw stuff, cabbage that's properly cooked." When my daughters and daughters-in-law arrive at our place they all bring something, salads especially. Grrh.'

Meads enjoys winding people up about their dietary fads. He knows that too much fat is not good, and he applauds the greater variety of foods available. Even so, he enjoys telling people of going to a champagne breakfast in Whangarei attended by hundreds of guests. All the food was out on trestles — 'there was Rice Bubbles, corn flakes, muesli, yoghurt, Weet-Bix . . . then they had all the goodies, sausages, scrambled eggs, bacon. People were coming back and forth with plates of sausages and eggs. The caterers couldn't keep up. You know, not one person took a Weet-Bix.'

———◄o►———

15.
LIFE AND LEGEND

'I'll never forget when we made the first ad. Before I went up to Henderson, I said to them that I'd carry five posts. Geez, three was enough, my knees were just about buckling. You do 25 takes with three wet posts and see how you get on.'

OVER THE YEARS MEADS HAS OFTEN BEEN AMAZED BY THE EXTENT OF THE INTEREST IN HIM. HE WOULD NEVER SAY RUGBY HAD BEEN UNIMPORTANT TO HIM, OR THAT IN A NEW ZEALAND CONTEXT RUGBY IS A TRIVIAL MATTER, BUT HE WOULD SAY IT IS — OR SHOULD BE — STILL ONLY A GAME.

For that reason he has sometimes been incredulous when learning of the lengths some people have gone to come and visit his home patch. Verna recalls a young woman ringing and saying that she was soon to be married, and she wanted to give her new husband a special, surprise wedding present. She said she had told him she wanted to spend a night in Te Kuiti on their honeymoon. Could she, she asked, bring him along to meet his hero, Colin Meads?

Another time, in the 1980s, a busload of Japanese rugby players drove up to the farmhouse especially to see where Colin Meads lived. Colin took loads of them up to the high point on the hills of the farm in his ute, and Verna put on a spread for them.

Teams from all over, curious to see the hallowed locality of the All Blacks' 'Player of the Century', continue to visit Te Kuiti to enjoy Waitete's ambience. Perhaps the most unusual, idiosyncratic visitors of all were a team comprising members of Dunedin's zany 'No. 5' club, a band of devoted Meads admirers formed in the 1970s by a group of rugby fanatics of the famed University of Otago Rugby Club in Dunedin. Members of the club have met every year since on 3 June to mark Colin Meads' birthday.

The club flew Meads and Brian Lochore down to celebrate Meads' 60th birthday in 1996. On the Sunday morning, a group of them were having a glass of champagne in the house bar of the Shoreline Hotel when a priest got up and read a passage from 'The Bible', Alex Veysey's 1974 book *Colin Meads All Black*. 'I thought that was taking things a bit too far,' says Meads. But it was testimony to the religious reverence for Meads in the south. The Dunedin lawyer and former senior rugby player, Warren Alcock, recalls being required to get to his feet at the Dunedin Rugby Football Club's 125th jubilee and drink a toast to The Patron Saint of the No. 5 club.

When Meads was in Dunedin for the celebration, No. 5 club stalwart Paul Dwyer told him that they intended to bring a team of past and present players to Te Kuiti and play a match against Waitete to mark the occasion of Meads' 65th birthday in 2001. 'We were a bit worried that he mightn't have taken it seriously, even that we wouldn't come. We flew to Auckland, picked up a few former Otago University players there, drove down to Tauranga and grabbed another there. When we got to Te Kuiti, Colin had teed it all up. We watched Waitete play a club game on the Saturday, played our game on the Sunday and had a great time afterwards.'

Verna Meads said it was extraordinary. 'TV2 and TV3 were there, and reporters from several newspapers. Colin kicked off. There were 200 to 300 spectators, more than they get at a senior club match.'

Meads remains amused by it all. 'They always ring, without fail,' says Meads, 'usually quite late in the evening, after they've obviously had a fair few beers, and talk nonsense down the phone. They've sometimes rung as late as one in the morning. They're a bunch of characters, all right.'

'Yes,' says Verna, 'and there've been times when Colin's not been home, so they talk to me instead. It doesn't seem to matter.'

'All such clubs have to have a bit of a fanatic behind them, and Dwyer's that man,' says Meads. 'Nowadays I'm usually home when the phone goes, and when I say I've been in bed for an hour or two they say, "Aw, you're slipping, old fella."'

Meads himself is a little bemused by the good-natured reverence behind it all. 'But if they take the trouble to call then I think it's only right that I should have a yarn to them.'

There was also a Wellington branch of the No. 5 club known as 'The Cambridge No. 5s'. This group of fans, members of the 'King Colin's Country Club', met in The Corner Bar and Grill of the Cambridge Hotel close to the Basin Reserve in Wellington. Verna remembers a tanalised post standing in a corner. Every time the club met, members' names went into a hat and the person whose name was drawn was called Colin for the rest of the night, and his wife or partner was addressed as Verna.

The family of famous people can sometimes feel dwarfed, mere appendages

RON PALENSKI COLLECTION

Forever five. Members of Dunedin's 'No 5' club toast Meads on the occasion of his 60th birthday in 1996. and not always individuals in their own right. Verna is blunt: 'I married Colin: our kids didn't. When our son Kelvin was a little kid — before he went to Te Kuiti High School — people were always asking him if he was going to be an All Black like his father. Kelvin didn't know what they were talking about. He'd say, "Yes." The same sort of thing happened to our eldest girl, Karen, when she was at netball trials. My father was a great dog trials man, and the kids knew that because dog trials were mentioned often. So once, when Colin wasn't at Karen's netball trials, she asked, "Is Dad away at the dog trials, Mum?"

'When Colin was away, I never said to the kids that he was off playing for the All Blacks, I just said he was playing rugby.'

The Meads children were all keen on sport and good at it. According to Verna, the oldest, Karen, was 'very shy. She went to Australia for two and a half years and I'm quite convinced it was to get away from being a Meads. She went to a remote part of Western Australia where iron ore was mined. Kelvin played rugby at high school and encountered one kid who wanted to clock him one in the lineouts because he was Colin Meads' son. Unfortunately, Kelvin got injured in a motor bike accident when he was 19 and couldn't play any more. Glynn got some of the same sort of reactions as Kelvin had. Rhonda went away in the New Zealand netball team in the early 1980s. She and Rita Fatialofa were New Zealand's second-string goal shoots behind Margaret Matenga and Margaret Forsyth. When they got injured, both Rita and Rhonda played in a test. We were still on a party line at

191

that stage when we got a call from overseas. There was a guy on the line who wanted to talk to Colin — he wouldn't talk to me. My first reaction was that something had happened to Rhonda, and he wasn't prepared to tell me. It turned out he was a press guy who wanted Colin to agree that he must be very proud of his daughter. He was saying that Rhonda was very good at jumping for the ball, and he wondered if it was because Colin had taught her how to go about it, schooling her up on lineout tactics and all that. I guess he was looking for an angle. But Colin wouldn't agree to that sort of talk. Actually, Colin went along to some of Rhonda's games when she was a schoolgirl, and if the team lost then his superstitious side took over and he wouldn't go to the next game. He felt that his presence caused the team to lose. Colin is a very superstitious man when it comes to sport. In ordinary life he doesn't appear to be, but in sport he certainly is.'

Their son Glynn was a talented player who progressed to Emerging Players teams and All Black trials. A tall, stringy player, he captained and played for his father's own provincial union, King Country, for several seasons as a No. 8 and sometimes as lock.

And the Meads' youngest girl, Shelley, born in 1971 and nine years younger than Glynn, played for the New Zealand women's basketball team. 'Not many people know that,' says Verna, 'because the women's game is very low profile. The men get all the money as far as I can see. We even had to buy her New Zealand uniform. The team went to Scotland and Taiwan. Shelley also made trips to Australia with club and rep teams and to Tahiti with the New Zealand Under-21 side. We had to pay for everything. Shelley was only a toddler when Colin gave up playing rugby, so in some ways she was unaware of the extent of the attention paid to Colin when he was playing for the All Blacks.' But both Shelley and Rhonda, according to Verna, were competitive like their father, 'in every sense. Watching them play was like seeing the look in Colin's eyes.'

Ask Meads if his involvement in rugby took him away from his family more often than he would have liked, and if he feels some regret about that, and he says it's easy to be wise in hindsight. He has always seen his as 'a fairly close family. But there are times when I've thought that I wasn't all that great as a father. There were times when I wasn't around when they perhaps needed their dad. But both Verna and I really like having the family and the grandchildren round. It's a lot of fun. I suppose a lot of adults say this, but in some ways I think I've been better with the grandkids than I was with my own.'

There are 13 grandchildren in all, 10 of them girls. Karen has three children (one boy); Rhonda has three (one boy); Kelvin a boy and a girl; Glynn three girls, and Shelley two girls. Meads says, 'I guess I'm going to be a netball fan.' One day he had four grandkids with him on his farm bike when a traffic policeman went by. 'I thought I was for it, but all he did was give me a toot.'

Both Rhonda and Karen live in Hamilton and their children have stayed on Colin and Verna's farm for weeks at a time. About three years ago, he and Verna took four of their grandchildren for a holiday, renting a house at Mount Maunganui for over a week. 'We paid for that from the proceeds of over 100 wild goats that the kids and I rounded up close by. On holiday, I seemed to be in the water, getting knocked around by the surf, three and four times a day. I've often thought that our own children weren't so lucky.'

For some years, Colin and Verna lived virtually alongside son Glynn and his

Opposite page
Verna and Colin with
11 of their grandchildren
Back row, from left
Juliana and Lara Wilcox
(Rhonda's two girls)
Karen's children Hayley
Stockman, with Clinton
and Kasie (far right)
On Colin's knee, Baylee
Mitchell (Shelley's eldest)
Front, from left: Hannah
and Mitchell Mead
(Kelvin's children), Abbey
and Christy Meads
(Glynn's eldest two) and
Jacob Wilcox (Rhonda's
youngest). Since this photo
was taken in 1999, Shelley
and Glynn have both had
daughters, Jamie
and Ruby.

TERRY WINN

family. Then in 1994 it was mutually agreed that there ought to be more space between them — Glynn in particular was looking for greater independence — so Colin and Verna moved to their present house a few kilometres away. They concede it is far from ideal, not what they had in mind for this stage of their lives. Verna is fairly caustic about it at times. She tells of how the plumbing was so bad, and the flow of water so pitiful, that she used to turn the tap on over the sink and walk away and do something else for a few minutes while the sink filled up. One day she misjudged the timing and the sink overflowed and flooded the room. 'We've been meaning to do the place up for ages, but we never have,' she says meaningfully.

It is clear to most that while Meads has made an immense contribution to New Zealand rugby, and to other areas of life in this country, the benefits to him and his family personally have not been proportionate. Their income from farming has

The Meads' home on the outskirts of Te Kuiti.

never been substantial. And Colin's long and frequent absences in the service of rugby, and for charitable work, made it difficult to run a profitable farm. In the past decade, their son Glynn did his share of the work and more at times.

Verna says that when one considers the length of Colin's career, and the honours bestowed upon him, their walls have little to show for it. There are bits and pieces stacked in corners around the house, she says, but if it hadn't been for their kids what little is on display would not have been there. 'When we went away for a few weeks in 1999,' Verna says, 'the kids came in and hung up a few pictures and other items to greet us on our return. Actually, that momentarily inspired Colin. He dug out a few other things, got out his hammer . . . and I told him not to. The walls aren't too solid. But he wouldn't listen. He hammered a four-inch nail in and knocked a hole as big as his fist in the wall.'

Meads has lived his entire life on a farm. Once or twice, he and Verna have thought of buying a house in town — Te Kuiti — and continuing to farm, but they never have. Meads says he finds it easier to relax out of town. He would miss not hearing dogs bark occasionally in the night. He doubts he could get used to going outside and looking over the fence at neighbours. 'It's just not me.' He dislikes having to dock sheep on frosty mornings, but looks forward to the birth of lambs and calves. Once a farmer, always a farmer. 'It will be a sad day when we've got to leave the farm.'

There are, in Meads' rural parlance, 'natural farmers and textbook farmers. When you grow up on a farm you can tell at a glance when stock need shifting. Not all do, by any means. When I was young I was into farming in a more intense way,

PHOTOSPORT

now I'm a lot more casual about it. I stock lightly now — on this farm, you could probably carry half as many stock again.'

Ask Meads what he would have done, or liked to have done, if he hadn't been a farmer, and he finds the question an awkward one to answer. 'Most likely it would have had to have been an outdoor job. Sitting in an office all day wouldn't have appealed. I was always a country kid, and my life was rugby. That's what it seems like: everything was rugby. I never went pig-hunting, but as a kid chased goats and shot possums. I liked animals, and Verna's father, who was keen on dog trials, gave me a few dogs. I even went to a few trials myself, but wasn't much good at it. Like most things, you have to put the time in. I didn't have it.'

Nowadays Meads fattens about 200 heifers a year, seldom straying too far from Aberdeen Angus or Hereford cattle.

With Colin Meads, then, for a long time it was either the farm or rugby. Verna occasionally wondered at the numbers of people from Wellington and Auckland who drove all the way to the Chateau on Ruapehu to go skiing. She and Colin never did anything like that. When Meads was starting out in representative rugby, he and Stan used to do some shearing and other farm work around the district to supplement the family farm's income. He and Stan treated their time away with the All Blacks as holidays, and the minute they got home they put in long hours on the farm to catch up. Which meant Meads was never inclined to wander on the hills experiencing a kind of Arcadian bliss; nor did he find time to lie in the grass and watch the clouds float by.

At present Colin and Verna run sheep and cattle on 120 acres of their own, and on a few hundred acres that they lease on a property nearby. The 120-acre property had to be fenced when they moved on to it, an expense they would rather not have had to bear.

Verna says, 'We've worked hard over the years. Colin and Stan did the sort of work guys just wouldn't do these days. And although Colin had some marvellous trips around the world with the All Blacks, the only time he ever set foot off the farm was to play rugby. We never had holidays — I can think of only two family holidays in our lifetime. One was after he had broken his back, and was in plaster; the other was after the hernia operation. I'm a bit sorry now that I never took the kids away. But because Stan and his father and mother were working on the farm when Colin was away playing rugby, he felt he owed it to them to work when he got back. I think that was bad for the kids and I regret that. Kids can sometimes pay a penalty for having a famous father.'

At one time, Verna and Colin bought more land, and borrowed money overseas via a local bank to pay for it. But it turned into a nightmare, and they battled with the bank for 14 years. They discovered one morning that 'we owed half a million more than we thought'. By their own admission they never recovered from it, and says Colin, 'I'm not on any rich list in New Zealand and never will be.' Part of the farm was sold to repay some of the debt.

Losing a major part of their farm meant they were dejected and, at times, angry and despairing. But there was nothing for it but to soldier on. Then, in many respects, they received worse news when, in 1999, Verna learned she had breast cancer. Her father had died of lung cancer in 1979, possibly attributable to the fact that he was a heavy smoker.

After surgery and the removal of two lumps, Verna was told that one of the lumps was cancerous. This was two days before she and Colin were due to fly to Ireland to attend a wedding. They went anyway and had a wonderful time. From Ireland they went to South Africa for three weeks where Colin, Willie John McBride and Frik du Preez were to take part in a three week fund-raising tour.

FOTOPRESS

Tough rivals on the international rugby fields of the world, now they're just good mates — Meads, Ireland's Willie John McBride and South Africa's Frik du Preez

McBride, the Irishman, and du Preez, a South African through and through, and Meads himself, are widely considered to have been among the finest locks to have played rugby. All three are good friends. The others were, in Meads' view, 'tough buggers, but fair'.

Verna had met McBride before, and could see why Colin thought highly of him. She says that on the trip to Ireland and South Africa she 'never let the shadow of cancer interfere with my holiday in any way. Two days after we got home I went into hospital and had my lymph nodes removed. They were okay.'

Four months of chemotherapy followed; then radiation treatment began in January 2000.

Just as she thought she was clear, in 2001 a lump was found in her other breast. A scan showed that the earlier cancer had disappeared. Her second cancer was, she was told, a different form and required different treatment from the first. She has had radiation and chemotherapy treatment simultaneously and has had a rough time with a chest infection and a blood transfusion. She says, 'Underneath it all, I feel very positive about it. I've had two primary cancers, not secondaries. I'm not lying down and giving up. I've got wonderful grandchildren; there's lots to look forward to. I'm determined to beat it. Rightly or wrongly I feel a lot of the cause of the disease relates to stress brought on by the loss of much of the farm and our dispute with the bank. I have good days and bad days. But the bank never got the better of me and this cancer isn't going to either. I'm not giving in.

'Friends and family have been fantastic. Colin's been great. He does most of the meals. Our daughters and daughters-in-law have brought casseroles out to us too.'

Verna Meads sees herself as a King Country person through and through. 'The King Country's always been home to me. Someone described Te Kuiti perfectly to me the other day as a little town with long arms. They wrap those arms around you when things aren't going too good. It's the only town we have known. We are treated no different to anyone else, and I like that. Occasionally people will joke, as they did when Jim Bolger was Prime Minister, and say that this isn't Jim's town, it's Colin's town.'

When she was young, Verna played badminton and tennis. And she enthusiastically followed her daughters' fortunes in basketball and netball. She began playing badminton when Colin was still playing rugby and they had young children, 'and the game really got a hold on me. It was played in town on Mondays and Wednesdays, so it could be fitted in because Colin's rugby practice was on Tuesdays and Thursdays. I played some games for the rep team; not that I was that good, but it was one sport I might have done well at if I'd put my nose to the grindstone. Once I beat a woman who was much better than me, purely because I decided that she wasn't going to win. If I had taken that attitude more often, which was what Colin and Shelley and Rhonda and Glynn had, I might have done better.'

But that's all in the past now. They had a family from the outset, and they shared a car with Colin's brother Stan. Says Verna, 'Someone had to stay home.' Verna never joined the Women's Division of Federated Farmers, for instance, but she was secretary of the local Parent Teachers' Association and secretary for an over-55s Internet Club. But for a time, a decade or more ago, Verna felt a lack of self-esteem. 'I couldn't see that I'd done much. Like Colin I'd left school before my fifteenth birthday, I had no qualifications, but then I realised I'd brought up these lovely children. I'd been secretary for Waitete club jubilee celebrations and for other rugby-related things for Colin during his career, and I'd done most of the farm accounts, and it dawned on me that I had done worthwhile things with my life that I hadn't sat down and thought about before.'

All of this accounts for why having to sell off some of their farm has been so upsetting to them. Nevertheless, both of them believe in trying to vanquish resentment. In this regard, they point to their friendship with the Irish referee, Kevin Kelleher, he who infamously sent Meads from the field at Murrayfield in 1967. Kelleher came to New Zealand and appeared on the television *This is Your Life* tribute to Meads. Verna liked that for, in her view, 'holding grudges sours you'.

When Colin was touring and playing rugby for the All Blacks, both in New Zealand and overseas, Verna always felt 'so much a part of his family as well as mine. I think it may have made life a lot easier for me than it may have been for some other players of his era. I don't think I felt as lonely as some All Black wives. I felt I got on so well with Colin's side of the family — with Vere and Ida, his parents — and in all the time we were working in close proximity, we only ever had one falling out, and that was my fault. Even then it was fairly minor. The farm was run as a family farm until it was sold to Colin and Stan in 1969. So, living so close — within calling distance of each other's houses — for all that time, I think we did pretty well.'

Colin Meads knows that it hasn't been easy for Verna to have been married to a man seen as having an all-consuming commitment to rugby. He is unreservedly grateful to her, and their children, for their tolerance and support in this regard. For his part, he found that, often as not, he ended up in administrative posts

Meads was the subject of a This Is Your Life *programme in 1988. Joining Colin and Verna for the big night in Wellington were: Back row — JB Munro (former IHC chief), former Minister of Maori Affairs and good friend of Colin's, Koro Wetere, Wilson Whineray, Irish referee Kevin Kelleher, Willie John McBride, Stan Meads, Brian Lochore and Kel Tremain. Front row: Joan Daniel (Colin's sister), host Bob Parker, Colin and Verna and Colin's father Vere.*

NZ Rugby Museum/TV One

198

Colin and Verna at the
Waitete Rugby Club
grounds, May 2002.

PHOTOSPORT

because he was persuaded to take them on.

And before that, says Meads, 'There were times when it seemed that every second person with an interest in rugby was saying it was time Colin Meads retired. They were saying I was over the hill. But never once did Verna side with them. She said that if I wanted to keep playing I should go for it.

'The fact was that a lot of the time, Dad — me — wasn't here. She had to juggle things, take the girls to netball, the boys to rugby. Fortunately, she enjoyed sport, but even so it must have been an ordeal at times.

'But there were bonuses. We had some good trips away — Verna calls them "plums" — and one of the first and more memorable was when the chairman of the NZRFU, Cuth Hogg, a marvellous man, shouted Verna a trip with me to the English Centennial in 1971.'

Both Colin and Verna feel it's a pity Stan isn't spoken of to near the same extent as Colin is, but they know that fame is a fickle thing. Verna says Colin's reputation snowballed after he was named Player of the Century, and since then the number of his speaking engagements has proliferated. She thought that after he stopped playing in the 1970s, his reputation would die a natural death. There was a time, she says, when the Kentucky Fried Chicken (KFC) outlets had a special called a Number Eight. Colin was asked to front the advertisement for this delectable. The advert was to feature Colin and a number of young schoolboy rugby players. KFC came back, embarrassed, and told Colin that they didn't want to use him after all. It was all to do with name recognition — that is, the lack of it. The youngsters all asked, 'Who's Colin Meads?' So the advert featured the much younger Michael Jones, the great Auckland and All Black flanker.

Meads was amused, not offended, to be told he was not wanted; that he was, in

PHOTOSPORT

At the 1999 Steinlager Awards dinner in Auckland, Meads was the NZRFU's inaugural recipient of The Steinlager Salver. The award was made to 'a legendary All Black who epitomises the All Black values of excellence, humility and respect.'

According to Verna, Colin's reputation snowballed after he was named New Zealand's Player of the Century at the end of 1999.

PHOTOSPORT

MEADS FAMILY

the eyes of the youngsters, a has-been who hadn't been. Verna smilingly talks of Colin's 'comeback'. 'He became an All Black selector, then manager. So he sort of reinvented himself.'

Back in the late 1970s, Meads was approached by the makers of tanalised timber and asked if he would make a television commercial for them. He thinks his nickname Pinetree appealed. At the time rugby was devotedly, unswervingly amateur. Any proceeds had to be lodged in a trust, as they had after the publication of Alex Veysey's *Colin Meads All Black* in 1974.

Those who thought they were seeing a commercial of Meads lugging tanalised posts around his farm were mistaken. The filming was done on a 10-acre block in Kumeu, West Auckland. Meads smiles about this marriage of muscly man mountain and tough, rugged, durable tanalised posts; about the black singlet, shorts and boots. 'When I first agreed to do it, I had no idea what it entailed. Talk about Take One, Take Two, and so on. We were up to about Take Twenty-five and I was getting pretty pissed off with it by then. They're pretty pedantic people — the producer would say, "That's not quite right, more emphasis required on . . ." this word or that one.

'When the treated posts first come out of the kiln, they are heavy as hell. It's all the moisture in them. The posts you get on the farm should have been out of the kiln for a couple of months. I'll never forget when we made the first ad. Before I went up to Henderson, I said to them that I'd carry five posts. Geez, three was enough, my knees were just about buckling. You do 25 takes with three wet posts and see how you get on. It was interesting, but I wasn't a natural.'

Meads has appeared in other adverts, one promoting Nissan utility vehicles especially. These were filmed in the South Island on what Meads regards as wild and rugged tracks, miles out the back of Gore, say. 'A group of possible buyers would arrive and stand around waiting until Colin Meads appeared out of nowhere driving a ute. I enjoyed it. It was quite a challenge at times.

'There was this Hustler model that was very high off the ground. One of the first promotions for the Hustler was held in Marlborough and I was parked up in some scrub over a hill from where all the people were gathered. Next thing a helicopter flies over the top of the crowd with a great wooden container dangling beneath it. Then from high above it drops the container behind the ridge and near to me. That was my cue to drive over the ridge, and make a dramatic entrance. I came bursting out of the scrub a few moments later, pulled up alongside the people, got out of the cab and said something like, 'That's one tough vehicle.' In those days, Meads donated his fees for tanalised timber and Nissan advertisements to the IHC Society.

At the time Meads recalls that the rugby union 'was terribly hot on amateurism'. It seems niggardly now when the pendulum in respect to payments appears to have swung wildly to another extreme. Production crews, when they heard the fees being paid for Meads, often said to him that he came very cheap, that it was 'no wonder' they got Meads, 'the last guy we used was getting two or three times what's being charged for you'. Meads has never had an agent and he still doesn't. 'I always say, "Verna's the boss, ring her," and she can get brassed off because I'm hard to get. I'll be out on the farm from early in the morning when I'm home. Verna will say, "Well, he'll be home for lunch," but she can't tell them when that will be. Sometimes it's 12, sometimes it's one, sometimes it's three o'clock. That's farming.'

Opposite page: Meads gets star treatment during the filming of the tanalised timber commercial at Kumeu in 1978.

'Well, Wilson didn't turn his down.'

Meads was created an MBE in 1971, and was chosen as a distinguished companion of the New Zealand Order of Merit in the 2001 New Year's Honours List. He knew people who had declined to accept such awards, and he thought long and hard before deciding to accept his. 'I had always looked up to and admired Wilson Whineray. He was a kind of tutor for me. Here was Wilson, educated and assured, but tough with it, and here was me, who had left school at 14. And yet we got on well, there was mutual respect. Wilson had got an OBE before I was ever offered the MBE, so when I was offered an award I probably said to myself, "Well, Wilson didn't turn his down."'

He recalls that, 'for several years in the late 1990s there were all these articles saying that Colin Meads should have been knighted. It all seemed a bit over the top to me. And then I learned that my name was being put forward.

It was then I remembered something that Kevin "Monkey" Briscoe had said when Wilson got the OBE: Monkey said it means "On his Bloody Ear". So I realised that if I accepted another award, I'd get the raspberry from some people. In the end I decided to take it, even though when people ask me what it is exactly I'm likely to forget the precise wording. The press then asked me if I was disappointed that I hadn't got a knighthood. Not in the least; I'd have been embarrassed to be called Sir Colin, I really would. I'm sure that Wilson Whineray and Brian Lochore have been embarrassed to be called "Sir" in many circumstances. I've said that I was thrilled to get the honour, that it was good for rugby and for sport in general. I mean, what the hell, if the award is equivalent to a Sir in the old system, I'm glad it's not the old system. When I went to receive the award, Dame Silvia Cartwright said that it was as much to do with my work for the IHC as it was for rugby. Dame Silvia's husband, Peter Cartwright, has a handicapped brother, and he was on the South Auckland branch of the society when I was.

'To me, anyone who goes looking for awards is doing their work for the wrong reasons.'

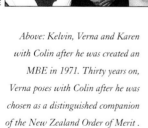

Above: Kelvin, Verna and Karen with Colin after he was created an MBE in 1971. Thirty years on, Verna poses with Colin after he was chosen as a distinguished companion of the New Zealand Order of Merit.

16.
THE 'MODERN GAME'

'We nearly always had a few beers with the opposition after a game, and we nearly always had a dinner. Some of those were among the most memorable occasions of an All Black's career . . . We formed great friendships. Those friendships don't exist between international players today. It's sad.'

I F YOU VISIT THE WAITETE CLUB'S HEADQUARTERS TODAY IT LOOKS AND FEELS SOLID, SPACIOUS. THERE'S NOTHING ELABORATE, NOTHING PRISSY, BUT THE AMENITIES — THE BAR, TABLES, SHOWERS, AND SO ON — ARE MORE THAN ADEQUATE.

The walls are adorned with memorabilia, photographs of club greats including long and loyal and distinguished servants, club teams of note from the various grades, and, of course, of former All Blacks, Kevin Boroevich, Stan Meads, and the Titan himself, Colin Meads. Of especial note is a long line of framed jerseys of international teams from all round the world, most donated by Colin Meads.

It is all a reminder of the convictions of rugby stalwarts like Fred Allen, Noel McQuilkin and Meads, the belief that the clubs have always been the cornerstones of the game in New Zealand. They fear those stones are crumbling. Allen speaks sadly, and with irritation, of the struggles clubs are having. 'Much of what we knew is gone. The players don't mix the way they used to. Too much money goes direct to the players. Half should go to the clubs. Clubs with proud histories — take my Grammar Old Boys in Auckland — are walking away from their rooms and being forced to combine with others.'

It is true that all unions are having difficulty in maintaining their base of players, keeping the more talented youngsters from gravitating, or being lured, away to the cities. Sponsorships and payments are hard to come by, and people and financial resources are spread too thinly around unions such as King Country, so the locals believe. Both Meads and McQuilkin say it's getting harder to persuade the young to commit themselves to a club, and even to play rugby itself. The young aren't flowing through into administration, the chain of succession isn't there as it once was. There's unemployment, competing sports, changing attitudes to life and work generally, fewer jobs available in meat works and hardly any in forestry and sawmilling around the district as there used to be.

On a Saturday in mid-January 2002, I wander along to the Waitete ground adjacent to Rugby Park, Te Kuiti, to watch the first pre-season training session of the year. It's fine but a blustery wind is blowing and the ground is sprinkled with newly cut long grass. The temperature's such that it could be early winter, the season about to begin in earnest. I think I recognise the solid Samoan who is running a game of touch football. I'm right, it's Peter 'Fats' Fatialofa, the former Auckland and Manu Samoa prop. Fats has been given the job of lifting King Country from the depths of the third division to which it has descended. His plan is to get King Country back into the second division, and then take it from there. One gets the feeling that the local rugby fraternity is rueful and a bit shamed to have been relegated. King Country is proud of its rugby past, feels it is better than that — not first division material anymore, perhaps — but second division certainly. Ox Wightman, Noel McQuilkin and others confirm that, and so does Craig McKellar, another King Country man originally from Alexandra in Central Otago.

Fats has put the squad of players through a beep test and had them bench press a few weights. While it's obvious that a few need strengthening up, he tells the squad that he doesn't want them becoming obsessed with weights. Wightman and McQuilkin are pleased to hear him say, 'I don't want you looking at mirrors, get out and do the hard yards in training.' McQuilkin is especially glad of that, because he thinks that in some quarters it's made a bit too easy for some players today. 'They get money for not turning up' when their injuries are fairly minor sometimes, he says.

Pinetree Meads himself arrives and we go inside and have a beer and a chat to Fats. Most of the squad are outside eating chops and sausages and white bread and tomato sauce off the barbecue, but Meads is introduced to a few of the younger, newer players. He says to one, a highly promising flanker who has been playing in the UK, 'You're not as solid as your old man.' It's said with a smile, but it contains a mild challenge.

Fats is wearing a Legends jersey, one with the message 'Serious Rugby Played for Fun' on it. It's possible to say that, in large part, that summed up the approach of both men to rugby generally. Meads reminds Fats of the 1988 Ranfurly Shield challenge when Auckland came down to Rugby Park and played King Country in days when the King Country's mascot was 'Boris the Boar'. 'Some bugger

*Colin Meads'
international rugby
jerseys make an
impressive display
at the Waitete
Rugby Club.*

released a boar on the paddock and the game got held up while they chased it around trying to catch it,' says Colin. (The story goes that the pig was elusive and camped inside the Auckland 22 for much of the second half.) 'Remember that?' Fats did, nods and grins. 'Nowadays the team's known as the "King Country Rams",' says Meads, and then he's silent. 'Nah, I think Boris the Boar fitted us, King Country, better.'

As we finish our beers and are about to leave, Colin draws my attention to a bloke standing at the bar. 'See that big fat fella at the bar. He's the build for a good rugby player, but he's lazy. A few beers is fine. But you have to do the work. He sums up the attitude of too many these days.'

There was no malice in Meads' tone. Simply bald, truthful as he saw it. The voice of one who'd been there, done the hard yards, knew what it took and takes.

Colin became chairman of King Country in 1987 and was elected to the NZRFU's council in 1992. On the playing field, he views that as 'another golden period for King Country. Divisional rugby had started and King Country won promotion to the first division. Unheard of for such a small union, as I understood it.' Meads was overseas for a time when involved in the TV Mud and Glory programme, and was delighted to learn that his union had beaten Bay of Plenty to gain a place among the provincial elite. He recalls that 'no one ever thought that we would stay in the first division in 1991. We were seen as one-year wonders. But Noel McQuilkin, our selector-coach, had other ideas and we won enough games to stay up. Under Noel we scored wins against Hawke's Bay, Canterbury and North Auckland in 1992. And if we could get a game in Te Kuiti, boy, any team had a hard road there. We had a vocal, antagonistic crowd, and they were right on the sideline. I can always remember Jeff Wilson and Marc Ellis saying, "Geez, you've got some rough so-and-sos round here, Piney. You can hear every bloody word they say on the sideline and they're not all too complimentary."'

He is aware of a rumour that circulated saying that he was behind moves to prevent television coverage of matches in Te Kuiti. When Meads was on the NZRFU Council, the council did a deal with TVNZ. It meant, says Meads, that there would be no coverage of games played in Te Kuiti. He was not happy about that and the King Country union approached TV3 to see if it was willing to televise rugby from Te Kuiti. 'But we got stopped, told we mustn't do that.'

For years Colin Meads was spoken of as The Big Cheese of King Country rugby. Just as All Black and Colin Meads were deemed synonymous by many, the same applied when mention was made of King Country. It was complimentary, and while Meads never sought accolades he was aware of them and, justifiably, quietly proud of the ways his contributions were received. Friends in the King Country decided that it was time Meads was made a Life Member of the union to which he had brought such fame and, occasionally, notoriety. Ewen MacLachlan of the Waitete club rang Meads in 1983 and said that the club was keen to put him up for life membership of the union. Colin's response was to say that he would be honoured to be a Life Member but that he was not looking for it. 'If people wanted to put me up I wasn't going to say don't do it,' says Meads. Proposals for life memberships went before the annual general meeting of the union. Meads thinks there was a requirement that 75 per cent of the vote be in favour for the applicant to succeed. According to Meads, the chairman of the time, Des Graham, told clubs throughout the union that if Pinetree was made a Life Member he would no longer be able to serve in the variety of official capacities that he had filled in the past, and was still filling. Meads laughs: 'So a lot of the clubs didn't vote for me. But they did vote for old Joe McGovern, who was a good old guy. He crowed and told me, "I beat you that time, boy. You didn't get picked."

'It was a terrible shock and my club was terribly upset. The media nationally made a thing of it, talked of a snub and some, possibly, read more into it than there was. I told my club that it didn't worry me. Then a lot of people said I should tell King Country where to go; but I said, "Who's it going to hurt?" So I just carried on as if nothing had happened.'

Afterwards, Meads found that a lot of the small clubs — Turangi for one — told him that they had been given to believe that making him a Life Member would automatically debar him from further truly useful functions in the union.

They thought he would no longer be eligible to sit as a member of the union, either. 'You only make Piney a Life Member when he's finished; he's too young to be a Life Member, that was the message they had been given. King Country copped a backlash in a way and I just wanted the whole business to go away.'

A few years later, the union did make Meads a Life Member, but only after he had told his proposers that he would not consent to his name going forward unless he was assured that there would be 'no debacle like the last time'. The rules had been changed so that the board approved of such nominations in advance of the AGM, and would not put a name forward without unanimous support.

These days, King Country languishes in the third division nationally. It is not something that pleases Meads one little bit. He accepts that King Country's halcyon days are in the past, and that it is unreasonable to expect a union like his to foot it in the rugby bigtime anymore. And yet . . . he thinks the King Country must strive to get back into the second division and stay there. He believes country unions have more ups and downs than the major unions, mainly because they have fewer resources all round and the loss of two or three key players can have a dramatic effect. For that reason he is keen on promotion-relegation systems. 'When teams have their golden patches they should have a right to go up to the next division. We all know the chances of them staying there are remote. But I will always fight for the promotion-relegation system. I opposed those in administration who wanted to have a set number of teams — and the same unions each time — in the first division.

'I have always wished — and though I would like to see it happen, I know it won't — to see a second-division side win the Ranfurly Shield. The gap in standard has grown so wide, and continues to widen, that it seems out of the question now. It is a huge worry for country districts, the way that when we get a good player, there is no way we can keep him.' As Meads sees it, King Country's demotion to the third division was mainly because after the 2000 season 'we lost four of our top players'.

He knew, when his son Glynn was coach of King Country in 2001, that people were comparing the two of them — were saying that Piney was a better coach than 'Pinecone'. The word in some quarters was that if Glynn had done a better job, King Country would still have been in the second division. Meads senior says he 'kept away from that. A lot of people were reluctant to talk to me about it, so I kept away from the team entirely.' Nevertheless, he thinks the critics 'were really missing the bus. We had been heading that way for three or four years. I'm not saying Glynn can escape taking some of the blame. But there's nothing to be gained from saying Piney was a better coach — he's well past that. After my experience with the Cavaliers team in South Africa, I lost most of my ambitions to coach. I decided that I ought to face the fact that I had my limitations there, and while I could see myself more as an administrator, I still liked being involved with teams as fully as possible.'

To Meads, the main reason for the decline in the competitiveness of the country unions is the population drift to the big urban maws. When he was a gung-ho young player in the 1950s and 1960s, every little town or village had a mill. Many of these villages are gone now. As Meads says, his eyes twinkling, 'In a mill there is half a rugby team. Some of them were real tough, hard men. Pureora used to have a team; there was a whole village there, and two or three sawmills all within about 10 miles of each other. Now there's nothing. To play out there was one of the great occasions of King Country club rugby. You knew you had played 80 minutes of football. The same applied to those little places in the south of the King Country — Owhango for instance — they all had teams. They have gone. Instead of sawing logs in local mills the logs are all transported elsewhere.'

Changes in farming have also meant the loss of young men who used to be employed on farms. 'I often remark,' says Meads, 'that every four-wheel farm bike in the country represents the loss of one young fella that used to work on the farms. Technology has replaced workers. If I didn't have my four-wheel bike, I'd be unable to get around and do the work I do.'

The variety of recreational pursuits available to young people has also taken them away from rugby, but Meads sees that as far more noticeable in the cities. Rugby and cricket still dominate in the King Country, although the ease with which youngsters can hop in a car and buzz off to Hamilton or Rotorua makes it harder to get them to commit themselves to regular participation in team sport especially.

As well as the external pressures on rugby, Meads sees many changes surrounding the game itself that have diminished it in his view. Take the relationship between players and administrators — 'always an awkward one', says Meads. Players take to some administrators and not to others. Meads thinks that, 'In many ways the gap could be widening. One reason may be that there aren't the after-match functions like there used to be. Players don't stay around and meet officials in the same sorts of social environments. From provincial level to tests the players just don't know the rank-and-file administrators the way they used to. Even in King Country now, there would be people on our Board that the players wouldn't know. Perhaps there's a bit too much of the "them and us" situation today. We do keep up the old traditions in King Country to a degree, but in the Super 12 quite a lot of players don't even turn up to after-match affairs, or when they do they pop in for a few minutes and then they're away.'

To Meads the same thing applies often after tests. When a young Argentine side came here and played against the All Blacks early in the 2001 season, 'there was no after-match function as such. All they wanted to do was meet the All Blacks, pat Jonah on the back, swap a tie with the guy they'd marked . . . but they never met the All Blacks. To me that was tragic. This is not what sport is about. Sport is bigger than simply what occurs on the field of play. Today's players are hell-bent on parading round the ground and thanking the crowd; what about the poor buggers you've just beaten? Wouldn't the purpose of sport, the essence of sport, be better served by having a beer afterwards in your opponents' dressing room?

'The Argentine players had no mementoes to go home with. We nearly always had a few beers with the opposition after a game, and we nearly always had a dinner. Some of those were among the most memorable occasions of an All Black's career. We had some fabulous dinners with the French; I can remember swapping all my gear, my All Black blazer for a French one. We formed great friendships. Those friendships don't exist between international players today. It's sad.

'The excuse for not meeting the Argentine side was that the All Blacks had a test next Saturday. So they were whipped away. Nowadays they are more worried about making sure they have a pool session, have their bananas and nuts and sandwiches and all that stuff in the dressing room, stuff that we never saw.'

Are there too many international matches played today? Meads thinks the easy answer is, Yes. But then he knows that internationals are where the money is. He thinks touring sides don't play enough games against provincial teams. One result

Glynn 'Pinecone' Meads.
Colin believes there was
much misguided criticism
of his coaching in 2001.

PHOTOSPORT

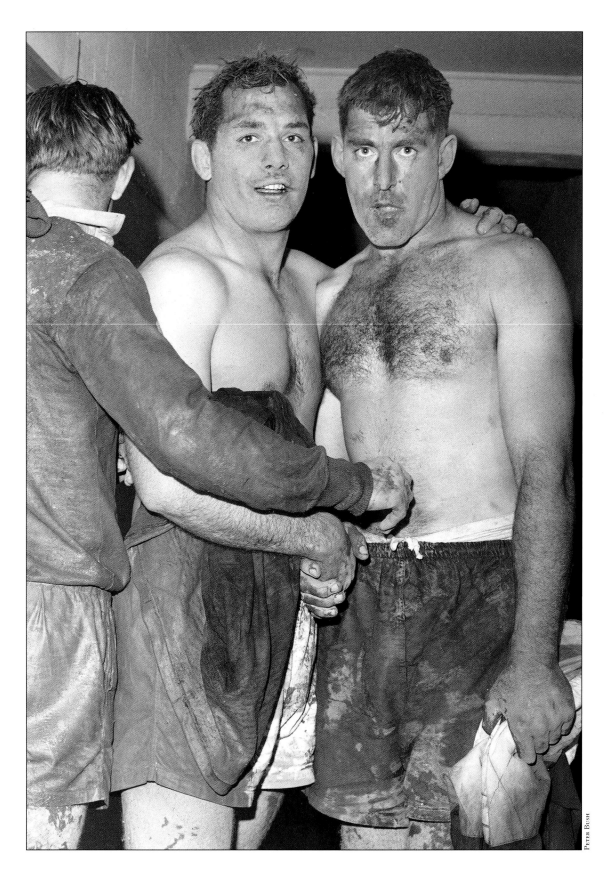

PETER BUSH

Swapping jerseys after test matches was always part of the All Blacks tradition in Meads' day. Left: Meads and South Africa's Andy MacDonald after the third test of the 1965 series at Christchurch — a match the All Blacks lost 16–19. Right: Meads swaps his final test jersey with great rival Willie John McBride after the fourth test in 1971.

PETER BUSH

is that very few rugby players get an opportunity to play against touring sides. He thought there was something special about the fact that players from Oamaru, Nelson, Wanganui or Otorohanga were able to say they had played against Australia, or South Africa. 'Some of those players became All Blacks.' He laments that so much of what pertained when he was a player has been lost, but he is also prepared to admit that this 'is a fact of life'.

The fact that Meads thinks the All Blacks are not physically or technically, or tactically for that matter, dominant in the way they were for a time when he was in his pomp irritates him even now. And it is one of the reasons why Meads has stuck with rugby. It is almost as if, in his heart of hearts, Meads wants to believe, or at least help continue to assert, that there is something termed The Divine Right of All Blacks. As if, when All Blacks stride up to the Pearly Gates, a true All Black will be waved on, allowed in as a matter of course. The lapses Meads thinks have been apparent in the last decade or so is something that makes him quaver within, and stirs a resolve that has never died, a belief that the name All Black should mean The Best a Rugby Player Can Be. Hallowed talk, of course. And laugh if you will, but Meads' rugby philosophy has always been that a rugby player must be the best he can be, and he must fight to remain there. That's what lifts the overall standard, that's what makes players strive and look up, and when you get up there, Meads would gruffly intone, 'you fight to stay there'.

Good and bad press

Meads doesn't see himself as a media authority, partly because he doesn't take a close look at it. His inclination is to say that the New Zealand rugby media compare more than favourably with their counterparts elsewhere. He feels that 'No matter what sport it is', the Australian media finds it hard to make unfavourable comparisons between their representatives and players from other nations. 'It must be hard for them to accept that they are not always the best.'

For years, Meads and a few of his team-mates were amazed at how accurate the renowned New Zealand sports journalist Terry McLean was at predicting who would be selected in the All Black team. 'He was often only one off. We all thought he must have had inside information. People say that today about Wynne Gray of the *New Zealand Herald*. Overall I think that the New Zealand press is pretty fair.'

When Meads was a player he thought that some overseas journalists seldom had a good word to say about the All Blacks. 'John Reason never said a good word about us. If I'd whacked someone it was the biggest tragedy that had ever happened.' Meads saw Reason as making out that most of the players from Great Britain and Ireland were imbued with ultimate fairness and untarnished noble virtue, those in whom butter wouldn't melt in their mouths, and to whom on-field transgressions were not only abhorrent but unknown. To everyone else, Reason's stance induced remarks like, 'Pull the other one'.

'J.B.G. Thomas saw the Lions as the greatest team in the world. When he came out here he never saw a Lion do anything untoward. Either Don Clarke was responsible for beating them by kicking penalties, or we indulged in foul tactics.' In Meads' view visiting journalists from the UK lost most of any sense of objectivity they may have possessed the minute they arrived in New Zealand.

The media do have an effect on players, Meads is sure of that. Players are often told not to read reports, not to listen to what is being said. But in his experience, most

Meads with veteran rugby scribe Sir Terry McLean, years after the two men had departed the playing fields and the press boxes.

players do read and listen to what is being said by the media. 'Good and bad things are said about players. I got some good press and some bad press; no doubt some of it was deserved. I think the media should avoid being too aggressively critical. Bad press used to make me grit my teeth and swear to do better next time. I may have been in a minority there. In 90 per cent of cases fair criticism will work for the benefit of a player. Praise that is excessive is not all that helpful, and nor, for that matter, is condemnation.'

17.
PLAYERS — THEN AND NOW

'New Zealand has always been lucky to have had a large pool of very fine players.'

No one who played with or against Colin Meads saw him as anything but astute and alert. He may not have had much of a formal education but when it came to rugby football his peers awarded him a doctorate. The citation in the dressing room reads, 'He was a cunning and clever big bugger, as keen a student of the game as there has been. He may not have read a textbook in his life, but he could have written one on the basics of rugby football, and forward play especially.'

Meads prepared well; he was a shrewd and careful observer of what other players did, and he grafted bits of their stock onto his tree of rugby-playing knowledge. He aspired to be better than the best of those he played with and against.

Meads feels that while it is hard to compare players of different eras, partly because the game is different now, 'basically it's still rugby'.

In Alex Veysey's *Colin Meads All Black* he talks at length about many of the finest All Blacks of his playing days. That is the place to go too if you want his observations on the likes of South Africans Martin Pelser, Frik du Preez, and others; and if you want to read of his assessment of the likes of Lions Dickie Jeeps, Barry John, J.P.R. Williams, and others.

Australia has thrown up a number of excellent players who loom large in

Meads' Hall of Fame. He thinks immediately of the unpredictable brilliance of wing David Campese and the all-round accomplishments of lock John Eales. 'And the midfield back Tim Horan, he was one of the greats from anywhere. Michael Lynagh and Nick Farr-Jones were very good, and of today's crop, George Gregan is outstanding.'

Says Meads, 'The French too have always had some great players. Philippe Sella in the backs, he was great. And they've always had some good forwards, big, robust buggers.'

The South African Danny Gerber wasn't as well known as he should have been, because he was at his best during a time when South Africa was isolated, but in Meads' book he was a great player. The English lock forward Martin Johnson struck Meads as having a lot of potential when he played a couple of seasons for King Country and became a New Zealand Colt. 'When he left here, he was just another up and coming young player, but he developed into a first-rate international footballer.'

Another player who has impressed Meads, although his opinion is based solely on television observations, is Lawrence Dallaglio. 'He's a competitor. He's got that extra bit of yardage when he goes. In some ways he plays as if he's been schooled by the best of the All Blacks.'

As for Meads' feelings about how he related to those he played against, and what their reaction to him was, he says, 'I was never censured by my own team-mates. But when they were in the opposition, the odd one tried things to the limits — including the likes of Ken Gray, the greatest prop I ever put a shoulder on. I loved playing with or against Kel Tremain and Brian Lochore, had great friendships with them.

Meads says Ken Gray was 'the greatest prop I ever put a shoulder on.' Here, Gray leads a raid against the French in the second test of the 1968 series at Athletic Park. Other All Blacks are, from left: Meads, Kel Tremain, Alister Hopkinson and skipper Brian Lochore.

Together in black for the last time. Brian Lochore — who was brought out of retirement — and Meads locked the All Blacks' scrum in the third test against the Lions at Wellington, 1971.

PETER BUSH

'And Wilson Whineray helped me right from the start when I was the shy country boy wondering what to do next, where to go, what not to do. I often wonder what they thought of me, straight from the sticks. I'd hardly been out of Te Kuiti. I'd been to Auckland only once in my life, and twice to Hamilton when I first got in the New Zealand Colts team in 1955. I'd never been to the South Island.'

Meads had a lot of time for most of the All Black forwards he played with in the 1950s and '60s. 'I admired John Graham, for instance, for his ability with words, with management and so on. More latterly, I developed a respect for the likes of Jock Hobbs. Jock was a good player and a good guy.'

According to Meads, 'Sean Fitzpatrick epitomised All Black rugby in many ways. A great leader and a tough player. A no-nonsense rugby player. I've always admired him. Fitzpatrick stood out for his attitude, competitiveness, and never-say-die attitude.' Say that Fitzy was renowned as one of the best player-referees and Meads agrees. With a smile he says, 'He was always into that . . . and Colin Meads was one to let the referees know when there was a knock-on and the like too.'

Others that Meads admired include 'Buck' Shelford, 'an aggressive type of player. He came of age as captain of our Wednesday team on the Cavaliers tour of South Africa in 1986.' And Zinzan Brooke impressed Meads from the beginning. 'I was lucky enough to be manager for a time when he was playing. Zinny was one of the great tourists. He'd have been great in my day. His sheer competitiveness, allied to the mercurial things he could do around the field and with the ball.'

Below: Sean Fitzpatrick, who, says Meads, 'epitomised All Black rugby in many ways.'
Opposite page: Zinzan Brooke . . . 'he'd have been great in my day.'

PHOTOSPORT

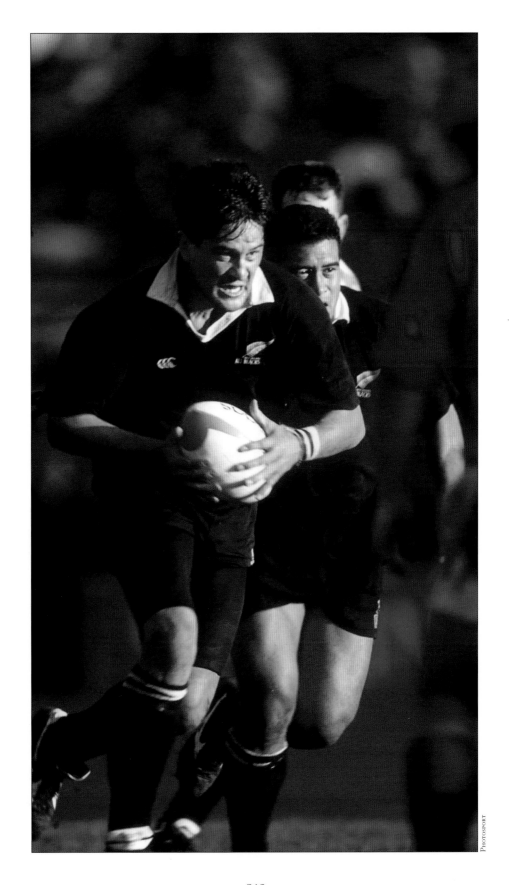

PHOTOSPORT

PHOTOSPORT

Left: Stu Wilson — 'good guy, gifted footballer.'
Below: Dave Loveridge — 'brilliant player, wonderful thinker.'

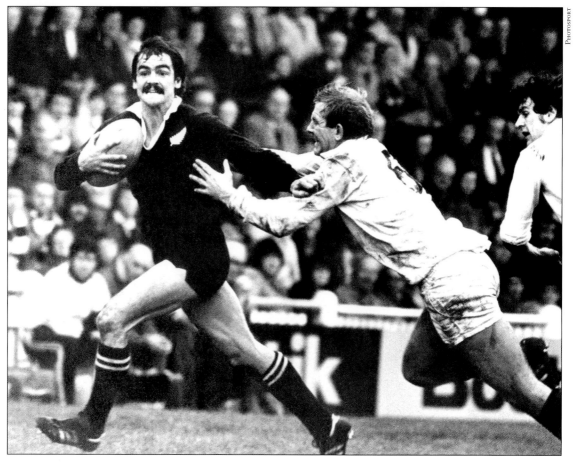

PHOTOSPORT

Meads is aware that some of those on Zinzan's last tour, to the British Isles in 1997, felt he didn't pull his weight in the playing department. 'Well,' says Meads, 'that's money. He'd have been planning other things, like where he was going the next year.'

What of Graham Mourie? Meads feels he and Mourie never gelled, although he 'gets on all right with him', perhaps because they had opposite views on playing against South Africa. But that shouldn't have made much difference for, as Meads says, 'People often thought that I and others thought less of Ken Gray for not going to South Africa with us in 1970, but we never held it against him. It's a personal thing. Everyone has a right to make those sorts of decisions. I had a feeling that Graham may have thought that, because he wouldn't go to South Africa, I'd hold it against him.'

Brian Lochore shared Meads' belief that players had a right to go with their consciences when it came to such matters. In fact, he says that after Gray had declared his unavailability, 'I rang Ken personally and said that while we'd have loved to have had him, it was his right to make that decision, and I wanted him to know that he had the support in that respect from all of his former team-mates.'

Meads admits it took time for him to adjust to the differences in outlook and behaviour of the players who followed him: 'They became more sophisticated,' says Meads. Stu Wilson is a case in point. 'A good guy. So much was a joke. He'd say things tongue-in-cheek. Stu liked to say he wasn't a tackler, but he could tackle when he had to. A gifted footballer.'

Meads had close friendships with forwards. He says, 'One seems to form a stronger rugby bond with forwards, if you're a forward. It's the same with backs.' Nevertheless, he says he had some great times with backs too. From his era he cites Kevin 'Monkey' Briscoe of Taranaki. 'Monkey was a great friend, and a great character. Terry Lineen was a favourite, and Pat Walsh was one of those whom I loved listening to. A wonderful speaker, he could sing a song just like that, was very talented all round. Pat's a godfather to one of our children; Terry O'Sullivan's a godfather to another. (Kel Tremain was another.)

'John Kirwan was a favourite of mine, and I admire Mehrtens. I just love little Mehrtens. He's cheeky. I know he's had his problems at times, but what a player. Actually, he's not so little anymore. He's obviously been working on it. Mehrts is the best first-five I've seen since I played. What a punt he has too. That is just so valuable.'

Meads says that 'New Zealand has always been lucky to have had a large pool of very fine players.' In 1971, his last year in the All Blacks, a number of new players were introduced. Meads remembers the lock Peter Whiting who was 'to become a great player, in my view'.

Meads' list of outstanding All Blacks since 1971 includes the halfback Dave Loveridge, 'a brilliant player. A wonderful thinker. I rate Graeme Bachop very highly too. He was strong in himself and would have had no trouble adapting to today's game. I rate Justin Marshall and Byron Kelleher. They are tough buggers. They may not be quite as skilful as some former All Black halfbacks, but if only more of our forwards had their aggression.'

Apart from Mehrtens, among the first-fives Meads singles out Grant Fox, Wayne Smith and Duncan Robertson. 'Foxy was a fine technician. Sure he was no tackler, but he was a great general. And while he may not have been noted as a runner, the outside backs scored a lot of tries when Foxy was playing. Smith set up play nicely. He had good vision and was an incisive runner. Robertson was good tactically and a fine all-round footballer.'

Of the second-fives, 'Warwick Taylor was the best for me. Another heady player, he could bust it up if he had to. He may have helped make Smith. Walter Little got mucked around a lot, picked then not picked, and though he had crook knees he was tough. He and Frank Bunce were tough and good together. Bill Osborne was another strong and accomplished footballer. And I like the look of Aaron Mauger. He's pretty complete for his age.'

Among the centres, Meads can't go past Bruce Robertson. 'He was gifted and wonderful at running wings into position. Some say he may have found it tough in today's highly physical environment. I don't know. A great player though.

'Buncey — Frank Bunce — was another I had a lot of time for. He didn't become an All Black until he was 30, which says a lot for his attitude. Other players liked playing with Buncey, he organised and controlled a backline. He had a lot of heart, and opposition backs rated him. Joe Stanley was another very good player, similar to Bunce in many ways.'

In Meads' book, New Zealand has always had talented wings: Kirwan, Bryan Williams, Jonah Lomu, Stu Wilson, Grant Batty, Craig Green, Jeff Wilson, Tana Umaga, Bernie Fraser. 'Bryan Williams stood out. He may have been the best winger of all. No one in New Zealand saw the real greatness of Williams, you had to have been in South Africa in 1970 to have seen that. Phenomenal, unbelievable.

'The opposition worry when Jonah's in the team, so his influence is considerable. His form is variable but he's turned on some big games. He gives centres some scope. Batty was a feisty little fella who gave it everything. As for Umaga, I think he's a wing, and a very good one.

'Green was like Malcolm Dick in my day, a gifted all-round player who was a bit underrated. Resolute, reliable and faster than some thought. Very good on the blind side too.

'Jeff Wilson is a complete rugby player when his mind is on it. Too good a footballer to leave out of the All Blacks. And Bernie Fraser, when focused, was very talented.'

Talk of fullbacks and Meads finds it hard to go past Christian Cullen. 'At his best, brilliant, mercurial. I also had a lot of time for Glen Osborne. He was one of the best counter-attackers in the modern game. When he bulked up a bit he seemed to lose some of his speed.'

In the forwards, at No. 8, Meads adds Murray Mexted to the list that stars Zinzan Brooke — who had 'everything' — and Buck Shelford. Mexted was mobile and very good in the lineouts. And he was at his best when playing alongside Mark 'Cowboy' Shaw.'

Meads thought Michael Jones was a tremendously talented openside flanker especially. He was, incidentally, 'one of the most forgetful of all the players I've ever had anything to do with managing,' says Meads. 'He'd arrive at the ground without his boots. Then there would be a panic, taxis flying to go and get them. Injuries caught up with him, but in his early career he was a brilliant player.

'Jones and Josh Kronfeld were the best. They suffered terrible injuries, but were quick and never gave up trying. Josh was a character. Sure, he was different, and had other interests, but no one tried harder when it mattered. He valued the jersey all right.' Jock Hobbs appealed to Meads as both a fine player and person whose

Meads rates Michael Jones as a tremendously talented openside flanker — even if a little forgetful.

PHOTOSPORT

Forwards of favour.
Above: Mark 'Cowboy'
Shaw — 'a good-'un.'
Left: Anton Oliver —
'gives his absolute all.'

career, unfortunately, was cut short through concussion.

'When I was coach of the New Zealand Colts team in the mid-eighties, I was terribly impressed with Mike Brewer, who played on both sides of the scrum in his career, as well as at No. 8 on a few occasions. Brewer was clearly an All Black captain of the future, but unfortunately for him injuries ruined his chances of becoming captain. I'm sure he would have been outstanding in that role. 'Bruiser' liked to theorise, always had tactical ideas.

'Alan Whetton was a top blindside flanker, and Cowboy Shaw was a good-'un. Uncompromising, fit, the opposition rated him. Jamie Joseph was good and strong. No one messed with Jamie.'

Meads thought Andy Haden and Gary Whetton — 'a great athlete'— were impressive locks, and he also saw the Wellington lock Murray Pierce as 'a great battler. Not flamboyant, not as naturally talented as some others, but he always played the whole 80 minutes.

'Ian Jones always guaranteed you your ball in the lineouts and he was more robust than many thought. Robin Brooke also did a good job for the All Blacks, although he may have played on a bit too long.'

Mention props and Meads smiles. It's not that he sees them as naturally mischief-makers, but he knows they get up to mischief at times. 'I saw Olo Brown as a top tighthead prop, one of the best and underrated. Fitzy owed him a lot. Gary Knight was a fine prop too.

'John Ashworth may have looked a bit awkward with his long back but he did the job at loosehead. He, Knight and Dalton at hooker were a good front row. At his best, Craig Dowd was useful and very good around the field.

'As for Richard Loe, Loey could play either side. He could be a bit naughty but he was a good player and a good man to have in one's team.

'The hookers — I've spoken of Fitzy. And Andy Dalton was a quality player and a quality person in my book. Hika Reid and Norm Hewitt were alike in some ways and both were very good players. They were unlucky to have been playing at the same time as Dalton and Fitzpatrick. I rate Anton Oliver very highly. He gives his absolute all. He's a good captain, but there are leaders and there are captains. He may be one of those who is more valuable as a player than a captain. He's more pissed off to lose than anyone.'

And that was true of Meads himself, surely.

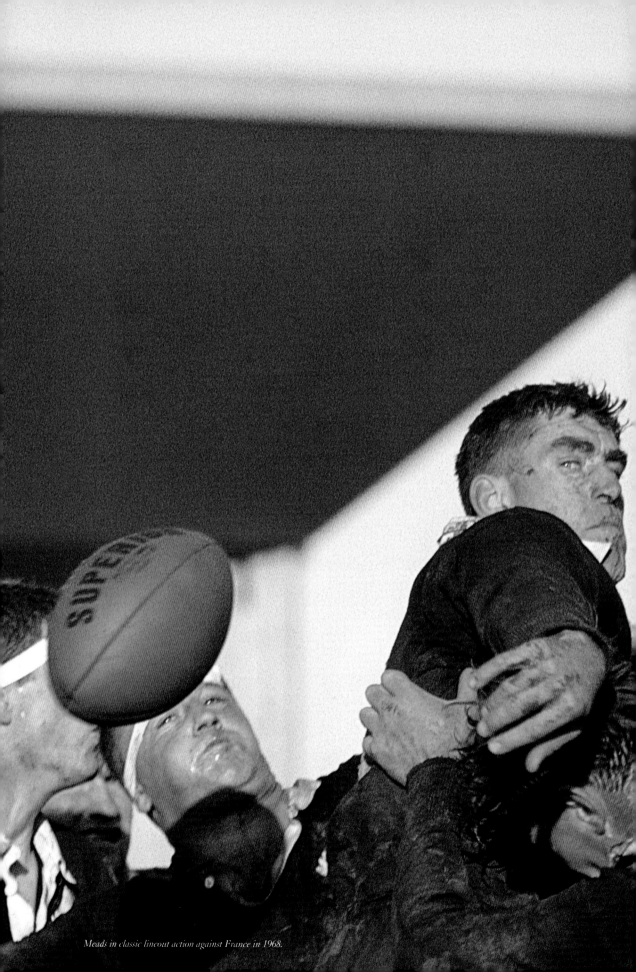

Meads in classic lineout action against France in 1968.

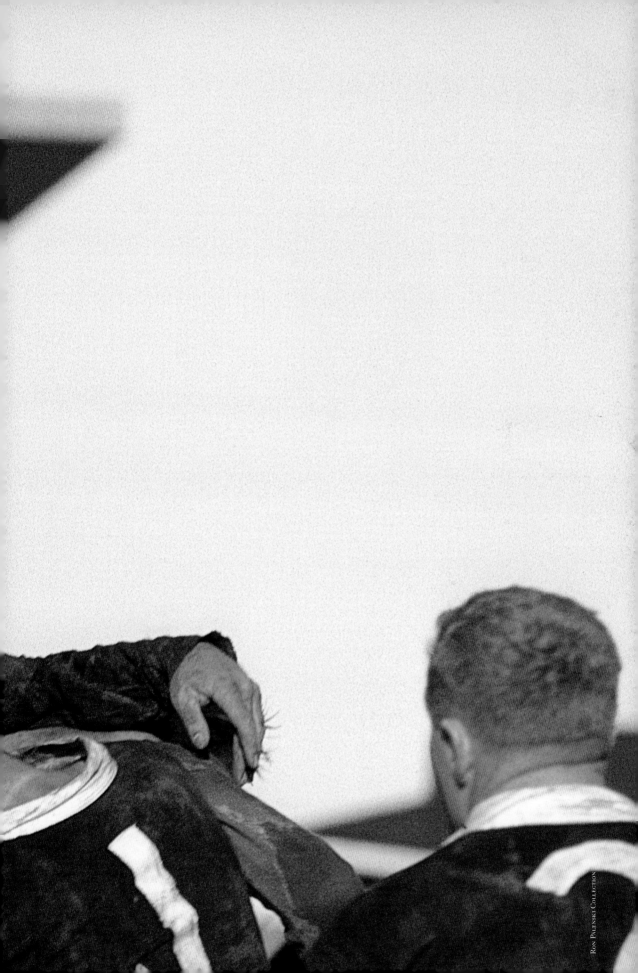

COLIN MEADS —
15 YEARS IN BLACK

COLIN MEADS' 133 APPEARANCES FOR THE

ALL BLACKS REMAINS A RECORD, MORE

THAN 30 YEARS AFTER HIS RETIREMENT.

SEAN FITZPATRICK (128) IS SECOND

ON THE ALL-TIME LIST.

MEADS SCORED 28 TRIES FOR NEW ZEALAND

AND KICKED ONE CONVERSION FOR A

TALLY OF 86 POINTS.

19**57**

Match 1 v N.S.W. at Sydney, won 19–3

Match 2 v AUSTRALIA at Sydney, won 25–11

Match 3 v AUSTRALIA at Brisbane, won 22–9 (try)

Match 4 v New England at Gunnedah, won 38–14

Match 5 v South-West Zone at Grenfell, won 86–0 (try)

Match 6 v A.C.T. at Canberra, won 40–8 (try)

Match 7 v Australian Barbarians at Sydney, won 23–6

Match 8 v Riverina at Wagga Wagga, won 48–11

Match 9 v South Australia at Adelaide, won 51–3 (2 tries)

Match 10 v Canterbury at Christchurch, lost 9–11

All Blacks to Australia, 1957 — the first of many such photo sittings for Colin Meads. Here, he is seated at the far right of the front row.

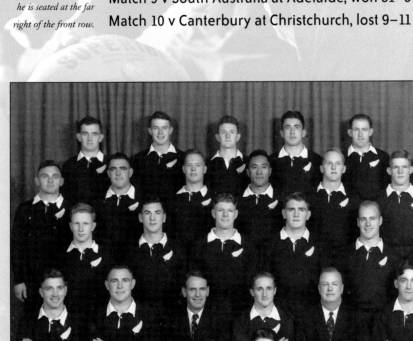

NZ RUGBY MUSEUM

19**58**

Meads delivers lineout ball during the first test against Australia at Athletic Park, Wellington, 1958. At Meads' right is his locking partner, Nev MacEwan.

Match 11 v AUSTRALIA at Wellington, won 25–3

Match 12 v AUSTRALIA at Christchurch, lost 3–6

Match 13 v AUSTRALIA at Auckland, won 17–8 (try)

News Media Auckland

19**59**

Meads (right) follows hooker Des Webb's progress in the second test of the 1959 series against the Lions at Wellington.

Match 14 v BRITISH ISLES at Wellington, won 11–8

Match 15 v BRITISH ISLES at Christchurch, won 22–8 (try)

Match 16 v BRITISH ISLES at Auckland, lost 6–9

News Media Auckland

1960

Match 17 v N.S.W. at Sydney, won 27–0 (try)

Match 18 v N.S.W. Country at Orange, won 38–6

Match 19 v Natal at Durban, drew 6–6

Match 20 v Griqualand West at Kimberley, won 21–9

Match 21 v South-West Africa at Windhoek, won 27–3 (try)

Match 22 v Boland at Wellington, won 16–0

Match 23 v Northern Transvaal at Pretoria, won 27–3

Match 24 v SOUTH AFRICA at Johannesburg, lost 0–13

Match 25 v Rhodesian XV at Kitwe, won 13–9

Match 26 v Rhodesia at Salisbury, won 29–14 (try)

Match 27 v Orange Free State at Bloemfontein, lost 8–9

Match 28 v Junior Springboks at Durban, won 20–6

Match 29 v Western Province at Cape Town, won 20–8 (try)

Match 30 v South-Western Districts at Oudtshoorn, won 18–6

Match 31 v SOUTH AFRICA at Cape Town, won 11–3 (try)

Match 32 v Eastern Transvaal at Springs, won 11–6

Match 33 v Transvaal at Johannesburg, won 19–3 (try)

Match 34 v Western Transvaal at Potchefstroom, won 28–3 (try)

Match 35 v SOUTH AFRICA at Bloemfontein, drew 11–11

Match 36 v North-Eastern Districts at Aliwal North, won 15–6

Match 37 v SOUTH AFRICA at Port Elizabeth, lost 3–8

Match 38 v Transvaal XV at Johannesburg, won 9–3

Match 39 v Rest of New Zealand at Wellington, won 20–8

19**61**

Try time. Meads crashes through the tackle of fullback Claude Lacaze to score in the All Blacks' rout of France in the third test in 1961.

Match 40 v FRANCE at Auckland, won 13–6

Match 41 v FRANCE at Wellington, won 5–3

Match 42 v FRANCE at Christchurch, won 32–3 (try)

NEWS MEDIA AUCKLAND

19**62**

Match 43 v Central-Western Districts at Bathurst, won 41–6 (try)

Match 44 v N.S.W. at Sydney, lost 11–12

Match 45 v AUSTRALIA at Brisbane, won 20–6

Match 46 v Northern N.S.W. at Quirindi, won 103–0 (try)

Match 47 v AUSTRALIA at Sydney, won 14–5

Match 48 v South Australia at Adelaide, won 77–0 (conversion)

Match 49 v AUSTRALIA at Wellington, drew 9–9

Match 50 v AUSTRALIA at Auckland, won 16–8

Meads feeds his halfback Des Connor in the drawn test with Australia at Wellington in 1962. Supporting Meads is Waka Nathan and Kel Tremain.

NZ RUGBY MUSEUM

19**63**

Match 51 v ENGLAND at Auckland, won 21–11

Match 52 v ENGLAND at Christchurch, won 9–6

Match 53 v Oxford University at Oxford, won 19–3

Match 54 v Newport at Newport, lost 0–3

Match 55 v Neath and Aberavon at Port Talbot, won 11–6

Match 56 v Abertillery and Ebbw Vale at Abertillery, won 13–0

Match 57 v London Counties at London, won 27–0

Match 58 v South of Scotland at Hawick, won 8–0

Match 59 v Cardiff at Cardiff, won 6–5

Match 60 v South-Western Counties at Exeter, won 38–6

Match 61 v Midland Counties at Coventry, won 37–9 (try)

Match 62 v IRELAND at Dublin, won 6–5

Match 63 v Swansea at Swansea, won 16–9

Match 64 v WALES at Cardiff, won 6–0

Match 65 v Combined Services at London, won 23–9 (try)

Match 66 v Llanelli at Llanelli, won 22–8 (try)

A forward of many parts. Meads displays his punting style against the English at Christchurch in 1963. All Black team-mates, from left, are: Dennis Young, Ian Clarke, Don Clarke and Allan Stewart.

PETER BUSH

1964

Match 67 v ENGLAND at London, won 14–0 (try)

Match 68 v North-Eastern Counties at Harrogate, won 17–11

Match 69 v SCOTLAND at Edinburgh, drew 0–0

Match 70 v Leinster at Dublin, won 11–8

Match 71 v South-Eastern Counties at Bournemouth, won 9–6

Match 72 v France B at Toulouse, won 17–8

Match 73 v FRANCE at Paris, won 12–3

Match 74 v South-East France at Lyon, won 8–5

Match 75 v Barbarians at Cardiff, won 36–3 (try)

Match 76 v British Columbia at Vancouver, won 39–3 (try)

Match 77 v AUSTRALIA at Dunedin, won 14–9

Match 78 v AUSTRALIA at Christchurch, won 18–3

Match 79 v AUSTRALIA at Wellington, lost 5–20

Two sets of brothers on the 1963–64 tour of Britain, France and Canada. At left, the Clarkes — Ian and Don — and Stan and Colin Meads.

1965

Colin and Stan battle it out with the great Springbok lock Frik du Preez during the second test of the 1965 series at Dunedin.

Match 80 v SOUTH AFRICA at Wellington, won 6–3

Match 81 v SOUTH AFRICA at Dunedin, won 13–0

Match 82 v SOUTH AFRICA at Christchurch, lost 16–19

Match 83 v SOUTH AFRICA at Auckland, won 20–3

SUNDAY TIMES JOHANNESBURG

1966

Meads leaves a trail of Lions in his wake as he sprints to score a try in the second test at Wellington in 1966.

Match 84 v BRITISH ISLES at Dunedin, won 20–3
Match 85 v BRITISH ISLES at Wellington, won 16–12 (try)
Match 86 v BRITISH ISLES at Christchurch, won 19–6
Match 87 v BRITISH ISLES at Auckland, won 24–11

BARRY DURRANT

19 67

Meads in possession against France B at Toulouse in 1967. Other All Blacks in the action, from left, are: John Major, Ken Gray, Sid Going, Earle Kirton (partially obscured), Wayne Cottrell, Graham Williams, Brian Lochore and Ian Kirkpatrick.

Match 88 v AUSTRALIA at Wellington, won 29–9

Match 89 v British Columbia at Vancouver, won 36–3

Match 90 v North of England at Manchester, won 33–3

Match 91 v Midlands/London/Home Counties at Leicester, won 15–3

Match 92 v ENGLAND at London, won 23–11

Match 93 v West Wales, at Swansea, won 21–14 (try)

Match 94 v WALES at Cardiff, won 13–6

Match 95 v South-East France at Lyon, won 16–3

Match 96 v France B at Toulouse, won 32–19

Match 97 v FRANCE at Paris, won 21–15

Match 98 v SCOTLAND at Edinburgh, won 14–3

Match 99 v Barbarians at London, won 11–6

NZ RUGBY MUSEUM

19**68**

Match 100 v Sydney at Sydney, won 14–9

Match 101 v Tasmania at Hobart, won 74–0

Match 102 v Junior Wallabies at Adelaide, won 43–3

Match 103 v Victoria at Melbourne, won 68–0

Match 104 v N.S.W. at Sydney, won 30–5

Match 105 v N.S.W. Country at Newcastle, won 29–3 (try)

Match 106 v AUSTRALIA at Sydney, won 27–11

Match 107 v Queensland at Brisbane, won 34–3

Match 108 v AUSTRALIA at Brisbane, won 19–18

Match 109 v F.R.U. President's XV at Suva, won 33-6

Match 110 v FRANCE at Christchurch, won 12–9

Match 111 v FRANCE at Wellington, won 9–3

Match 112 v FRANCE at Auckland, won 19–12

French captain Marcel Puget has the unenviable task of stopping a rampaging Meads in the second test of the 1968 series at Wellington.

PETER BUSH

19**69**

Meads takes it to the Welsh in the first test at Christchurch in 1969. Support comes from Bruce McLeod and Ken Gray.

Match 113 v WALES at Christchurch, won 19–0

Match 114 v WALES at Auckland, won 33–12

BARRY DURRANT

19**70**

Match 115 v A.R.U. President's XV at Perth, won 52–3

Match 116 v Border at East London, won 28–3 (try)

Match 117 v Paul Roos' XV at Bethlehem, won 43–9

Match 118 v Griqualand West at Kimberley, won 27–3

Match 119 v North-West Cape at Uppington, won 26–3 (try)

Match 120 v Eastern Transvaal at Springs, won 24–3

Match 121 v South-Western Districts at George, won 36–6

Match 122 v Western Province at Cape Town, won 29–6

Match 123 v South African Country at East London, won 45–8

Match 124 v Natal at Durban, won 29–8

Match 125 v Southern Universities at Cape Town, won 20–3

Match 126 v SOUTH AFRICA at Port Elizabeth, lost 3–14

Match 127 v Northern Transvaal at Pretoria, won 19–15

Match 128 v Gazelles at Potchefstroom, won 29–5

Match 129 v SOUTH AFRICA at Johannesburg, lost 17–20

Tempers flare in the fourth test against South Africa in 1970. Here, Meads and Hannes Marais go at it. All Blacks No. 7 is Tom Lister

NEWS MEDIA AUCKLAND

19**71**

*End of the road.
Meads with Lions'
skipper John Dawes,
manager Dr Doug
Smith, coach Carwyn
James and lock Gordon
Brown after the drawn
fourth test in 1971.*

Match 130 v BRITISH ISLES at Dunedin, lost 3–9

Match 131 v BRITISH ISLES at Christchurch, won 22–12

Match 132 v BRITISH ISLES at Wellington, lost 3–13

Match 133 v BRITISH ISLES at Auckland, drew 14–14

ABOUT THE AUTHOR

Brian Turner is a poet with a sporting problem. The oldest member of a prominent New Zealand sporting family, his many books include the best-selling *On the Loose*, which he wrote with the former All Black flanker Josh Kronfeld; *Opening Up* and *Lifting the Covers*, both written with his brother, former New Zealand cricketer Glenn Turner; and eight volumes of poetry. His writing awards include prestigious fellowships and the New Zealand Book Award for Poetry. Apart from rugby and cricket, his sporting interests include golf caddying, sailing, trout fishing and cycling. At one time he played hockey for New Zealand.